Elizabeth D. Leonard is a professor of history and the director of women's studies at Colby College in Waterville Maine. She is the author of *Yankee Women: Gender Battles in the Civil War*.

———— ❋ ————

### Praise for *All the Daring of the Soldier*

"*All the Daring of the Soldier* belongs to the select list of essential books about America's Civil War. . . . All historians and enthusiasts of the war owe it to themselves to read this magnificent work."
—Stephen B. Oates, author of *A Woman of Valor: Clara Barton and the Civil War*

"Engaging tales of valor, patriotism and dedication through letters and contemporary accounts."
—*Denver Post*

"Elizabeth D. Leonard adds important and fascinating information to Civil War scholarship."
—*Atlanta Journal & Constitution*

"*All the Daring of the Soldier* is an important contribution to Civil War history, with its meticulous research and breadth of vision. . . . Leonard has performed an astounding feat in pulling sources together to create a vivid picture of these extraordinary characters."
—*New Statesmen*

"[Leonard's] book offers a wealth of documentary evidence and just a bit of sound conjecture as well. It's an eye-opening, absorbing study, however, which examines the various roles of women—spies, camp followers, artillerists—while probing thoughtfully into their motives, whether for patriotism or profit and perhaps presaging enlightened feminism."
—*The State* (Columbia, SC)

"As interesting as they are varied, Leonard has collected here the stories of real women who 'put their lives on the line and engaged in the traditionally manly profession of war' as spies and soldiers."
—*Civil War Book Review*

"Even the battlefields of the Civil War aren't safe from women's history! Elizabeth Leonard's engaging inventive history of the many roles women played in America's formative war is a wonderful addition."
—Ellen Carol Dubois, author of *Women Suffrage and Women's Rights*

"Our understanding of the women who went to war as spies and soldiers in the 1860s is greatly enhanced by Elizabeth Leonard's latest book . . . her research has revealed numerous new and fascinating stories of women whose bravery and patriotism equaled or exceeded that of many men on the battlefield, and whose contributions were vital to the Union and Confederate war efforts."
—Lauren Cook Burgess, author of *An Uncommon Soldier*

"Elizabeth Leonard has done an exceptional job of bringing the story of army women to light. I believe this book will become a standard resource for anyone interested in women in the Civil War."
—DeAnne Blanton, military archivist and Civil War historian

"A welcome addition to the growing body of literature showing that women's roles in war have always gone beyond the conventionally feminine. Civil War women did knit socks and nurse—but they also soldiered."
—Linda Grant De Pauw, author of *Battle Cries and Lullabies: Women in War from Prehistory to Present*

"This important new book humanizes the stories of women who fought on both sides during the Civil War. Reflecting the diversity and complexity of the war itself, these women shed new light on the average people whose lives were absorbed into that colossal conflict."
—Kathryn Kish Sklar, author of *Florence Kelly and the Nation's Work*

# All the Daring of the Soldier

## Women of the Civil War Armies

### ELIZABETH D. LEONARD

PENGUIN BOOKS

PENGUIN BOOKS
Published by the Penguin Group
Penguin Putnam Inc., 375 Hudson Street,
New York, New York 10014, U.S.A.
Penguin Books Ltd, 27 Wrights Lane, London W8 5TZ, England
Penguin Books Australia Ltd, Ringwood, Victoria, Australia
Penguin Books Canada Ltd, 10 Alcorn Avenue,
Toronto, Ontario, Canada M4V 3B2
Penguin Books (N.Z.) Ltd, 182–190 Wairau Road,
Auckland 10, New Zealand

Penguin Books Ltd, Registered Offices:
Harmondsworth, Middlesex, England

First published in the United States of America
by W.W. Norton and Company, 1999
Published in Penguin Books 2001

1  3  5  7  9  10  8  6  4  2

THE LIBRARY OF CONGRESS HAS CATALOGED
THE HARDCOVER EDITION AS FOLLOWS:
Leonard, Elizabeth D.
All the daring of the soldier: women of the Civil War armies/
Elizabeth D. Leonard.
p.  cm.
includes biographical references and index.
ISBN 0-393-04712-1 (hc)
ISBN 0 14 02.9858 4 (pbk.)
1. United States—History—Civil War, 1861–1865—Women.
2. United States. Army—Women.   3. Confederate States of America.
Army—Women.   4. Women soldiers—United States—History—
19th Century.   5. Women Spies—United States—History—
19th century.   I. Title.
E628.L45   1999
973.7'082—dc21      98-52304

Printed in the United States of America
Set in Iowan Oldstyle

# Contents

# Acknowledgments

One of the most pleasurable but at the same time most humbling moments in the writing of any book comes when the author sits down to consider the many individuals who have been instrumental in bringing to fruition—in the form of a completed manuscript—what began as nothing more than a vague idea.

I would like to express my very deep gratitude to all who have contributed in various ways to the making of *All the Daring of the Soldier*, first and foremost the archivists without whose expertise and support I would have been stymied from the start. I offer a special word of thanks to DeAnne Blanton and William E. Lind of the National Archives in Washington, D.C., who pointed me in the direction of a great deal of evidence about women soldiers and spies that I would otherwise have been hard pressed to locate; and Anthony Thorson of the Dwight Historical Society of Dwight, Illinois, for the mountain of material he sent me on Jennie Hodgers. I thank also Sunny Pomerleau and the rest of the Interlibrary Loan staff at Colby College, as well as Peggy Menchen and our other splendid reference librarians, for bringing so much of the material I needed right here to my desk in Waterville, Maine.

My student workers at Colby have been very helpful as well: Maylene Cummings, who provided me with photocopies of all of the relevant material from the *Official Records of the Union and Confederate Armies*, and who also gave me some valuable feedback on other sources early on in the project; and Anna Denisova, who, although she initially knew nothing of the topic on which I was writing, bravely took up the task of reading the manuscript in a much more cumbersome earlier version and then tracked down, in libraries and archives across the United States, most of the photographs that are included here.

All of the scholars before me who have done important and difficult research and writing in this field deserve my appreciation. I am personally grateful in particular to Jane E. Schultz and Lauren Cook Burgess, whose seminal research and writing on women soldiers (and, in Schultz's case, also spies and army women) lies very much at the foundation of the work I have tried to do here. I also thank the many other scholars—among them James McPherson, Michael Fellman, Nina Silber, Judy Giesberg, and Kirstie Ross—who have participated in professional conference panels with me over the course of this project and have provided useful insights, guidance, and criticisms. I thank others known and unknown to me who have attended my talks and presentations to Civil War roundtables and other audiences and have shared their thoughts with me on the subject of women in Civil War military service. And I thank Judith Bielecki, historian and friend, for her invaluable perceptions regarding the difficulties that posing as a man entailed for the women I have described here, perceptions drawn from her own experiences reenacting in the guise of a Civil War woman soldier.

I am grateful to Colby for providing me with a pretenure sabbatical that gave me the necessary time to write my first crucial draft of this manuscript, and to my Colby colleagues for encouraging and supporting me so graciously in my work.

For her faith in this book, and for her sometimes stern but always wise advice on the manuscript in its several incarnations, I thank my wonderful editor at W. W. Norton, Amy Cherry. I also thank my amazingly precise and painstaking copy editor, Amy Robbins. This book has been improved immeasurably by these individuals' efforts.

For showing me over and over that being a historian and a writer is damned hard work, but work well worth doing nonetheless, I thank my mentor, friend, and colleague, John A. Phillips. John's sudden, cruel passing in January 1998 has left a multitude of us with a personal and intellectual emptiness that we shall spend the rest of our lives trying to fill.

Finally, I thank my two young sons, Anthony and Joseph, who bring enough joy to my life to inspire a thousand books.

# All the Daring of the Soldier

# Introduction

She was seized with horror at the idea of having to dedicate
her entire life to housework.

> *Rudolf Dekker and Lotte van de Pol*, The Tradition of Female
> Transvestism in Early Modern Europe, *1989*

Dashing, charming, fearless, yet lady-like, she combines in
herself all the daring of the soldier with the tenderness and
modesty of the woman.

> *F. L. Sarmiento*, Life of Pauline Cushman, the
> Celebrated Union Spy and Scout, *1865*

It was with some trepidation that Aletta Jacobs, fifteen years
old in 1870, contemplated the employment opportunities that
were available to young women in her time.[1] Aletta, who had
no desire to marry and become a housewife, was distressed to
discover that she might have to spend her life doing housework
anyway, for domestic service continued in the late nineteenth
century to represent the primary waged occupation for women.
Trying to imagine what her alternatives might be, Aletta began to
fantasize about dressing as a man and running away from home,
perhaps signing on as a ship's mate and sailing to a place where
no one was likely to recognize her. There, Aletta thought, she
might find a job as a coachman and so establish herself as an
independent and self-supporting individual. As a man, Aletta

knew, she would enjoy economic and other freedoms that her natural sex denied her.

As it turns out, Aletta Jacobs did not pursue her teenage fantasy. Instead, this daughter of a surgeon went to university and became a medical doctor. Jacobs was able to escape a life of drudgery and dependence because she was able to get a professional education—a privilege long denied to women—and because she could put that education to use in a field that had until very recently been open only to men. Aletta did not need to take on the trappings and the identity of a man to wrest from the world a living wage in an occupation of her choice. Gender expectations prevalent in her society and culture had shifted sufficiently by 1870 to provide some women with at least a few new alternatives. Aletta's initial fantasy of seeking financial security in the guise of a man, however, linked her with the very real experience of women in the past who had done precisely what she had imagined herself doing. Long before 1870 there were women in Aletta's native Netherlands and elsewhere, including America, who refused to let their biology dictate their destinies, instead assuming male identities in order to take jobs and to achieve forms of independence otherwise unavailable to them.

Almost a century before Aletta Jacobs dreamed of becoming a coachman, a young native of Massachusetts named Deborah Sampson, who had already spent many years earning her keep as a domestic servant, donned a suit of men's clothes, cut her hair, assumed the name of Robert Shurtliff, and enlisted in General George Washington's Continental army. Sampson was joined by thousands of other working-class Americans who saw military service during the Revolutionary War not only as a means to express their devotion to the patriot cause but also as an opportunity to earn a living (or so they thought).[2] Needless to say, the fact that Sampson was a woman made her decision to join the Continental army unusual. It did not, however, make her decision unique, either in the context of the Revolutionary War or in the history of American warfare. Sampson is merely one of the best-known women to have posed as a man and served as a soldier in American history. There were others who fought for the same cause; there were others, too, who followed in her footsteps in the next major American war, the Civil War.

When Joan Baez published a collection of her best-loved songs in 1964—only two decades after women gained permanent official status in the United States Army and Navy as WACs and WAVES—she included the traditional Anglo-American ballad "Jackaroe," which tells the story of a young woman whose love for a sailor named Jack drives her to assume a male identity and become a sailor herself.[3] In search of Jack, Jackaroe bravely goes off to war, where she finds her beloved badly wounded. With uncommon strength, Jackaroe carries her dying lover in her arms to a physician who heals him. At some point Jackaroe dispenses with her disguise: at the end of the song she and Jack are married, sure to live happily ever after. Notes Baez, the "Jackaroe" theme is an old one in English balladry, the theme of a girl or woman who assumes the identity of a soldier or sailor in order to be with the one she deeply loves.

It is a theme that recurs in literature as well as in song, and among the most recent renditions of this theme in American literature is Rita Mae Brown's 1986 best-selling novel, *High Hearts*, the story of fictional Geneva Chatfield of Albemarle County, Virginia, who in April 1861 assumes a male identity and a soldier's uniform in order to follow her new husband, Nash, into the Confederate army.[4] Geneva Chatfield is no simple retread of Jackaroe, however. What is interesting about Rita Mae Brown's heroine is that although, like Jackaroe, she is drawn into the war purely out of her devotion to Nash, this initial impulse quickly gives way to an even greater devotion to the Confederate cause and to the excitement of war itself. Unlike in "Jackaroe," as her story progresses, Geneva's love for Nash is overshadowed by her eager desire to demonstrate her daring and her dependability as a soldier, and she ultimately distinguishes herself from her much more ambivalent soldier husband by her extraordinary valor. In Geneva Chatfield we have a version of Jackaroe with an apparently modern twist: a mid-nineteenth-century woman masquerading as a soldier who is celebrated by her creator not for seeking out her male beloved and healing his wounds, but for outshining—and in fact outliving—her husband on the battlefield.

A study focusing on Jackaroe and Geneva Chatfield alone could yield an interesting discussion of the ways in which the differences between these two literary figures reflect changing popular expectations for women's behavior over the past century or so. The discussion becomes much more interesting, however, when one acknowledges that neither Jackaroe nor Geneva Chatfield can be fairly dismissed as a mere symbol detached from historical reality. In fact, scholars have compiled a list of over a hundred women who served as soldiers during the American Civil War alone, and the actual figures undoubtedly go much higher.[5] Women soldiers fought on the battlefields of the American Civil War just as Deborah Sampson and other women had done in the American Revolution. Moreover, as was true of the historical Sampson, the women who chose to serve as soldiers during the Civil War often did so for reasons rather different from those which have been attributed to their literary counterparts both traditional and modern. Patriotism and the love of a good man may have driven some women into the armies of the Civil War, but so, too, did their quest for adventure and their hope for a different sort of paying job than was typically available to them.

Although it highlights a few better-known individuals, such as Sarah Emma Edmonds, Jennie Hodgers, and Sarah Rosetta Wakeman, for whom the documentary evidence is more complete, *All the Daring of the Soldier* describes a panoply of women who disguised themselves as soldiers and fought in the American Civil War. This book is about Civil War women soldiers, but it is also much more, for it embeds its discussion of Edmonds, Hodgers, Wakeman, and others like them in a more expansive discussion of the multitude of women who served the armies of the Union and the Confederacy in other seemingly unconventional ways: women such as Belle Boyd and Pauline Cushman, who engaged in a range of espionage and resistance activities, and women such as Kady Brownell and Bridget Divers, who served the Union and Confederacy as army women and daughters of the regiment. In addition, the book links all these women of the Civil War armies to their predecessors in the American Revolution—notably Deborah Sampson, but also Mary Ludwig Hays McCauley, Margaret Corbin, and Lydia Darragh—as well as to their counterparts in American fiction from the period, as it searches for common ground and for cultural messages. *All the Daring of the Soldier* closes with a discussion of the reasons why women made the decision to put their lives on the line and engage in the traditionally manly profession of war.

Chapter One

# "The Ladies Were Terrific"[1]

*A Handful of Civil War Women Spies*

[At first] it was not deemed possible that any danger could
result from the utterances of non-combatant females. . . . That
this policy was a mistaken one was soon fully proved. . . .
*Allan Pinkerton,* The Spy of the Rebellion, *1883*

Lydia Barrington was born in Ireland in 1729.[2] In 1753, at the
age of twenty-four, she married William Darragh, the son of
a clergyman and himself a teacher. Not long thereafter the
couple immigrated to colonial Pennsylvania, where they produced nine children, four of whom died in infancy. In
Philadelphia, Lydia Barrington Darragh established not only her
family but also her career as a combination midwife, nurse, and
undertaker, by means of which occupations she served as her
family's primary wage earner. Throughout her four decades in
Philadelphia, Darragh provided important personal services to
the members of her community, particularly its women; she also
provided important services of a different sort to the army of
George Washington during the American Revolution.

*Lydia Darragh, bringing word of the British army's plans for attack on the Continental army.* Reprinted from George Barton, *The World's Greatest Military Spies* (1918).

In 1827, almost forty years after Lydia Darragh's death in 1789, an anonymous author published in the new historical journal, the *American Quarterly Review*, what amounted to a summary of direct testimony received from Darragh and others regarding her activities on behalf of the patriot cause during the Revolutionary War. According to the article—whose segment on Darragh in turn became the core of most later published treatments of her story—once the British army occupied Philadelphia in September 1777, Darragh began on a regular basis to provide her son Charles—an officer in Washington's Continental army—with bits and pieces of information regarding the enemy army's plans, which she gathered primarily from eavesdropping on the conversations of the several officers who were stationed at the headquarters of the British commander, General William Howe, near her home. These items of information were written in a simple code on scraps of paper that Darragh then typically hid inside the large buttons of the garments she and her trusted messengers wore, to be conveyed at strategic moments to the proper authorities.

Several weeks after she had taken up the role of a regular intelligence operative serving the patriot army, the significance of Darragh's surreptitious activities increased exponentially when she and her family became unwitting hosts to Howe's chief administrative assistant, the Adjutant General. One evening in early December 1777, the Adjutant General informed Darragh that her family must retire early as he needed the back room of her house for an extended private conference with other British army luminaries. As ordered, Darragh sent her husband and children to bed. But her own curiosity had been aroused by the apparent seriousness of the meeting, and she positioned herself outside the door of the conference room, where she overheard a plan for a surprise attack on General Washington's troops, stationed about ten miles north of town at a place called White Marsh.

Determined to convey this information to the general as quickly as possible in order to save not only her son's life but the lives of many others, Lydia Darragh returned to her own room, where she remained in bed until the officers knocked at her door to let her know they were leaving. When they knocked, Darragh rose slowly in order to convince them that she had been deeply asleep all the while. Then, on the following day when the time seemed right, Darragh told her family that she had to go to a mill some distance away to purchase flour—a trip for which she persuaded General Howe to grant her a pass through the British lines. Once beyond the pickets, Darragh hastened towards the Americans' encampment, encountering one of Washington's subordinate officers—a Lieutenant Colonel Craig—to whom she disclosed what she had heard. Craig then saw to it that Darragh was fed while he himself proceeded to transmit the information to Washington, who gave it full credence and set about undermining the plot. Back home, Darragh anxiously awaited the consequences of her deed. When the British troops returned to Philadelphia, she quickly learned that her efforts had successfully foiled their plans. The Adjutant General's suspicions fell for a time on members of the Darragh family, but they fell most lightly on Lydia, who, he recalled, had been sound asleep when he and the others had concluded their conference. In the end, he remained mystified and frustrated, and Darragh escaped detection.[3]

It is not known whether Darragh continued to provide information to Washington's army in the wake of this incident, or whether she instead counted herself lucky for not having been caught and subsequently retired for the duration of the war to care for her family and pursue her own work. An obituary from January 1790 suggests the latter, for it pays no attention to Darragh's wartime espionage activities, focusing instead on her many contributions to her community's health and welfare, particularly in her capacity as a midwife.[4] Still, it is beyond question that Lydia Darragh had at a crucial moment performed dangerous

*Belle Boyd, as she looked in 1861.* Reprinted from George Barton, *The World's Greatest Military Spies* (1918).

service as a spy on behalf of the patriot cause. Even in the early twentieth century, one source fondly lifted her up as "the Brave Quakeress" whose timely act "Saved Washington's Army from Destruction."[5]

Whether or not they personally knew the story of Lydia Darragh's intelligence activities on behalf of the Continental army during the American Revolution, an untold number of women of both the North and the South bravely upheld the tradition of American women's engagement in spy work during the Civil War. Undoubtedly the most famous of these female Civil War spies—in her own time and in historical memory—was Maria Isabella ("Belle") Boyd, born near Martinsburg, Virginia (now West Virginia), in 1843.[6] By 1861 this childhood tomboy—known for climbing trees, racing her horse through the woods, and relentlessly bossing her playmates around—had grown into a compelling young woman whom many considered beautiful, and who many more insisted had an uncanny knack for making the most of her numerous charms to win the hearts and confidence of men. At least as important, when the Civil War broke out, the teenage Boyd (whose family, although not wealthy, was well connected to the Confederate leadership) proved herself, in the words of one contemporary Northern journalist, "insanely devoted to the rebel cause."[7] For this reason above all others, Belle Boyd dedicated herself immediately to doing what she could on the Confederacy's behalf.

On July 3, 1861, prior to the Union and Confederate armies' first real engagement at Bull Run later that month, federal troops occupied Martinsburg. Soon after, a number of drunken soldiers barged into her family home and attempted, among other things, to hoist a United States flag on the roof. In the process, one of the soldiers seems to have insulted Boyd's mother, who refused to see the Stars and Stripes raised over her home. In response to the soldier's rudeness, Boyd took out a pistol and shot him. Whether or not Boyd killed the young soldier is unclear, but her violent action nearly provoked a riot, and the Union forces' commanding officer subsequently demanded that she appear before him in connection with the incident. However, persuaded by powerful cultural notions that prevailed throughout most of the war deeming it unchivalrous to adopt, unless absolutely necessary, any "resolute measures . . . toward those of the weaker sex" regardless of the odiousness of their activities,[8] the officer failed to find Boyd guilty of any punishable offense. The only significant consequence of Boyd's action was the posting of a guard at her home to forestall similar occurrences in the future.[9]

If he hoped to encourage the eager young Boyd to take an early retirement from her prosecession activism, the federal commander at Martinsburg was destined for disappointment. Instead, Boyd's attack on the Union soldier marked the beginning of her career as a Confederate operative determined to provide the Southern army with whatever information she could obtain about the movements and plans of the enemy's troops. In her

1865 memoir, *Belle Boyd in Camp and Prison*, Boyd recalled that her residence within the federal lines and her acquaintance with so many federal officers gave her easy access to important strategic intelligence. "Whatever I heard I regularly and carefully committed to paper, and whenever an opportunity offered I sent my secret dispatch boy . . . [to] some brave officer in command of the Confederate troops."[10] Working initially without a cipher and apparently without even trying to disguise her handwriting, Boyd almost immediately found herself in trouble again when one of her notes ended up in Union hands. This time federal authorities promptly took Boyd into custody and warned her that her actions were treasonable. Once again, however, traditions of chivalry—combined with a general shortage of prison facilities considered appropriate for housing a woman with even a modicum of social standing—led authorities to release her, thereby unavoidably allowing Boyd to continue her spy work. Gradually learning the use of a cipher, Boyd continued to ride through the countryside on horseback transmitting her encoded messages until March 1862, when she was again arrested. This time frustrated federal officials in Martinsburg held her for a week in a converted hotel while they pondered her case. As before, however, at the end of the week she received her release from General John A. Dix, the commander of the Union's Middle Department. Dix sent Boyd to join her family at Front Royal, about forty miles south, with nothing more than a stern admonition to cease and desist.

At Front Royal over the next several weeks, Boyd continued to operate in opposition to the Union army, eavesdropping—like her Revolutionary predecessor Lydia Darragh—on federal war councils being held at her aunt's hotel in town or even in her own home, and compiling bits of information from seemingly informal conversations with federal officers and soldiers who were as yet both unfamiliar with her face and growing reputation and perhaps also foolishly naïve about the curious young woman's motives. Whatever information she gathered over the

course of the early spring Boyd faithfully transmitted to significant figures in the Confederate military.

It was in late May 1862, in connection with Confederate
General Thomas J. ("Stonewall") Jackson's campaign to defend
Virginia's Shenandoah Valley against further Yankee encroach-
ment, that Boyd performed what has come to be known as her
most important piece of work for the Confederacy. Having accumulated, through various channels, a cache of information she
believed relevant to Jackson's strategy, on May 23 Boyd raced out
on horseback to notify the general in person at his headquarters
several miles away. Major Henry Kyd Douglas later recalled
Boyd's daring venture, in which he became an unexpected but
enthusiastic participant. Boyd, Douglas wrote, was dressed in
white as she hurried in his direction, and she "seemed, when I
saw her, to heed neither weeds nor fences, but waved a bonnet as
she came on, trying, it was evident, to keep the hill between herself and the village." Under orders, Douglas rode out to meet this
"romantic maiden whose tall, supple, and graceful figure struck
me as soon as I came in sight of her." Boyd, he wrote, was nearly
breathless as she gasped out her message for Jackson: "Go back
quick and tell him that the Yankee force is very small—one regiment of Maryland infantry, several pieces of artillery and several
companies of cavalry. Tell him I know, for I went through the
camps and got it out of an officer. Tell him to charge right down
and he will catch them all." With that, she was gone. Moments
later Douglas conveyed her words to Jackson, noting that even as
he spoke with his commanding officer, "I saw the wave of her
white bonnet as she entered the village and disappeared among
its houses."[11]

As tradition has it, Boyd's maneuver allowed Stonewall
Jackson and his men to claim an important victory that day, driving the Yankees garrisoned in Front Royal back across the
Potomac River towards Washington. For her timely deed the general expressed his gratitude by rewarding Boyd with a note of

acknowledgment that became one of her most treasured possessions. "I thank you," Jackson wrote, "for myself and for the Army,
for the immense service that you have rendered your country today."[12] Indeed, as a result of this and her other exploits, by the
summer of 1862 Boyd's reputation as a spy was well established.
"You have heard or read of 'Belle Boyd,'" wrote one federal officer
to a relative towards the end of June; "a lady of considerable
notoriety all over the valley. . . . [T]hat she is a precious rogue I
think no one questions though no one can prove it." The troublesome Boyd, wrote another, had a flair for crossing federal lines
"with perfect ease and impunity, whenever she wished, in spite of
their efforts to the contrary. They say," he added, "she is a won-
derfully keen intriguer."[13]

At the same time that word of her deeds was spreading, federal
officials were growing weary of treating Boyd's interference in
their plans for the region as nothing more than a minor inconve-
nience. In late July 1862, following one of Boyd's expeditions to
carry dispatches, they took her into custody again, this time with
the intention of bringing a halt to her activities. On July 30
Brigadier General Julius White, at Winchester, Virginia (about
twenty miles north of Front Royal and the same distance south of
Washington, D.C.), wrote to Assistant Secretary of War C. P.
Wolcott to inform him of Boyd's arrest and to request further
orders. "Mr. [Alfred] Cridge is here with Miss Boyd as prisoner,"
wrote White. "What shall be done with her?" Later that day
Wolcott responded succinctly: "Direct Cridge to come immediately to Washington and bring with him Belle Boyd in close custody,
committing her on arrival to the Old Capitol Prison. Furnish him
with such aid as he may need to get her safely here."[14]

Formerly a boardinghouse, the Old Capitol Prison was a three-
story building made of "dingy brick," which one Washington
provost marshal, William E. Doster, later described as "one of the
many makeshifts to which an unexpected war had driven the
authorities," where the "real walls were necessarily the bayonets,

the bullets, and above all the incorruptibility of the soldiers who guarded the premises. . . ."[15] There, nineteen-year-old Boyd underwent a brief investigation, culminating in her bold refusal to take the oath of allegiance. Boyd then began a monthlong imprisonment, during which she enjoyed the admiration and affection of many of her fellow inmates. On August 1 fellow prisoner William F. Broaddus described Boyd in his diary as a "graceful" person and a "remarkable character," whose dress was "simple," whose manners were "easy," and whose "style of conversation" was "interesting." Of her secessionism Broaddus noted approvingly that "she spoke in the most fearless manner [of] her determination to work while she lived for the Southern cause, and to die, if need be, in its defense."[16]

Sometime later D. A. Mahony—a Northern journalist imprisoned at the Old Capitol for his own secessionist proclivities—similarly described Boyd's defiant attitude towards the Yankees. This she displayed, among other things, by her frequent singing of the anthem "Maryland, My Maryland," whose words, "stirring enough to Southern hearts, were enunciated by her with such peculiar expression as to touch even sensibilities which did not sympathize with the cause which inspired the song." According to Mahony, Boyd was kept confined in her room most of the time, but had permission to keep both her door and her window open. Her appearance at either the door or the window simultaneously exposed her to the worshipful gazes of her admirers and the abuse of her detractors. Federal prison guards and soldiers stationed near the prison in particular treated Boyd rudely, as if to suggest that her imprisonment in and of itself placed her beyond the pale of chivalry's protection. Treating her instead as a "common woman," soldiers and guards taunted her with pretended jabs with their bayonets and with "coarse jests, vulgar expressions and the vilest slang of the brothel . . . made still more coarse, vulgar and indecent by the throwing off of the little restraint which civilized society places upon the most abandoned

*A more mature Belle Boyd.* Courtesy of the Library of Congress.

prostitutes and their companions." Boyd refused to break down in the face of such defamatory behavior, and instead responded in kind, "hurrahing for [Confederate President] Jeff[erson] Davis and Stonewall Jackson," mocking those who insulted her with comments such as "How long did it take you to come from Bull Run?" and indicating her disdain for soldiers who were stationed on guard duty rather than at the front: "Go meet men, you cowards. What are you doing here in Washington?" By the time she left the Old Capitol, Mahony recalled, Boyd's irrepressible nature had won over many of her sworn enemies, so that there was "not one, Federalist or confederate, Prisoner of State, officer of the Old Capitol, as well as prisoner of war, who did not feel that he was about to part with one for whom he had at least a great personal regard." As if to confirm the truth in Mahony's words, former provost marshal Doster—who knew her while she was imprisoned at the Old Capitol—later recalled Boyd with fondness. "During the whole stay," he wrote, "she was never, to my knowledge, found in ill-humor, but bravely endured a tedious and companionless imprisonment."[17]

Her irrepressible nature aside, evidence suggests that the challenges of her captivity—not least of all the oppressive late-summer heat in the capital—wore Boyd down physically. Late in August, in part, apparently, because of her physical suffering, federal officials decided to release Boyd, banishing her to Richmond, where they hoped she would leave her spy career behind once and for all. On August 29 Brigadier General James S. Wadsworth, stationed in Washington, wrote to General Dix at Fortress Monroe—the headquarters of the Union's Department of Virginia, located on the tip of the Virginia peninsula—directing him to place Boyd beyond the federal lines at the first opportunity.[18] Shortly thereafter, Boyd enjoyed a rousing welcome in the Confederate capital, where her exploits on the nation's behalf had become well known.

Determined not to let enemy officials restrict her movements in any way, however, Boyd soon left Richmond for an extended tour of the South, ending up in occupied Martinsburg again sometime in early 1863. By the late summer she was arrested anew for being within federal lines in contempt of the orders pertaining to her banishment. She was subsequently returned to Washington and imprisoned at the Carroll Prison—an annex of the Old Capitol—this time for three months. As before, Boyd's health declined under the stress of her confinement, and again she was

*Belle Boyd: probably a promotional photograph for a postwar stage performance on the subject of her career as a Confederate spy.* Courtesy of the State of South Carolina Confederate Relic Room and Museum.

sent south. When doctors in Richmond suggested that she take another long trip to improve her health, Boyd conceived what became the final work of her espionage service to the Confederate military: bearing dispatches from the Confederacy to its supporters in England. According to one source, Jefferson Davis provided her with five hundred dollars to cover her expenses.[19]

In May 1864, at Wilmington, North Carolina, Boyd boarded a blockade runner called the *Greyhound* and set sail for Europe. Her venture and her spy career, however, were cut short by the *Greyhound*'s swift capture by the USS *Connecticut* and its forced return to Fortress Monroe hundreds of miles up the Atlantic coast. As it turns out, the incident did not prove a total loss to Boyd: among the *Connecticut*'s crew was a young ensign named Samuel Harding who seems to have fallen in love with her on the journey back to Fortress Monroe. On August 25, 1864, the two married in England, having found their way there by separate routes following Boyd's final release from federal custody and Harding's dismissal from the navy "for neglect of duty."[20] In England, Boyd composed and began to market her memoir, in part to raise funds to support herself after Harding returned to the United States—possibly carrying Confederate dispatches—where he was arrested and imprisoned as a Southern spy. The two reunited briefly, only to be torn apart again by Harding's sudden early death.

After the war, the young widow took up a theatrical career in England and America, centering many of her performances on her exploits as a Confederate spy. Boyd supplemented her income by giving lectures at veterans' gatherings across the United States where, according to one source, "many an old soldier remembered her as the most daring woman in the Confederacy."[21] In addition, Boyd bore three children over the course of two subsequent marriages—first to a former officer of the British army named John S. Hammond, with whom she went to live in California, and, after their 1884 divorce, to the son of a Toledo, Ohio, clergyman named Nathaniel R. High, with whom she lived until her death.[22] In the early 1870s a tired and careworn Boyd briefly spent time in a mental hospital in Stockton, California, her unexpected disappearance from the public eye leading to the publication of a number of false reports of her untimely death. On November 12, 1874, the New York Times reprinted an article that had originally appeared in the Atlanta News a few days earlier, describing a woman who was traveling the country posing as Belle Boyd and giving lectures. This article alleged that Boyd's "stormy career" had landed her in a California lunatic asylum in 1872, where she had died. "It is cruel," the article lamented, "this attempt to drag from her grave in California the poor woman whose many faults were more than atoned for in her

*A youthful Rose Greenhow.* Courtesy of the Library of Congress.

tragic end, and whose unwomanly career deserves forgiveness and forgetfulness in its really ardent and patriotic devotion to the South."[23] Boyd's actual death came in 1900, at the age of sixty-seven, in Kilbourne, Wisconsin, apparently the result of a heart attack. In 1929 the United Daughters of the Confederacy arranged to have her remains removed from the cemetery in Kilbourne and transferred to the town of her birth.[24]

Boyd was by no means the only American woman during the Civil War to take up the sort of spy work that Lydia Darragh had performed during the American Revolution. Rather, she was joined in her Civil War espionage operations by a host of other women, among them four who left sufficient records for us to flesh out their stories in some detail: Rose O'Neal Greenhow, Antonia Ford, Elizabeth Van Lew, and Pauline Cushman.

Born in 1817 in rural Montgomery County, Maryland, Rose

O'Neal—like Belle Boyd—came from a family of limited financial resources and little education.[25] Far more so than was the case with Boyd, however, O'Neal's humble beginnings failed to inhibit her climb up the social ladder. As a teenager Rose O'Neal traveled with her sister Ellen Elizabeth to Washington, D.C., where they stayed with an aunt who maintained a boardinghouse in the Old Capitol building (later, ironically, to become the Old Capitol Prison). There, the attractive young sisters had the opportunity to associate with a number of their aunt's male boarders, many of them up-and-coming politicians, and Rose in particular developed a taste for living an active social life and rubbing shoulders with people in power. Some years later, when, at the age of twenty-six, she married forty-three-year-old Dr. Robert Greenhow, Rose O'Neal demonstrated her determination to leave behind what she considered the dull country life of her childhood. Dr. Greenhow, a Virginian, was both wealthy and socially well placed; marriage to him promised Rose continued access to the sort of world to which earlier visits to her aunt's boardinghouse had accustomed her.

Indeed, by the time she was in her mid-thirties, the mother of four daughters, and living with her husband and family in the nation's capital, Rose O'Neal Greenhow had not only established strong connections with the Washington political elite but had herself become a person of significant social influence—and cunning. Surrounded by the many advantages that her prestigious husband could offer her, wrote one contemporary, Greenhow became well known for "her beauty, the brilliance of her conversation, her aptitude for intrigue, the royal dignity of her manners, and the unscrupulous perseverance with which she accomplished whatever she set her heart upon."[26] In 1850 Greenhow and her husband left Washington for four years, heading west, where the doctor thought he saw the opportunity for great financial gain. Instead, an injury led to his early death in San Francisco. His widow returned to Washington, moved with her daughters into a small home near the White House, and resumed all the valuable contacts that she had established prior to the family's western sojourn, presumably living off her late husband's wealth. As the 1850s gave way to the 1860s, Greenhow enhanced her independent status as a premier Washington hostess and socialite, as well as her reputation as a woman to be reckoned with, thanks to her ability to obtain favors, influence members of Congress, and advance her friends' careers.

As sectional tensions increased, Greenhow, like Boyd, openly revealed herself to be a woman of "pronounced rebel proclivities,"[27] and at the war's outbreak she immediately became an activist on the Confederacy's behalf. She linked up with Lieutenant Colonel Thomas Jordan (alias Thomas John Rayford) of Virginia, a former quartermaster in the United States Army who was in the process of developing an elaborate Confederate spy network in the federal capital. From Jordan, Greenhow learned the use of a simple, twenty-six-symbol cipher, and she began to exploit her connections with prominent Unionists for the purpose of eliciting information that she then transmitted in code to relevant figures in the Confederacy.[28] Greenhow and Jordan also invented an elaborate system by which she could convey significant information to him or to their trusted assistants by raising and lowering the shades of the windows on one side of her house. Over time, Greenhow and Jordan enlisted the regular help of various others, forming an extensive spy ring that included both men and women.

Greenhow became most famous for her spy work that gave the Confederate army the edge in its first major confrontation with the soldiers in blue at the battle of Bull Run in July 1861. An 1863 letter written by General P. G. T. Beauregard—second in command to the Confederate army's ranking officer, General Joseph E. Johnston, in the summer of 1861—confirms that on July 10 Greenhow sent an attractive young woman named Betty Duvall to Beauregard's post at Fairfax Court House, just a few miles from Bull Run, bearing—tightly wound in her chignon—a message concerning Union commander Irvin McDowell's preparations to advance on the Confederacy six days later. General Milledge L. Bonham of South Carolina received the message and transmitted it directly to Beauregard, who notified President Davis and then immediately began preparations to undermine McDowell's advance. On the sixteenth, Greenhow communicated a second time with Beauregard, who was now encamped with his army near Bull Run. With the help of George Donellan, a former Interior Department clerk, Greenhow sent Beauregard an encoded dispatch containing the news that, as Beauregard later wrote, "the enemy—55,000 strong, I believe—would positively commence that day his advance from Arlington Heights and Alexandria on to Manassas [near Bull Run], via Fairfax Court-House and Centerville." This news Beauregard also forwarded by telegraph to President Davis, who ordered General Johnston, stationed fifty miles away, to bring his troops into the area as reinforcements. While awaiting Johnston's arrival, Beauregard shifted his own troops to meet the advancing federals, and on July 21 the Union suffered a stunning and humiliating defeat. The following day Greenhow received from Thomas Jordan an expression of Jefferson Davis's gratitude for her loyal service, similar to that which Boyd later received from General Jackson. Wrote Jordan: "Our President and our General direct me to thank you. We rely upon you for further information. The Confederacy owes you a debt."[29]

Over the next several weeks Greenhow continued to gather and transmit information to her contacts in the Confederate army. "I was urged to leave the city by more than one," she later wrote, "and an escort offered to be furnished me if I desired; but, at whatever peril, I resolved to remain, conscious of the great service I could render my country, my position giving me remarkable facilities for obtaining information."[30] With relative ease Greenhow seems to have gotten her hands on valuable military secrets, including details about Union military strength in and around Washington. However, even as Greenhow moved about with apparent impunity, federal officials were growing determined to put an immediate halt to all leakage of strategic military information. In connection with this goal, they reached the conclusion that the influential and outspoken Greenhow must be a key player in the suspected ring of prosecession intelligence operatives functioning in the capital. By late July the head of the federal government's newly formed secret service organization, Allan Pinkerton, ordered the close surveillance of the Greenhow home and—despite his wariness about angering Greenhow's many powerful friends in the United States Congress—the investigation and arrest, where appropriate, of any and all persons entering or leaving the house. Finally, on August 23, having gathered what he believed to be sufficient evidence of her treasonable behavior, Pinkerton placed Greenhow herself under house arrest. He immediately stationed a number of men inside the house as guards, authorizing them to arrest any of her coconspirators who might unsuspectingly come to call.

The thorough search of the house that followed initially produced little incriminating evidence, thanks to Greenhow's timely destruction of a number of relevant papers. Over the next few days, however, the men who tore apart her clothes, furniture, and other personal belongings found copies of eight intelligence reports dating from July and August which clearly demonstrated the extent of Greenhow's knowledge about Northern military plans and fortifications. "No more troops have arrived," Greenhow had written on August 21. "Great activity and anxiety here, and the whole strength concentrating around Washington, and the cry 'The Capital in danger,' renewed. I do not give much heed to the rumors of [Union General Nathaniel] Banks' command arriving here, although he has advanced this way." Greenhow's reports also implicated a number of her cohorts and heaped suspicion upon some decidedly prominent Unionist figures who had come under her sway, not the least of whom was the powerful senator from Massachusetts, Henry Wilson, who seems to have been one of Greenhow's primary—if foolishly unwitting—sources and perhaps even her lover. (Many interpreters of Greenhow's papers believe that Senator Wilson was the author of a stack of love letters also found in her home.) Although the evidence on this score is not conclusive, that Wilson provided Greenhow with important military information is indisputable. "Wilson told me last night," Greenhow mentioned in her August 21 report, "that they had . . . fifty guns of heavy calibre,—confirmed by my scouts. Wilson goes on [Union General George B.] McClelland's [*sic*] staff today as aid and adviser. I regret this. . . ."[31] Meanwhile, Greenhow was outraged by the intruders' treatment of her things. "Everything showed signs of the contamination," she wrote later. "Those unkempt, unwashed wretches—the detective police—had rolled themselves in my fine linen; their mark was visible upon every chair and sofa. . . . Every hallowed association with my home had been rudely blasted—my castle had become my prison."[32]

Word spread quickly that federal agents had captured a major figure in Confederate espionage, and a woman. On August 26 both the *New York Times* and the *New York Herald* smugly reported Greenhow's arrest, and many—as in Boyd's case—cheerfully cast aside traditions of chivalry when faced with the spectacle of a woman actually being taken prisoner for spying. Some suggested that she would soon be tried for treason. Instead, Greenhow remained under house arrest with her youngest daughter, "Little Rose," and two of her female couriers, Lillie Mackall and Betty Hassler (Betty Duvall had been removed from service in the wake of her delivery of the July 10 dispatch to General Beauregard: she was considered too attractive not to be noticed a second time). Over the weeks ahead, federal officials confined at "Fort Greenhow" a number of other women also suspected of intelligence work on behalf of the Confederacy, but none of the prisoners achieved Greenhow's level of celebrity. According to one source, "Crowds passed the house hoping for a glimpse of the lady, and thousands talked of the new prison. . . . An official assured her that he could have made a great deal of money by charging the public ten dollars for each peep at her."[33] Greenhow attempted to make good use of both her political connections and the popular interest in her case. In November she wrote to United States Secretary of State William H. Seward complaining of the conditions of her imprisonment and comparing her situation to that of Marie Antoinette. Needless to say, the letter failed to bring about her release. In the meantime, however, the disgruntled Greenhow continued to serve as a conduit of information to the Confederacy. Federal officials made various attempts to stop the flow of information in and out of the house, searching the rooms on a regular basis, restricting Greenhow's use of writing materials, sealing the windows, and denying her any opportunities for communication with suspected coconspirators. But Greenhow was doggedly persistent (she even claimed to have put her hands on the minutes of President Abraham Lincoln's cabinet meetings), and as a result, on January 18, 1862, authorities transferred her, with Little Rose, to a more secure spot, namely the Old Capitol.[34]

For about five months Greenhow and her daughter remained at the Old Capitol, now prisoners in the same spot where as a teenager Greenhow had acquired her first taste of the whirl of life in Washington. During this time Greenhow continued to try to provide information to Southern loyalists whenever the opportunity presented itself. She also continued to write angry letters to political contacts and family members on the outside complaining about the conditions of her imprisonment. On March 15, 1862, she wrote to one of her daughters, now living in California, grumbling about the filth and vermin she contended with daily, and also about the presence on the prison grounds of contraband slaves, whose growing numbers left Union army officials scram-

*Rose Greenhow and her daughter, "Little Rose," while imprisoned at the Old Capitol.* Courtesy of the Library of Congress.

bling for places to house them. "We cannot open our windows without the stench from over 100 negroes," Greenhow wrote with predictable racist contempt towards those she considered subhuman, adding nastily, "If you have ever been in the neighborhood of a negro meeting-house in summer you can fancy what odors reach us when our door opens. . . ."[35] That same month, perhaps as a result of the intervention of some of her prestigious connections, Greenhow underwent not a trial for treason but an appearance before a commission consisting of General John Dix (who later examined Belle Boyd) and United States Secretary of the Treasury Judge Edwards Pierrepont. As officials would later do with Boyd, Dix and Pierrepont decided that Greenhow should be banished south, where presumably she could do less harm and also draw less attention to the whole project of Confederate espionage. Still, it was June 2 before the *New York Times* recorded her release and her removal, under close custody, to Baltimore. There, supporters of the Confederacy greeted her with the same enthusiasm that Richmond residents would accord Boyd a year later.[36]

Traveling on to the Confederate capital, Greenhow enjoyed further adulation from various dignitaries, including President Davis and General Beauregard, who praised her for her contributions to the cause of the South. Wrote Greenhow:

On the evening after my arrival our President did me the honour to call upon me, and his words of greeting, "But for you there would have been no battle of Bull Run," repaid me for all that I had endured, even though it had been magnified tenfold. And I shall ever remember that as the proudest moment of my whole life, to have received the tribute of praise from him who stands as the apostle of our country's liberty in the eyes of the civilised world.[37]

From that point on, Greenhow continued her activities on behalf of the South as best she could, in the last resort assuming the role of a blockade runner, in connection with which she traveled, with Little Rose, to England and France. There, she socialized, tried to drum up foreign support for the Confederacy, and produced her memoir, *My Imprisonment, and the First Year of Abolition Rule at Washington*, a provocative work that brought the loyalty and good sense of a number of important Union men into question. As the months passed, however, Greenhow yearned to return to America, where she still owned property,[38] and where she could feel more connected to the events of the war and possibly serve the Confederacy more effectively. With this in mind, and with two thousand dollars in gold in her possession, in September 1864 Greenhow boarded a blockade runner, the *Condor*, bound for North Carolina.

Greenhow failed to make it home to the Confederacy alive. Spied by a Union gunboat in the waters just off the coast near Wilmington, North Carolina (the site of Belle Boyd's embarkation for England in 1864), the *Condor* raced ahead up the Cape Fear River, the captain hoping to avoid confrontation. Instead, he ran the *Condor* aground on a sandbar. Desperate to escape, Greenhow demanded that she be allowed to board a lifeboat, although the weather was ominous. Against the captain's wishes and advice, Greenhow and two other passengers struck out for shore. Their lifeboat capsized in the rough water, and within moments Greenhow, weighed down by her cache of gold, drowned. When her body, which washed up on the shore the following day, arrived by steamer in Wilmington, she was laid out in state in a hospital chapel with a Confederate flag for a shroud. On October 1 Greenhow was buried. Sometime later a monument was erected to commemorate her deeds on the Confederacy's behalf.

Belle Boyd and Rose O'Neal Greenhow dedicated themselves to the Confederacy and served it by gathering and transmitting information relevant to their nation's military operations whenever and by whatever means they could. Federal officals during the war clearly considered both women sufficiently dangerous to the Union cause and sufficiently accomplished in their efforts against it to merit incarceration—despite strong Victorian resistance to the use of such action against women. They felt much the same about Antonia Ford, a young Virginia native whose espionage services, like those of Boyd and Greenhow, contributed significantly to one of the Union's more embarrassing, and costly, military misadventures.[39]

Antonia Ford was born in Fairfax Court House, Virginia—the site of General Beauregard's headquarters prior to the first battle of Bull Run—in 1838. Unlike Boyd and Greenhow, Ford came from a wealthy family: her father was a well-known and prosperous local merchant. Like Boyd and Greenhow, however, as soon as the war broke out, the decidedly prosecessionist twenty-three-year-old Ford—whom contemporaries universally described as beautiful, refined in her manners, and widely courted—proved herself to be spunky, independent, and determined to lend her many talents to the cause of the South. By the fall of 1861, Ford's patriotism and loyalty had carved out a place for her in the affections of J. E. B. Stuart, already a well-respected general in the Confederate cavalry thanks to his courageous performance in leading a crucial charge on the federal forces at Bull Run in July. On October 7 of that year, Stuart issued a document naming Ford an honorary member of his staff. "She will," wrote Stuart, "be obeyed, respected and admired by all the lovers of a noble nature." One Confederate soldier who witnessed Stuart's presentation of the commission to Ford later insisted that the document "was not only signed but it bore the impression of the General's signet ring, and there is no sort of doubt as to its genuine character." Still, he noted that General Stuart's intentions were more lighthearted than serious—that the commission was "meant to produce good humoured laughter from a young lady" and was handed to Ford with only "mock formality," as might be expected given standing proscriptions against women's formal connection to the army. Whether issued in jest or in earnest, however, Stuart's commission to Ford would later figure prominently in the trajectory of Ford's spy career.[40]

Though numerous bits of evidence tie Ford loosely to both the first and second battles of Bull Run (the second encounter of the armies occurred there in August 1862), her name and her reputation as a Confederate intelligence operative are most close-

ly linked to the humiliating capture of the Union's General
Edwin H. Stoughton in March 1863, the event that in turn led to
her arrest and imprisonment. In the early months of 1863, to for-
tify the federal capital, the Union command began sending an
increasing number of troops to Fairfax Court House, under
Stoughton's authority. Lieutenant John Singleton Mosby, a tal-
ented and dangerous Confederate guerrilla fighter whom General
Ulysses S. Grant would—in vain—later order hanged without
trial if captured, greeted the federals' arrival with his typical tactics, harrassing the enemy with raids and assaults while effectively eluding all attempts to apprehend him or his men. Evidence
suggests that Mosby made the Ford home his base of operations
and colluded with Antonia Ford in particular to keep the federals
off-balance. She brought him vital information gained by means
of her seemingly innocent associations with admiring men in
blue and her independent observations of goings-on about town.
Mosby then utilized the information Ford conveyed to him to
formulate his strategy. Ford seems to have cultivated a particularly friendly relationship with Stoughton himself, riding so
often with him on horseback through the countryside that their
relationship became the source of considerable gossip and concern among Stoughton's troops. One of his soldiers wrote a pre-
scient letter to a friend in New York, which was subsequently
published in the *New York Times*, warning that "if Stoughton gets
picked up some night, he may thank her for it."[41] As it turns
out, on the rainy night of March 8, 1863, John Mosby and more
than two dozen of his raiders captured General Stoughton, along
with close to forty of his soldiers, over fifty of his horses, and all
of his weapons, while he was asleep—and possibly drunk—at
his headquarters.[42]

The reaction of the Union's Secretary of War, Edwin M.
Stanton, was intense. Stanton instructed Lafayette Baker, the
United States Secret Service's chief detective at this point, to
investigate the conditions of the capture and to arrest whoever

*Two views of Antonia Ford, as she looked in 1861.* Courtesy of the Library of Congress.

was responsible. For his part, Baker quickly became convinced
that a spy was to blame: "The time, circumstances, and mode of
this attack and surprise," he wrote in his report, "the positive
and accurate knowledge in possession of the rebel leader, of the
numbers and position of our forces, of the exact localities of officers' quarters, and depots of Government property, all pointed
unmistakably to the existence of traitors and spies within our
lines, and their recent communication with Confederate officers." Indeed, for Baker, the trail of evidence led directly to
Antonia Ford. Acting on his suspicions, Baker sent a woman
employed in his agency to the Ford home to test his theory.
Baker's operative, posing as a Confederate sympathizer, stayed
only long enough at the Ford residence to win her subject's confidence and to provoke her, in a moment of bravado, to display
her commission from General Stuart. This document, Baker
wrote, provided sufficient evidence of Ford's treasonable activities, especially when supplemented by Ford's admission to her
houseguest that she had, as the Union spy later reported it,
"made herself acquainted . . . of all the particulars relating to the
number of our forces there [at Fairfax Court House] and in the
neighborhood, the location of our camps, the places where officers' quarters were established, the precise points where our
pickets were stationed, the strength of the outposts, the names
of officers in command, the nature of general orders, and all
other information valuable to the rebel leaders," and that she
had, moreover, communicated all this information to Mosby
prior to the attack on Stoughton. Baker immediately ordered
Ford's arrest and transfer, first to Centreville, Virginia, a few
miles west of Fairfax Court House, and then to Washington
about fifteen miles to the northeast, where on March 16 she was
searched and found in possession of a stash of contraband correspondence and a handful of Confederate money. Baker relieved
her of these items and ordered her into confinement in none
other than the Old Capitol Prison.[43] Word of Ford's arrest

spread quickly, and on March 18, as it had done in the case of Rose Greenhow in August 1861, the *New York Times* condemned her without trial. "Miss Ford of Fairfax," read the article, "was unquestionably the local spy and actual guide of Capt. Mosely [*sic*] in his late swoop upon that village."[44] As before, now that Ford had been captured, northerners seemed happy to dispense with Victorian notions of female frailty and incapacity in order to pin the responsibility for yet another embarrassing federal defeat on a crafty and daring female enemy.

During her imprisonment at the Old Capitol, Ford had an apparent advantage that neither Boyd nor Greenhow had enjoyed, namely a federal officer willing to lobby feverishly for her release. Prior to her delivery to the prison, while undergoing an interrogation at the headquarters of General Samuel P. Heintzelman, the Union commander in charge of the defense of Washington, Ford encountered the young and handsome Major Joseph C. Willard, who, according to more than one source, immediately fell in love with her. Early in 1864 Ford herself fondly recalled their first meeting in a letter to Willard. "I think fate," she wrote, "has a good deal to do with us. . . . It seems I was literally thrown in your way by a power above us—call it Destiny. . . ."[45] Still, "fate" did not move too quickly, and even the intervention of others besides Willard could not force the bureaucratic wheels to move any faster. No less a figure than her earliest supporter, Confederate General Stuart, rose to Ford's defense, on March 25 requesting from John Mosby a statement exonerating Ford from complicity in the raid on Stoughton.[46] In the meantime, Willard steadily pressured the federal authorities, at the same time encouraging Ford to take the oath of allegiance. In return, she urged him to resign from the Union army.

It is unclear precisely how long Ford remained in jail. On May 30 the popular journal *Frank Leslie's Illustrated Newspaper* reported that she had recently been sent south with a group of exchanged prisoners, but an August 15 article in the *Southern Illustrated*

*News* indicated that Ford was still in Union hands. Certainly by the fall she was free, and the following spring, almost exactly one year from the date of Stoughton's capture, Ford married Joseph Willard, who a week earlier had resigned his Union army commission. A relative later recalled Ford's response to the question of why she had chosen to marry a Yankee. "I will tell you truly, Sallie," Ford replied, "I knew I could not revenge myself on the whole nation, but felt very capable of tormenting one yankee to death, so I took the Major."[47] In the next few years Ford bore three children, two of whom died in infancy. Far from tormenting her husband to death, it was Ford herself who died young, possibly as a consequence of her third pregnancy and delivery. In 1871 she left Willard a widower. He never married again.

In their time, Belle Boyd, Rose Greenhow, and Antonia Ford made names for themselves as Confederate enthusiasts who boldly and effectively took up the work of Civil War intelligence. It would be a mistake, however, to assume that only the South produced women who were willing to engage in such work. Love for the Union, too, generated female espionage operatives whose names became familiar both during and after the war, and for whom the historical record is substantial. Among these, the two whose lives and wartime activities are easiest to trace are Elizabeth Van Lew and Pauline Cushman.

Once lauded by the chief of the Union's Bureau of Military Information, General George H. Sharpe, for having represented for "a long, long time . . . all that was left of the power of the U. S. Government in the city of Richmond,"[48] Elizabeth Van Lew was born in 1818 into a family made wealthy by her father's successful hardware business.[49] Van Lew—who never married—lived her entire life in her family's elegant home high atop Church Hill in Richmond. As a young girl she had traveled for her education to Philadelphia, where her uncle was mayor. She returned to Richmond harboring strong antislavery sentiments which led her,

*Elizabeth Van Lew at the time of the war.* Courtesy of the Valentine Museum, Richmond, Virginia.

once she was able, to free the family slaves, reunite them with their spouses, and participate in the "Underground Railroad" for fugitives from other homes and plantations. Indeed, it was her long-standing and ardent abolitionism that underlay this middle-aged Virginian's support for the Union during the war. Long before the Confederate attack on Fort Sumter, such sentiments had led Van Lew's proslavery neighbors to consider her either daffy or dangerous, or both.

The exact origins of Van Lew's espionage activities are cloudy. Although her career peaked in connection with General Grant's 1864–65 siege of her city, other evidence—including two letters written in early 1864 by General Benjamin Butler, then commander of the Union's Army of the James—suggests that Van Lew was already an active and well-respected operative by this point. In the letter he wrote to Grant's adjutant general John A. Rawlins on April 19, 1864, Butler described Van Lew as "a lady . . . of firm Union principles, with whom I have been in correspondence for months, on whose loyalty I would willingly stake my life."[50] As with her Confederate counterparts Boyd, Ford, and Greenhow, Van Lew utilized numerous sources for collecting information. Despite her outspokenness on the slavery issue, her plush home had for some time served as a gathering place for Richmond's prominent citizens (as Greenhow's had in Washington), and it continued to do so during the war. She, along with her elderly mother and her brother John—both of whom seem to have been somewhat more moderate in their pro-Unionism than she, though they did not obstruct her activities—entertained various Confederate military officers and government officials who unwittingly revealed bits of information which she then forwarded faithfully to her Union contacts. Van Lew gleaned additional insights from the Union soldiers imprisoned in the Confederate capital whom she took under her care, she and her mother having gained entry to the prisons by virtue of their being among the few women in Richmond willing to express overt sympathy for the men in blue. Indeed, the Van Lews' attention to the Union soldiers provoked some anger among their townsfolk. Wrote one correspondent to the July 31, 1861, *Richmond Enquirer*:

> Whilst every true woman in this community has been busy making the articles of comfort or necessity for our troops, or administering to the wants of the many hundreds of sick, who, far from their homes, which they left to defend our soil, are fit subjects for our sympathy, these two women have been expending their opulent means in aiding and giving comfort to the miscreants who have invaded our sacred soil, bent on raping and murder, the desolation of our homes and sacred places, and the ruin and dishonour of our families.[51]

Despite such disapprobation, tending to the men housed in the infamous Libby Prison—which stood at the foot of the hill on which her home was perched—became Elizabeth Van Lew's avocation. There, as in other prisons, she consulted with the inmates about what they knew, making careful mental note of their observations, which she later committed to paper, possibly using the cipher that was found hidden in the back of her watch when she died.

The information Van Lew gathered by such means she then transmitted to her Union contacts via an elaborate series of relay stations and a number of trusted associates—many of whom were slaves and former slaves. "She had a farm in the country on the other side of the James River from us and below Richmond," explained Colonel D. B. Parker, a member of Grant's staff, in an 1883 interview.

> Every day two of her trusty negro servants drove into Richmond with something to sell—milk, chickens, garden-truck, etc. These negroes wore great, strong brogans, with soles of immense thickness, made by a Richmond shoemaker. . . . Shoes were pretty scarce in the Confederacy in those days, but Miss Van Lew's servants had two pairs each and changed them every day.

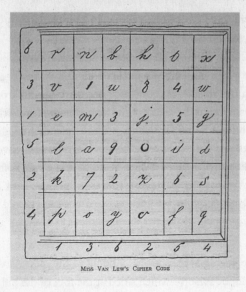

MISS VAN LEW'S CIPHER CODE

*Elizabeth Van Lew's cipher code.* Reprinted from William Beymer, *On Hazardous Service* (1912).

They never wore out of Richmond in the afternoon the same shoes they wore into the city in the morning. The soles of these shoes were double and hollow, and in them were carried through the lines letters, maps, plans, etc., which were regularly delivered to General Grant at City Point the next morning.[52]

Among the assistants Van Lew employed in her work was a former family slave named Mary Elizabeth Bowser, whom she had some years earlier sent north, as she herself had been sent, for schooling. In 1863 a friend of Van Lew's succeeded in persuading President Jefferson Davis's staff to hire Bowser as a maid in his official residence. Bowser's reports from inside the Confederate White House, which Van Lew conveyed to her contacts at City Point, were invaluable. According to Unionist Thomas McNiven, a baker who was also engaged in espionage in the Confederate capital, Bowser had a particularly keen memory, and when he made his regular deliveries to the Davis home, he could always count on her sharing some important information with him.[53]

One of the most interesting aspects of Van Lew's career as a Union spy was her adoption of a persona carefully devised to make her appear incapable of the work that she was in fact performing. Much like her Confederate counterparts, Van Lew paraded her political sentiments about for all to see, but unlike Boyd and Ford, at least, she did so in a context where expressing such sentiments could be extremely dangerous. Thus, she shrewdly cultivated an aura of innocent foolishness, tending towards mental imbalance. Van Lew commonly dressed in odd clothes—sometimes, according to one source, letting herself be seen in "buckskin leggings, a one-piece skirt and waist of cotton, topped off with a huge calico sunbonnet"[54]—and wandered through town singing nonsense songs and muttering to herself. Combined with her spinster status and her long standing (and to many, unfathomable) radicalism on the slavery question, Van Lew's behavior led many observers, who referred to her as "Crazy Bet," to conclude that she was incapable of being devious.

But deviousness was not at all beyond the bounds of Van Lew's nature, regardless of what most of her neighbors thought, and indeed, Van Lews's diary and papers indicate that as a result of her subterfuge, she believed herself to be under constant watch by authorities, and in constant danger. A 1915 *New York Times* article proclaimed that "there was not a moment during those four years [of Civil war] when Lizzie Van Lew could hear a step behind her on the street without expecting to have somebody tap her on the shoulder and say 'You are my prisoner.'" [55] Still, she persisted, transmitting whatever information she could lay her hands on to the federal officials outside Richmond. Van Lew also encouraged the use of a secret room in her home for hiding not just dispatches but also fugitive Union soldiers, possibly including some of those who were part of an elaborate tunnel escape from Libby Prison in February 1864 in which over a hundred federal officers made their way to freedom.[56] Van Lew played a key role, as well, in the theft and secret reinterment of the body of a federal officer, Colonel Ulric Dahlgren, who was killed while participating in a surprise raid on Richmond in March 1864. Learning through her secret channels that enraged Confederates had buried Dahlgren in an unmarked grave, Van Lew, with the help of a man who had witnessed the undignified burial, devised a clever plan that resulted in the rescue of Dahlgren's body and its proper burial beneath a peach tree at the entrance to a local cemetery.[57]

For those who during the war questioned "Crazy Bet's" significance as an intelligence operative for the Union army, the arrival of Grant's occupation troops in April 1865 provided proof. Officials immediately assigned a special guard to Van Lew's home for her protection, the assumption being that her townsfolk might seek revenge against her for Grant's victory. Tradition has it that Van Lew's home was the first to display a large federal flag—perhaps twenty-five feet in length—in recognition of the Union troops' arrival, and that Van Lew hoisted it herself. In any case, in the days to follow, numerous federal officers, and possibly Grant himself, visited the Van Lew mansion to pay their respects. Needless to say, the vanquished residents of Richmond treated Van Lew differently, viewing her as a shameless traitor. Evidence suggests that until her death, resentful townspeople encouraged their children to shower Van Lew with disrespect or to avoid her altogether.

Van Lew's final years were difficult for other reasons as well. Though she had possession of the family home, her financial resources were extremely limited—not least of all because she had spent so much money in connection with her various wartime efforts on behalf of the Union. In recognition of this, shortly after his 1868 election to the presidency, Ulysses Grant appointed Van Lew postmaster of Richmond, a position she held, at some peril to her own safety, throughout his two terms in the White House. Grant urged that his successor, Rutherford B. Hayes, allow Van Lew to continue in this capacity, but thanks perhaps to the lobbying of her many local opponents, Van Lew soon saw her status reduced to clerk and her location changed to Washington, D.C. There, her independent attitude and her unyielding temperament led to further demotions, until she resigned and returned home to Richmond virtually penniless. To the end of her life Van Lew remained financially dependent on others, including the family of at least one Union soldier—a descendant of Paul Revere—who had been housed at Libby Prison and for whom she had cared during his incarceration. Until her death in September 1900, Van Lew continued to fight for various causes—among them woman suffrage—while she coped with her relentlessly hostile community.[58]

Elizabeth Van Lew was an actress of sorts who cultivated the character of a daft, middle-aged spinster in order to cover her tracks as the leader of Richmond's Unionist underground resistance operation. She was joined in the work of spying for the Union by a professional actress, Pauline Cushman.[59] Born in 1833, by the time of the Civil War Cushman shared with Boyd, Ford, and Greenhow a reputation for physical beauty and personal appeal. Although a contemporary journal described her simply as "a handsome young lady," her 1865 biographer, F. L. Sarmiento, presented a more elaborate image of her "entrancing form and flashing eye" and her "overflowing . . . charms of a most wondrous beauty."[60] Cushman spent her early years in New Orleans, then moved with her family to Michigan, where the location of her frontier home allowed her to be in frequent contact with her indigenous neighbors. From early on Cushman, like Boyd, enjoyed the outdoors, and she soon exhibited a range of skills and interests including horseback riding, hunting and target shooting, canoeing, and other tomboyish sports. Out of this context

Cushman developed the yearning for adventure that later carried her as a young woman to New York City, where she embarked on a stage career. In early 1863 her career took Cushman to Wood's Theater in Louisville, Kentucky, the site of her first act of subterfuge on behalf of the Union, and the launching pad for her wartime service as a spy for the Union army.

It was while she was appearing at Wood's Theater that a group of admiring (and possibly drunken) Confederate officers dared Cushman to interrupt one of her performances to offer a toast in Jefferson Davis's honor. Promising to consider their proposal, Cushman secretly visited the Union army's local provost marshal, to whom she suggested that she might use the opportunity of such a public toast to convince the town's Confederate sympathizers of her hatred for the Union. Having thus created a smoke screen for her future activities, she explained, she could proceed to provide valuable service as a federal intelligence operative. The provost marshal agreed, asking only that Cushman guarantee her loyalty to the Union with an oath of allegiance. The following night, in the midst of her performance, Cushman spoke out on behalf of Davis and the Confederacy. She was immediately expelled from her Northern theater company and sent to federally occupied Nashville, where she reported to the Union's chief of army police for the Army of the Cumberland, Colonel William Truesdail, and awaited instructions for her first assignment.

Unlike in the cases of Boyd, Greenhow, Ford, and Van Lew, Cushman's name is not tied to any specific military successes or embarrassments. Nevertheless, an article that appeared in the *New York Times* about a year after her Louisville toast noted that "among the women of America who have made themselves famous since the opening of the rebellion, few have suffered more or rendered more service to the Federal cause than . . . Pauline Cushman, the female scout and spy."[61] During the previous year Cushman had busied herself gathering information about enemy fortifications and operations and, under cover of her reputation as a die-hard secessionist, engaging in effective counterespionage, compiling lists of those in the Nashville area and beyond who harbored dangerous anti-Union sentiments and identifying for Union officials the names of any local Confederate spies whom she could discover. Cushman had also served as a federal courier, and evidence suggests that her range of activities extended through Kentucky, Tennessee, northern Georgia, Alabama, and Mississippi as well. In the course of her work, Cushman seems to have assumed a variety of disguises—including, on occasion, men's clothes—to have spent much time on horseback, and to have wielded a pistol fearlessly. Despite her repeated professions of loyalty to the South, however, Cushman's activities had increasingly provoked suspicion among Confederate observers, leading to her arrest, late in the spring of 1863, near Shelbyville, Tennessee, by General John Hunt Morgan, like J. E. B. Stuart one of the Confederacy's leading cavalry commanders. Morgan's arrest of Cushman quickly gave way to a brutal interrogation by his comrade in the cavalry, General Nathan Bedford Forrest, who pronounced a sentence of death by hanging in her case. Although the generally mild treatment of women spies on both sides during the war makes it seem unlikely that Forrest would actually have executed Cushman—no woman was executed by either government for espionage or related activities during the war—the unexpected arrival of Union troops at Shelbyville prevented the setting of any such precedent and secured Cushman's reprieve and the continuance of her work for several more months.[62]

In June 1864 *Frank Leslie's Illustrated Newspaper* referred to Cushman as "Major Pauline Cushman," and there is evidence that at some point during her loyal service to the Union, Cushman, like Confederate Antonia Ford, received an honorary military commission in recognition of her brave service to her nation's army, possibly from General William S. Rosecrans or

*Two views of Pauline Cushman: probably promotional materials for her post-war career as an actress and lecturer on her Civil War adventures.* Photo of Cushman in civilian clothes, reprinted from Richardson Wright, *Forgotten Ladies* (1928); photo of Cushman in uniform, courtesy of the Collection of the New-York Historical Society.

General James A. Garfield, then both with the Union's Army of the Cumberland.[63] Cushman's counterintelligence days were cut short, however, as a consequence of the enormous attention she had received in connection with her arrest by Morgan and her condemnation by Forrest. After the war, she returned to the stage, where for a period of time, like Belle Boyd, she presented monologues on the war—sometimes dressed in full military uniform—on stages as far-flung as New York and San Francisco. Eventually, however, interest in Cushman's exploits began to fade and she turned to alcohol and other distractions to disguise the pain of her declining fortunes, and perhaps also to relieve some physical ailment associated with her wartime service. Recalled one Union veteran living in California:

> In 1872 Major Pauline Cushman, the spy of the Cumberland as she called herself, lectured in Watsonville, and there I got my first knowledge of her. She was selling pamphlets that gave a very thrilling account of her adventures in the war. After the lecture she went to a saloon that was kept by Charley O'Neil and became inebriated. This saloon was fitted up with card and billiard tables and had private rooms, and it was a great resort. During the night that Major Pauline was there the shutters were closed, and the occurrences were unfit to talk about, much less to relate in print.[64]

Having been married once before the war—to Charles Dickinson, with whom she had two children who died in infancy and who himself died of camp fever while in the army—Cushman, like Boyd, married twice more, in 1872 to August Fitchner, who died soon thereafter, and in 1879 to Jerry Fryer, from whom she subsequently separated. When the stage no longer welcomed her, Cushman turned to sewing for a living, supplementing her income with a small pension based on her first husband's military service. After falling ill, however, she became addicted to morphine, and on December 2, 1893, she died in San Francisco from an overdose of the drug.

From Boyd to Cushman, the women whose names are most prominently associated with espionage and resistance on behalf of their respective nations during the Civil War performed services which authorities who benefited from their work cheered, and which those on the opposing side deemed worthy of punishment. Contemporary Confederate sympathizers celebrated Boyd as the "Belle Rebelle" while hostile Unionists labeled her the "Cleopatra of the Secession" and condemned her for undermining federal war strategy. In August 1862 an angry journalist from the *New York Herald* denounced Boyd as the "notorious female spy . . . familiarly known as the betrayer of our forces at Front Royal," and noted that Boyd had "managed in divers ways to recommend herself to our officers," such that she was able to sustain "a pretty regular budget of intelligence" by means of which "the enemy was advised of our favorite designs." In 1864 *Frank Leslie's Illustrated Newspaper* identified Boyd simply as "the famous rebel spy," and an obituary published in the *New York Times* in 1900 commented that although Boyd's name had to a great extent already faded from memory, nevertheless "the time was when that name caused many a secret council at army camps and many a plan was hatched to place its owner where she could not add to the harm she had done."[65]

Similarly, contemporaries considered Rose Greenhow a brilliant, "dangerous and skillful spy" and a fierce enemy of the Union,[66] and to many Northerners only Antonia Ford's subterfuge could explain an incident so thoroughly humiliating to the federal forces as the capture of General Stoughton, his men, his horses, and his supplies. (To Southerners, of course, Ford's spy work proved the loyalty and the too-little-tapped cleverness of Confederate women.) Of Unionist Elizabeth Van Lew it is equally true that contemporaries presumed her espionage activities to have been of great significance during the war. Writing to

Colonel James Allen Hardie on April 5, 1865, General Benjamin Butler noted that "Miss Eliza [sic] Van Lew was my secret correspondent in Richmond and furnished valuable information during the whole campaign." Two years later he wrote warmly to Van Lew herself: "There is no lady in the Country whom I rather would meet than yourself. I retain a lively sense of your patriotism and fidelity to the Country in her darkest hours." And when General George H. Sharpe wrote to General Cyrus Ballou Comstock in January 1867, he urged that Van Lew be generously reimbursed for her uniformly valiant efforts on the Union's behalf. "I feel bound to recommend," Sharpe noted, "from a very considerable knowledge of the matter that the sum of fifteen thousand dollars be paid to Miss Elizabeth L. Van Lew for valuable information and services rendered to the U. S. Government during the war. . . ."[67] With respect to Pauline Cushman, we know that on December 3, 1893, almost thirty years after Appomattox, the *New York Times*'s notice of her death described her as a "female scout . . . well known on account of her services" during the Civil War.[68] Even more important, members of a local Civil War veterans group were determined to commemorate her work on the Union's behalf in proper style: they claimed Cushman's body from the local morgue and treated it to a military burial—complete with an honor guard and a gun salute—in the section of the city cemetery reserved for veterans. Cushman's military service was not forgotten, nor was her later reputation as a troubled, dissipated, and perhaps morally debased woman allowed to dim the lights on her final stage exit.

## Chapter Two

# "The Women Are the Worst of All"[1]

*The Broad Scope of Female Espionage and Resistance
during the Civil War*

"A woman in every plot" is almost a proverb among those
who have had much to do with successful conspiracies and
treachery.

*Lafayette Baker*, History of the United States
Secret Service, *1867*

Numerous biographies, biographical sketches, memoirs, and
other published and unpublished sources document the
exploits of Belle Boyd, Rose Greenhow, Antonia Ford,
Elizabeth Van Lew, and Pauline Cushman—the five women who
became best known both during and after the Civil War for what
opponents considered their treasonable behavior on behalf of their
respective armies. Even if we were to assume that only these five
women engaged in espionage and resistance during the Civil War,
we would still have to acknowledge their diversity: this handful of
spies and resistance operatives came from both the North and the
South, supported both the Union and the Confederacy, had their
roots among the wealthy as well as the not so well-to-do, and
ranged from late adolescence to middle age. They also performed a

variety of daring deeds that centered on information collection and transmission, but which also included blockade running, the conveyance of contraband correspondence and goods, and other activities of the sort.

The stories of these five women provide us with additional insights into the phenomenon of women's engagement in Civil War espionage and resistance, for they offer glimpses of other women—such as Betty Duvall, Betty Hassler, Lillie Mackall, and Mary Elizabeth Bowser—who assisted them in their work and whose far less detailed but incontrovertible appearances in the historical record lead us to question how widespread and how complex the phenomenon of women's intelligence and resistance activity truly was during the war. In order to answer this question, we clearly need to look beyond the stories of our five better-known female operatives and their trusted female associates, to the many other women who dedicated themselves to serving their respective nations in similar ways.

As it turns out, without even doing much digging we can unearth published accounts of the exploits of a number of other women who participated in similar sorts of activities during the war, including Charlotte and Virginia Moon, the two young daughters of a Virginia planter. The Moon sisters individually and cooperatively revealed themselves to be ardent Confederate sympathizers, appearing in disguise when necessary, and glad to lend their fine equestrian skills and their bravado to the work of delivering secret dispatches soliciting intelligence from federal soldiers dining in their apparently hospitable homes, and carrying contraband goods to the South.[2] Of the two, younger sister "Ginny" seems to have been the higher-spirited. One account claims that when Ginny was captured by some federal soldiers while serving as a courier of information and goods—in this instance carrying perhaps as much as forty bottles of morphine, seven pounds of opium, and between twenty-five and fifty letters on her person—she won her release by pulling a Colt revolver from the folds of her dress and threatening to kill any man who tried to search her. The story is also commonly told of Ginny that while she was a student at an Ohio school for girls in 1861, she was relentless about expressing her prosecession sentiments, and on one occasion used a small pearl-handled pistol to shoot out the stars of the United States flag one by one, and then used her ring to scratch the words "Hurrah for Jeff Davis" into the glass of a local store window. Although both sisters were arrested during the war, they both escaped long-term imprisonment.

On at least one occasion the three Sanchez sisters—Lola, Panchita, and Eugenia—daughters of a Cuban immigrant residing in Florida, similarly made their contribution to the Southern cause by conspiring to convey to Confederate authorities information unwittingly divulged to them by a group of Union officers.[3] Lola, the story goes, overheard a number of Union officers who were on the front porch of the family home discussing plans for a gunboat attack on Confederate fortifications in the area. Aware of the value of this information to the Confederates, Lola left her sisters behind to entertain and distract the Union soldiers while she saddled up her horse and rode through the dark woods lying between her home and the Confederate lines. The information Lola delivered reportedly allowed the Confederates to meet and capture the Union gunboat, which they subsequently renamed *The Three Sisters* in honor of the women's service. Like Charlotte and Virginia Moon, the Sanchez sisters avoided punishment for their deeds on behalf of the South, as did Olivia Floyd, a native of Port Tobacco, Virginia, who served the Confederacy as a spy and smuggler.[4] Over the course of the war Floyd—an unmarried woman in her early thirties—frequently conveyed through the lines both matériel (clothes, money, and letters) and information (which she, like the Sanchez sisters, gathered while entertaining Yankee soldiers in her family home). By November 1862 federal officials were convinced that Floyd was engaged in a variety of disloyal activities and ordered her arrest. Floyd evaded the order, however—or perhaps the federal authorities failed to carry it out. In any case, she continued throughout the war to serve as a link in what one historian has called the "great chain of spies and messengers that operated along the great spy route between Richmond and the Confederate agents in Canada." When she died in 1905, even the New York Times published the news of her death, calling her a "famous woman Confederate blockade runner."[5]

A number of published works suggest that a young Tennessean named Antoinette Polk was instrumental in making possible the escape from capture by Union forces of a group of Confederate soldiers who were socializing at her father's home, Ashwood Hall, outside of occupied Columbia.[6] Like so many Southern women, Polk was a skilled equestrienne, and one day while riding with a female cousin into town, she found a division of Union cavalry preparing to scour the outlying areas for Confederate sympathizers. Aware of the presence of the men in gray at Ashwood Hall, Polk determined to save them from discovery. With her cousin she raced home with the news of the Union soldiers' plans, arriving just in time—"breathless and nearly spent, her hat and whip gone, her blond hair falling all over her like a mantle"[7]—for the Confederate soldiers to get away.

A similar story is told of Roberta Pollock, a native of Warrenton, Virginia.[8] As the story goes, in December 1864 Pollock was busy eavesdropping on a conversation at the federal provost marshal's office, located not far from her home, when she heard federal officials discussing their plans for capturing some of Confederate guerrilla (and Antonia Ford ally) John Singleton Mosby's men, along with a mass of grain. Once she had heard all she needed to know, Pollock left the building, bribed a Union picket to permit her to pass through the lines, walked two miles until she came to the home of a friend where she was able to borrow a horse, and then, despite the bitter cold and an impending storm, rode through the night to convey her information to the nearest Confederate authorities. On the way, Pollock encountered a federal picket who threatened to arrest her. But whereas Ginny Moon had resorted to armed threats to avoid capture, Pollock called upon the same traditions of chivalry that so often protected female conspirators on both sides of the struggle: she informed her intended captor that he might shoot her on the spot, but that she would under no circumstances spend a night "unprotected" in the company of a bunch of soldiers. Pollock was released and subsequently delivered her message safely.

Stories such as those of Lucy Williams and Rebecca Wright[9] show that pro-Union women, too, did their part for their cause. Williams, a resident of Greenville, Tennessee, and the young wife of a Confederate soldier, in September 1864 took what amounted to treasonable action in conjunction with her own pro-Union sentiments, and quite possibly as well in conjunction with a romance that had blossomed between her and a wounded federal cavalry officer who was quartered for his convalescence in her home. On an evening when Confederate cavalry commander General John Hunt Morgan was dining at her staunchly secessionist mother-in-law's house, Williams engaged him in conversation, eliciting from him some important information about his immediate plans for an attack on a nearby Union encampment. Admitting to him that she was a known Unionist and claiming that she feared his troops might loot and burn her home, which was within the Union lines, Williams duped Morgan—who had captured Union spy Pauline Cushman the previous year—not only into granting her a pass with which to get by the Confederate pickets in order to see to her home's protection, but also into lending her a horse to expedite her travel. Instead of heading home, however, Williams rode through a driving rainstorm to the federal army's encampment, where she exposed Morgan's plan of attack. Reportedly, she then led the federals via a winding secret route back to Greenville, where they killed Morgan preemptively and sent his troops flying in all directions.

Rebecca Wright was a Quaker schoolteacher in Winchester, located in Virginia's much contested Shenandoah Valley, when the

Union's own cavalry commander General Philip Sheridan solicited her help in the fall of 1864 to provide information regarding the position and strength of General Jubal A. Early's forces, who were attempting to hold the region for the Confederacy. Taking advantage of her youth and of the personal interest one of Early's soldiers had taken in her, tradition has it that Wright gathered from her erstwhile suitor the information Sheridan needed in order to bring on the September 19 Third Battle of Winchester, the first salvo in Sheridan's ultimately victorious Shenandoah Valley campaign. Years later Sheridan honored Wright—like Elizabeth Van Lew the object of lifelong ostracism by her community for her Unionist views—with several tokens of his appreciation, including a watch, a personal letter of gratitude, and, also like Van Lew, a bureaucratic appointment in the federal government.

Better known among Unionists than either Williams or Wright is Harriet Tubman, who during the war served not only as an accomplished conductor of the "Underground Railroad" but also for some months as a spy and informer for the United States government.[10] Born a slave, Tubman became a federal espionage agent in March 1862 at Beaufort, South Carolina. Under the direction of Major General David Hunter, commander of the Union's Department of the South (which included South Carolina, Georgia, and Florida), Tubman served as both a spy and an organizer of scouts through the spring of 1863. She was an appropriate choice for an intelligence operative, as she knew the area well and could easily secure the confidence of other slaves and former slaves who knew the area even better than she. As an organizer, too, Tubman appears to have been quite skilled, selecting from among her contacts in the slave community a core group of loyal allies who became her scouts, and to whom she served as a liaison to the federal authorities. When she died in 1913, the *New York Times* remembered Tubman's work as a scout and a spy among her accomplishments.

Several of the many other women who supported their

*Harriet Tubman.* Courtesy of the Library of Congress.

nation's cause by such illicit activities and whose stories have surfaced are worth mentioning, if only to show the breadth of these women's wartime experiences. Because the war was primarily fought on their soil, Confederate women and pro-

Southern women of the border regions had particularly rich opportunities to engage in espionage and resistance on behalf of their cause, and therefore their exploits are often easier to track than those of their Union counterparts. Among pro-Southern women whose stories made them into local heroines of resistance to the Yankee invaders, we find Katie Beattie, who was arrested and charged with aiding Confederate prisoners to escape and with engaging in various acts of sabotage against the Union in and around her Missouri home. Louisa Bruckner, niece of federal Postmaster General Montgomery Blair, was arrested and briefly imprisoned at the Old Capitol for smuggling supplies—as much as a hundred ounces of quinine, sewed into her skirt— from Washington to Virginia. Like Rose Greenhow and Elizabeth Van Lew, the wife of a former diplomat, Belle Faulkner of Martinsburg, Virginia—Belle Boyd's hometown—used her reputation as a lavish hostess to cover the true, subversive purpose of her invitations to federal soldiers occupying the town to socialize at the Faulkner home. Effie Goldsborough, the daughter of a prominent Maryland family, was arrested and banished south late in 1863 on the general charge of being an "avowed rebel" and the specific charge of carrying letters to the South (Jefferson Davis later rewarded Goldsborough with a clerkship in the Confederate Department of the Treasury). Elizabeth Carraway Harland of New Bern, North Carolina, concealed a report detailing the Union's fortifications in her town in a bone of ham, which she then delivered at a crucial moment to nearby Confederate authorities. Mrs. Sarah Hutchings of Baltimore was convicted by a federal military commission in her hometown in November 1864 on the charge of supplying Confederate guerrilla Harry Gilmore with arms (Hutchings received a sentence of from two to five years' imprisonment in the Fitchburg, Massachusetts, House of Correction, from which Abraham Lincoln pardoned her in January 1865). Belle Jamieson was imprisoned at Fort Pickens in August 1862 after it was discovered by U.S. Army officials in

Florida that following her numerous horseback rides with charmed soldiers in blue, she had been making careful note of the federal fortifications there. Mrs. William Kirby was a Louisiana blockade runner who succeeded in evading the federal authorities for some time before they captured her, found two cavalry rifles hidden in her dress, and banished her to Ship Island off the coast of Mississippi for the duration of the war (Kirby died on the island). Hannah Larue, of New Orleans, was disinclined to conceal her anti-Union sentiments in the wake of Benjamin Butler's May 1862 occupation of her city (Butler's enemies dubbed him "the Beast"), and nearly incited a riot among her townsfolk by distributing slips of paper falsely claiming that Union General George B. McClellan and forty thousand of his troops had been captured by the Confederates. And Molly Tynes, from near Wytheville, Virginia, made a midnight horseback ride across the countryside in July 1863 to rally a force of about fifty young boys and old men who then staved off an attack on the town by a thousand federal soldiers under the command of Colonel John Toland.[11]

Brief published accounts of these and other predominantly pro-Southern women spies and resisters come quite readily to hand. Moreover, if we mine the primary materials that are available as well, we soon uncover an additional wealth of information about still other women who were similarly engaged during the war, among them Belle Edmondson, dubbed by the editors of her diaries and letters the "lost heroine of the Confederacy."[12] Born in 1840 in Pontotoc, Mississippi, to a local government land agent of limited financial resources and his wife, Edmondson— like Belle Boyd—early on earned a reputation of being an unruly and willful child. When she was a teenager, Edmondson's parents sent her to a local girls' finishing school, but their efforts to tame her were largely unsuccessful. Edmondson continued to seek adventure, and when the war came she quickly sized it up as an outlet for her frustrated energies. Her family having shortly before relocated from Mississippi to a farm outside Memphis, Tennessee, Edmondson found herself positioned near the heart of Union offensive operations in the region, and she immediately began her wartime service by tending to the sick and wounded soldiers in local hospitals. By 1862, however, Edmondson yearned to do something more exciting which would also serve as an outlet for her hatred of the Yankees, and thus she turned her hand to espionage, mail transportation, and smuggling in the Memphis area.

Mid-nineteenth-century elite and middle-class women's fashions played an important role in enabling them to convey various materials across military lines during the war. The hoop skirt in particular seems to have been designed as a hiding place, not only for letters and secret correspondence but also for drugs, medicines, and other goods. Some women, one source notes, also made use of their elaborate hairdos and their "reticules"—cloth bags designed to hold such necessaries as mirrors, powder, and perfume, which were carried on the arm and closed with a drawstring—for storing secret dispatches.[13] Confederate loyalist Mary Chesnut mentioned such devices in an August 29, 1861, diary entry in which she complained about the restrictions that Yankees were imposing on Southern women, who when traveling could now expect to have their hair searched for hidden papers, and their skirts and bustles searched for pistols.[14] Belle Edmondson must have been familiar with all these contrivances: on March 16, 1864, she described in her diary some of the tactics she used to make her work as a smuggler possible. "At one o'clock," she wrote, "Mrs Fackler, Mrs Kirk & I began to fix my articles for smugling [sic]. We made a balmoral [petticoat] of the Gray cloth for uniforms, pin'd the Hats to the inside of my hoops, tied the boots with a strong list, letting them fall directly in front, the cloth having monopolized the back & the Hats the side. All my buttons, brass buttons, Money &c in my bosom." Edmondson went on to record some of the difficulties these very tactics entailed, noting that she found walking with her load almost impossible—"Weight of contrabands ruled," she wrote—and as a result she had to take the risk of hailing a cab to take her to her destination. On this occasion she met with no trouble from the federal pickets, and arrived home near dark, tired but glad for having safely delivered her cargo.[15]

Although she was usually successful, sometimes Edmondson was searched, with the result that she lost all or part of her contraband. "Brought a great deal through the lines this eve," she wrote on March 23, 1864, but, she noted, "Yankee Pickets took our papers." A week later she wrote again in some frustration, "I did not smuggle a thing through the lines, except some letters."[16] Indeed, Edmondson's various activities eventually provoked sufficient suspicion on the part of the federal authorities that they decided to arrest her. News of the order for her arrest leaked out, however, inducing her to flee south to Mississippi in June 1864. There she remained until her unexpected death—possibly a suicide—in 1873.

The editors of her diaries and letters called Belle Edmondson the "lost heroine of the Confederacy," but Southern sympathizers might well have applied that sobriquet to Confederate enthusiast Eugenia Levy Phillips, who, during the early months of the war, became a symbol to the federal authorities of precisely the sort of unrestrained pro-Southern sentiment found among some female residents of the United States, or of federally occupied areas, that demanded suppression.[17] Eugenia Yates Levy was born in 1820 in Charleston, South Carolina. The daughter of a successful merchant, Eugenia married South Carolina lawyer and politician Philip Phillips in 1836. From Charleston the Phillipses moved to Mobile, Alabama, where seven of their nine children were born and where Philip's political career culminated in his election, in 1853, to the United States House of Representatives. As a consequence of his election, the family relocated to Washington, D.C., where they were living at the time the war broke out.

Just which event along the path to war first unleashed Eugenia Phillips's verbal fury is unclear. Evidence suggests, however, that from the outset the more moderate Philip repeatedly warned his wife to control her virulently anti-Union tongue, to no avail. Once the Union forces met with defeat at the first battle of Bull Run in July 1861 and frustrated federal authorities began hunting for all who might be held at least partly responsible, Phillips, like Rose Greenhow, fell under immediate suspicion. For too long she had expressed, in a most uncompromising manner, both her disdain for the Yankees and her support of the South. As a result, on the very same day—August 23, 1861—that he arrested Rose Greenhow, the federal Secret Service's Allan Pinkerton placed Phillips, her equally outspoken daughters Caroline and Fanny, and her sister Martha under house arrest on the charge of maintaining treasonable correspondence with the enemy. As in Greenhow's case, federal soldiers then searched Phillips's home, creating considerable chaos but finding little in the way of hard evidence against either her or her daughters, thanks in part to a trusted Irish maid's demonstration of her loyalty by dumping a stash of family letters, filled with expressions of anti-Union sentiment, into the kitchen stove. Phillips's experience of the intrusion into her home was as unpleasant as Greenhow's. "Our home," she later wrote, "became our prison. Our mail was opened before our indignant eyes, men occupied every room, friends were denied admittance. People viewed our well known abode with fear and we were completely shut out from the outer world."[18] Meanwhile, Northern newspapers immediately reported on Phillips's arrest and confinement, claiming that among other things she was guilty of "illuminating" her house in celebration of the Union defeat at Bull Run, a charge—like so many others—that she vehemently denied.[19]

After less than a week, for reasons of security and efficiency, federal officials decided to move Phillips, her daughters, and her sister Martha to "Fort Greenhow." For the next three weeks the Phillips women fought boredom and what they considered the intolerable conditions of their imprisonment at Greenhow's home: all four women, Phillips later wrote with disgust, were placed in "one filthy room in the attic, with a bed very soiled and innocent of any covering," making for a situation that was "appalling to dainty folk" like themselves.[20] During this period Philip Phillips worked avidly to secure the four women's exoneration from all charges by emphasizing to a number of his powerful Washington friends the innocence that they themselves proclaimed. "We begin to feel somewhat more reconciled to our position," Eugenia Phillips wrote in her journal on August 29, "and console ourselves in the consciousness that we have done nothing we should regret or which would warrant the indignity put upon us." Elsewhere in her journal, Phillips provided a more complex characterization of her "innocence." "Again I ask myself what is my crime?" she wrote.

> If an ardent attachment to the land of my birth and the expression of deepest sympathy with my relatives and friends in the South, constitute treason—then am I indeed a traitor. If hostility to Black Republicanism, its sentiments and policy—is a crime—I am self condemned—! If detestation of this unholy war, inaugurated by party lust—is deserving punishment, then am I worthy of its severest penalties—! and thus suffering I would shout Hosannas for the glorious cause of southern independence.[21]

On September 18, thanks to the intercession of Lincoln's future Secretary of War, Edwin Stanton, federal officials released the Phillips women, but only on the condition that the whole family would remove farther south, where presumably they could stir up less trouble. According to Phillips, the forced departure from Washington was hasty and cruel, requiring the sacrifice of many treasured possessions. Still, her banishment did not prevent Phillips from reasserting her loyalty to the Confederacy by agreeing to secrete among the goods she was allowed to carry with her a collection of papers and letters—possibly one from Rose Greenhow herself—to be delivered to Jefferson Davis at her earliest convenience.[22]

A new start for the Phillips family in the South failed to bring an end, however, to Eugenia Phillips's conflicts with the federal government. Indeed, her reputation among Union authorities as a troublemaker and a possible spy followed her to her new home in New Orleans, and soon after General Butler and his troops occupied the city in May 1862, Phillips found herself in trouble again. On June 30 "the Beast" issued his Special Orders No. 150, recalling Phillips's "traitorous proclivities and acts" while in Washington, accusing her of teaching her children to spit on Union soldiers, and charging her with viciously mocking the remains of a federal soldier, a Lieutenant De Kay, as his funeral cortege passed by her house. Butler's orders further demanded that Phillips—who continued to deny all charges against her—henceforth be regarded as an "uncommon, bad, and dangerous woman, stirring up strife and inciting to riot," and that she be confined in isolation (but with a female servant if she so desired) on Mississippi's Ship Island until further orders.[23]

If Phillips had complaints about the living conditions at "Fort Greenhow," she surely had them about her accommodations on Ship Island, where Louisiana blockade runner Mrs. William Kirby died—probably from illness—during her own imprisonment. Phillips's "cell," she later claimed, initially consisted of nothing more than a huge box resting on a pile of sand, lacking entirely in furniture or any normal comforts and infested with insects (she was subsequently moved to a slightly more hospitable building near the federal officers' headquarters). According to Phillips, the food she received was virtually inedible: rancid bacon, stale bread, and "something called Pea"; and she was allowed neither exercise nor direct contact with her family in New Orleans and was forced to "endure," as Rose Greenhow had been, the proximity of countless contraband slaves. Moreover, the treatment she received from the guards who watched over her defied all rules of decency and bitterly violated her class privilege. "The zeal displayed in forcing suffering upon me was worthy of a savage," she wrote in her memoir, taking a tone that forswore future forgiveness.[24]

In addition to being compelled to live under degrading conditions, Phillips claimed that she suffered personal humiliation in the form of "Beast" Butler's determination to depict her publicly not as an upstanding Southern lady but as a woman of questionable morality. Certainly Butler had set this tone when he openly called her an "uncommon, bad, and dangerous woman." And Phillips believed that Butler had reinforced public impressions of her moral depravity when he issued his Special Orders No. 151, condemning one Fidel Keller—another presumed desecrater of the Union dead—to Ship Island as well but forbidding him any communication with her.[25] In any case, she strove not to crack under the various pressures of her confinement, responding to Butler's weekly inquiries about her apparently frail health without complaint and doing all she could at the same time to minimize her husband's worries. Finally, thanks to the combined efforts of a number of prominent Washington friends on her behalf and official concerns about the unavoidable physical and emotional toll that a lengthy imprisonment might take on her, federal authorities decided to send her home, preempting any popular resistance to her release by hinting that she was pregnant.[26] Phillips was not pregnant, but she was stretched to the limit emotionally. She later recalled that as soon as she reached home her shattered nerves gave way to such an extent that she briefly feared that she would never regain her emotional equilibrium. Following her release, Phillips and her family picked up stakes again and removed for the remainder of the war to La Grange, Georgia, where she confined her war-related activities to managing a hospital for sick and wounded Confederate soldiers. The Phillipses eventually returned to Washington, where Philip took up his law practice once more. Though she and her husband remained in the capital from then on, when Eugenia Phillips died in 1902 she was still bitter towards the Union and resented its treatment of her during the war.

It is wise to remember that women's resistance activities in the Civil War South were not exclusively the purview of secessionists. Extensively covered in wartime newspapers was the story of a Cincinnati-born Unionist named Mrs. Patterson (Mary Caroline) Allan, who, like Elizabeth Van Lew, was a member of Richmond's social elite. Allan was arrested in July 1863 for a combination of offenses including providing Northern contacts (among them, Union General John A. Dix's brother, the Reverend Morgan Dix of New York) with strategic information and with the names of persons resident in the North whom she knew to be Southern sympathizers.[27] The *Richmond Daily Examiner* carried several articles pertaining to Allan's case, first following her arrest in July—when the paper described in detail Allan's system of conveying information through the mails by including letters to her intended contacts inside letters addressed to trustworthy Northern female friends and relations—and then as her case went to trial some months later. Allan's arrest was deemed particularly noteworthy in light of her social standing, although there was some dispute about whether she in fact merited elite status. The unsympathetic author of a July 20, 1863, article in the *Examiner* gave an account of Allan's rise to social prominence in which he made it clear that he considered Allan—the daughter of a poor Cincinnati family who had married into the Allan family's wealth—to be nothing more than a pretender and therefore, he mistakenly believed, theoretically far more likely to engage in subterfuge than a "real" Southern lady.

Particularly irksome to Southern journalists covering the Allan story was what appeared to be Allan's shameless exploitation of the Reverend E. M. Hoge, whom she had been visiting when she learned the names of various prominent New York clergymen and others in the North who eagerly supported the rebellion.

"Through the sacred amenities of friendship expressed for a worthy Minister of the Gospel and his household," one journalist wrote with undisguised contempt, "Mrs. Allan was received into the family—the deadly Northern asp in the garden of Southern hospitality."[28] Irksome as well was Allan's confinement, not in Richmond's Castle Thunder Prison (which housed political prisoners and individuals charged with treason) but in the St. Francis de Sales convent under the care of the Sisters of Charity. Reported the *Examiner*, another woman—Mrs. F. Mathias—had been arrested just days before on charges of using treasonable language and bribing a surgeon to discharge her husband from the Confederate army on false pretenses. Being without wealth or influential relatives, Mathias had been confined at Castle Thunder, while the socially superior Allan, though "charged with a crime tenfold more aggravated," had in contrast been made "invulnerable in her monastic retreat." Rather than justice bowing down "to the condition that gold imposes," the *Examiner* insisted, "the power of wealth ought to be, and will be, we trust, powerless to destroy [its] equipoise."[29] As it turned out, Allan's social connections continued to serve her quite well: although it took several months and several court appearances, she was released from confinement on $100,000 bail in February 1864. Subsequently Allan's undoubtedly well-paid lawyer, George Randolph, managed to get her trial postponed so many times that the war ended without a judgment in the case.

Contemporary newspapers devoted several columns to the Mary Caroline Allan story. Close attention to the newspapers of the Civil War period yields information—often, unfortunately, mere snippets—on other women activists as well: women such as a Mrs. Gwin of Washington, D.C., who, like Rose Greenhow and Eugenia Phillips, was placed under house arrest late in August 1861 on suspicion of maintaining dangerous connections with the federal government's enemies in the Confederacy; a Miss Hosler of Suffolk, Virginia, captured by Union soldiers in

May 1863 while attempting to pass through the lines with dia-
grams of federal fortifications and details about federal troop
numbers stashed in the handle of her parasol; Mrs. Matt Ward of
Louisville, Kentucky, arrested in April 1863 while on board a
southbound steamer for smuggling Confederate army uniforms,
and released "after a slight admonition that a future similar
transgression would be severely punished"; Emma Jones, a native
of Massachusetts who nonetheless had such strong prosecession
feelings that the governor banished her in June 1864—north to
Barnstable; and a Mrs. N. J. Reynolds, a Miss Shuller, and a Miss
Maggie Oliver, arrested on board the steamer *Mollie Able* bound
for Jackson, Mississippi, for smuggling medical supplies in the
false bottoms of their trunks.[30]

Clearly, various published secondary sources, contemporary
newspaper accounts, and unpublished personal papers attest to
the fact that the numbers of women who engaged in Civil War
espionage and resistance far exceed the most famous five. Even
so, such sources leave untold a significant portion of the story
of women's wartime involvement on this front, as a close study
of the original 130 published volumes (a total of more than
138,000 pages) of the *Official Records of the Union and Confederate
Armies* reveals. These dense volumes provide a mass of further
evidence pertaining to hundreds of additional women spies,
scouts, independent, surreptitious, or official gatherers and con-
veyors of military information, and subversive and/or resistance
operatives who came to the attention of authorities on both
sides of the conflict.[31]

About most of these women, unfortunately, we can know very
little beyond the fact that military officials on one side or the
other deemed their activities and the consequences of their activities sufficiently troublesome—or meritorious—to deserve comment. Among the women cited in the *Official Records* are many
who conveyed unsolicited military information to friendly authorities who proved glad to receive the information and did not hesi-

tate to put stock in it. In April 1862 one Mrs. Corner reported to the Union's Colonel E. P. Scammon on the nature of Confederate troop movements in and around federally occupied Raleigh, North Carolina, news that left him little hope of saving the nearby town of Princeton from Confederate capture. In February 1864 Confederate scout A. J. Lawson received a report from a Mrs. Banks regarding the presence near Meridian, Mississippi, of two divisions of Union General James B. McPherson's corps, who, she informed him, were prepared with seventeen pieces of artillery, a large number of wagons, and rations to last them twenty days. In September 1864 the Union's Major General Frederick Steele, stationed in Little Rock, Arkansas, pondered the intentions of a large contingent of the Confederate army that a Mrs. McCune had warned him were readying themselves for action near the Mississippi River. In December 1864 the Union's Lieutenant Colonel James F. Hall praised a Mrs. Hodges as "the most observing person I have found" after she brought him a report on the military situation in Savannah.[32]

Probably some of the most effective unofficial informers—for the Union at least—were black women, particularly slaves who found their way to Union army encampments. Wrote Major General James S. Negley to Lieutenant Colonel Flynt in September 1863: "My scout . . . reports having seen a negro girl near Lee's Mill [Tennessee], who came last night from La Fayette. She says she 'seen heaps of rebels between the gap and La Fayette;' that there was a very large army there."[33] Records of black women's reports are extremely difficult to trace, however, as their names—and even their persons—were rarely deemed worthy of formal notice by those who kept track of such things. Even Harriet Tubman, a paid spy in the Union army's employ and a well-known figure in her own time, receives no mention by name in the *Official Records*.

Needless to say, some of the unsolicited information brought by women to military authorities did not meet with ready official acceptance. In April 1863 Mrs. Lucinda Willard informed the Union's Brigadier General Francis B. Spinola that Confederates encamped near Tranter's Creek in North Carolina were planning an attack on the town. Spinola passed on Willard's news with the caution "I make the statement for what it is worth." Nevertheless, Spinola admitted that other sources had confirmed Willard's report, and he urged the erecting of defenses against the attack she had predicted. Some women also seem to have greatly over-estimated the quality of the information they chose to convey. A Mrs. Nottingham, the mother of a lieutenant commander in the Union navy, was the focus of a January 1864 letter from Benjamin Butler to Rear Admiral Lee, in which he relayed a rumor she was spreading, to the effect that Butler was about to commence a land attack on Richmond with the assistance of the United States Navy. Suspecting that Nottingham had confused the details concerning something her son had heard in a private meeting and then misguidedly reported to her, Butler called for an investigation into the rumor's origins. As he pointed out wryly in his letter, "The experiment has been tried of how the secret would have been kept if we had intended an expedition." Military officials rejected some women's reports, but they pumped others for whatever facts and figures they might be able to provide. Mrs. N. A. Wilson, a refugee from the South who came north in early 1863, ostensibly for the purpose of finding adequate medical treatment for her sick daughter (but in fact for the purpose of escaping the South's declining material conditions), gained the attention of the Union's Major General Joseph Hooker as one capable of giving much information of value, regarding the situation in the South generally and also regarding the Confederate military's plans and activities in and around Winchester, Virginia.[34]

Substantial numbers of women voluntarily or semivoluntarily gathered information and transmitted mostly accurate intelligence reports to their own military organizations. Large numbers of secessionist women in particular came to the federal authorities' attention as a consequence of their having carried on contraband correspondence with, and having conveyed strategic intelligence and matériel to, the Confederacy. Even an officer's wife was not beyond suspicion. In September 1861 Mrs. Elizabeth K. Baldwin, the wife of a United States Navy commander, became the subject of an investigation as a result of her habitual and overt expression of anti-Union sentiment, combined with her ongoing correspondence with an unnamed secessionist living in Philadelphia. Wisely or not, officials discontinued their surveillance of Baldwin's activities pursuant to her taking the oath of allegiance.[35]

As we already know, for women activists engaged in espionage and resistance, although the likelihood of more severe punishment seems to have been slim, the possibility of arrest and imprisonment (or banishment) was very real. It is not particularly surprising, therefore, to learn that on November 7, 1861, federal officials in Philadelphia took a Mrs. Ellen Boyd Kennedy into custody just as she was about to leave to join her husband, a Confederate army officer, in Virginia. According to the official report, Kennedy was suspected of having on her person contraband letters meant for transmission to the Confederacy. Charged simply with "intending to proceed to Virginia in violation of the rules and regulations prescribed by the military authorities of the United States," Kennedy was confined in Philadelphia for almost three weeks before she took an oath to remain within the boundaries of the United States and to cease all correspondence with the South. On January 4, 1862, officials arrested Mrs. H. M. Wood in Illinois and sent her to Washington on charges of having procured designs for a paper mill which she was intending to forward to the Confederacy. Wood was not confined, but officials kept her under surveillance until the middle of February and then sent her home to New York. Such incidents continued throughout the war: in May 1863 Colonel Joseph Morgan of the 90th New York State

Volunteers arrested a Mrs. Wilcoxen near Brashear City, Louisiana, after finding her in possession of a number of firearms that he believed she intended to smuggle into Confederate hands. In January 1864 Colonel Geza Mihalotzy of the 24th Illinois Infantry reported his arrest of a Miss Locke and a Miss Barnet, both of whom he charged with carrying contraband information to the Confederate army. In June 1864 General Ambrose Burnside received an order to arrest one Mrs. Jane Bowles and her daughter—both of whom were named in connection with the conveyance of information concerning federal movements in the area—and send them to the provost marshal general at the headquarters of the Union's Army of the Potomac.[36]

The *Official Records* document as well the active participation of women in sabotage, particularly against the federal army. In June 1864 Major Jeremiah Hackett of the 2nd Arkansas Cavalry (Union) reported from Cassville, Missouri, his capture of two women—a Mrs. and a Miss Gibson—whom he had discovered attempting to cut telegraph wires laid by the Union forces in their area. Secessionist women devised other ways of displaying their antipathy towards the Union cause. Also in Missouri in June 1864, a Unionist civilian in Williamstown wrote to Brigadier General Clinton B. Fisk regarding an incident at the local Methodist church, whose facilities Unionists and Confederate sympathizers in the community awkwardly shared. On a recent Sunday, R. J. Anderson wrote, when a "guerrilla rebel preacher" was scheduled to lead the pro-Southerners' service, some male members of the Unionist congregation sneaked in and nailed a United States flag to the front of the pulpit. When the service was over, the same men took the flag down and held it over the church door in an attempt to compel their secessionist counterparts to pass under it as they exited. Outraged at this affront, Anderson continued, some of the women made their way to a different door. But a Miss Martha Palmer chose to express her sentiments more directly by knocking the flag out of the hands of the intruders and into the street, and trampling it on her way out.[37]

Some Southern women drew official attention as a result of a combination of offenses. Considered a "violent secessionist," Jennie Smith of Baltimore was arrested in June 1861 for smuggling military goods, and a search of her undergarments yielded a stash of percussion caps and military buttons. This was not Smith's first arrest: federal authorities had taken her into custody at least once before for conveying contraband letters to the South. A whole group of women appears in a March 1863 letter from the Department of Missouri's Provost Marshal General, Lieutenant Colonel Franklin A. Dick, regarding their involvement in carrying on secret correspondence with the Confederacy themselves, and as agents for others. "Several rebel mails have been taken in the last few weeks," Dick wrote, "and I find that a large number of women have been actively concerned. . . ." Noted Dick, many of the women were the relatives of officers in the rebel military service, including Mrs. Frost, the wife of the rebel general D. M. Frost; Mrs. McPheeters, the wife of a rebel surgeon; Mrs. Cook, the wife of a rebel senator from Missouri; Mrs. Polk, the wife of a former United States senator, and her daughters; and Mrs. Bredell, the mother of a rebel army captain. "These women," added Dick,

> are wealthy and wield a great influence; they are avowed and abusive enemies of the Government; they incite our young men to join the rebellion; their letters are full of encouragement to their husbands and sons to continue the war; they convey information to them and by every possible contrivance they forward clothing and other support to the rebels. These disloyal women, too, seek every opportunity to keep disloyalty alive amongst rebel prisoners.

"I have been appealed to very many times by our loyal people," Dick continued, "to know why these disloyal women were not sent through the lines. . . . I respectfully suggest that such an order be issued by the Secretary of War."[38]

Probably no group was more conspicuous or annoying to the federal authorities for their various offenses against the Union than the Battle women—Fannie, Dolly, and Sallie (respectively the daughters and daughter-in-law of Confederate Colonel Joel A. Battle)—along with Fannie's cohort, Harriet Booker. Fannie and Harriet Booker, described by a sympathetic Confederate official as "refined and very excellent young ladies," were arrested in Tullahoma, Tennessee, in April 1863 for their outspokenness in favor of the Confederate cause. Officials also charged Fannie with spying, smuggling, and procuring a forged pass; they charged Harriet Booker similarly, noting nevertheless that they considered her less intelligent than Fannie, and therefore "obviously" under her control. Officials took Dolly and Sallie Battle into custody two years later on the charge of being part of a family of "spies and harborers of rebels and guerrillas since the beginning of the war." Wrote Major General Robert H. Milroy in a communiqué to General George H. Thomas, commander of the Union's departments of Tennessee and the Cumberland, the Battle women's mother and mother-in-law "boasts that they have done more good for the Confederate cause than a regiment of soldiers." Milroy also noted that daguerreotypes of Dolly and Sally were found on the body of a rebel guerrilla after he was killed. When Dolly and Sally refused to take the oath of allegiance, General Thomas ordered them banished south.[39]

Indeed, federal officials produced a stack of documents in which they described individual Southern women variously as "secessionists," "unsafe people," "improper persons," "enemies," "formidable characters," "bold, determined, unscrupulous" troublemakers, "she-rebels," "uncompromising and persevering rebels," and "prating rebels." They recommended a range of responses to such women's behavior, including surveillance, arrest and detention, and banishment. In some cases, simply refusing to take the oath of allegiance to the United States proved that a woman was dangerous and should be punished: Brigadier General Benjamin F. Kelley, whose principal responsibility during the war was to guard the Baltimore & Ohio Railroad in Maryland and West Virginia from attack by Confederate raiding parties, issued an order in August 1862 declaring that women who refused to take the oath had clearly demonstrated themselves to be disloyal. Thus, Kelley insisted, the "public interest" required that they be confined in order that they might no longer "be at liberty for the purpose of disseminating their treason among the citizens." Not even Abraham Lincoln's secessionist half sister-in-law (Mary Todd Lincoln's half sister) was exempt from punishment for her treasonable language and behavior. In August 1864 Lincoln wrote to the Union's commander of the District of Kentucky, Major General Stephen G. Burbridge, stationed at Lexington, instructing him that a previous order issued by Lincoln to shield Emily Helm from being arrested simply because she was the widow of a Confederate general (Benjamin Helm, killed at the battle of Chickamauga, Tennessee, in September 1863) and almost a relative was now to be superseded by a new order demanding retribution for her disloyal words and acts. Wrote Lincoln: "If the papers given her by me can be construed to give her protection from such words or acts, it is hereby revoked *pro tanto*. Deal with her for her current conduct just as you would with any other."[40]

At least one Union woman earned Confederate sanction for her general vexatiousness: a Mrs. Sawyer, whom the Confederate agent for prisoner exchange in July 1863 was holding as a prisoner in Richmond while he awaited instructions for her return to the North. But by far the greater number of documents refer to Confederate women, such as Kate and Ella Barnett, Laura Latham, Ellen Martin, and a Mrs. Moore, all cited in one December 1863 circular as worthy of forced removal beyond the federal lines for having "acted disrespectfully" towards the President, the government, and the officers, soldiers, and loyal citizens of the United States when they stomped out of an Episcopal Church in Vicksburg, Mississippi, in the midst of prayers for the welfare of the nation and its leadership.[41] Southern women in particular also made trouble for the Union by participating in guerrilla warfare. Historian Michael Fellman has argued that guerrilla warfare during the Civil War "blurred gender boundaries and gender decorum in often horrifying ways," not least of all, as he points out, because male guerrillas depended on their female allies for supplies, information, and shelter.[42] Indeed, a good number of pro-Southern women engaged in the guerrilla activity that ravaged the border states, especially Missouri. In November 1862 Brigadier General John McNeil reported from Palmyra his arrest and imprisonment of a Miss Powell and a Miss Creath, who, upon being searched, had both been found in possession of thousands of gun caps and other items of value to the local guerrillas. More important, wrote McNeil, was the fact that the young women's disloyalty took the form of exploiting their "beauty, talents and superior education" in order to persuade men to become involved in guerrilla warfare who "except for that influence would have been . . . honest." Creath and Powell, he insisted, were "openly and persistently disloyal" to the extent that he regarded them each "of sufficient importance to either justify a strict surveillance or banishment from the State." As late as February 1865 the Union's Lieutenant R. B. Kelley wrote to his commander from Rolla: "Colonel: I have the honor to report that . . . [I have] found the body of the man Sallee, but no trace of those who murdered him. I am informed, however, that one John Brown, a noted guerrilla, was one of the murderers. I arrested his wife for harboring him. I arrested Mrs. Fore for harboring guerrillas and bushwhackers. I also arrested John Lester, Widows Wright and Coleman, for the same reasons." [43]

*Nancy Hart.* Courtesy of the West Virginia State Archives.

The story of one female guerrilla, Nancy Hart, has appeared in a variety of published sources over the years. Hart, a native of the mountains of western Virginia, came to prominence during the war as a consequence of having led contingents of Confederate cavalry on a series of raids on federal outposts in her area. Union authorities put a price on her head, and subsequently captured her in June 1862 at Summersville. Apparently Hart shot the soldier who was assigned to guard her, however, and she galloped away only to return several days later with two hundred cavalrymen who seized a number of federal officers and enlisted men who offered no resistance.[44]

The *Official Records* make it clear that there were many others who, like Hart, participated in guerrilla activities beyond Missouri. In February 1865 the 75th Pennsylvania Infantry's Lieutenant Colonel Alvin Matzdorff wrote from Franklin, Tennessee, of a particularly heinous example of a woman's collusion with male guerrillas: a Mrs. Cherry, he wrote, had been hiding two "bushwhackers" in her home, but when federal soldiers on the scene demanded to know if she had seen the men she was hiding, she answered in the negative and politely invited the soldiers to search the house. Before the search got under way, however, the men hiding inside opened fire on the bluecoats, wounding several and then escaping themselves. As retribution, the federals burned Mrs. Cherry's house to the ground.[45]

The *Official Records of the Union and Confederate Armies* reveal much about the sheer numbers of women on both sides of the Civil War who engaged in the work of conveying intelligence to their own military organizations; of the Confederate women in particular whose treasonable activities—from the perspective of the Union—included the carrying on of illegal correspondence, smuggling, and aiding and abetting guerrilla fighters; and of the women in general who earned reputations and sometimes harsh punishment for being subversive in both word and deed. Increasingly it becomes clear that Boyd, Greenhow, Ford, Van Lew, and Cushman should be viewed as simply the most prominent among a vast multitude of women who showed their loyalty to their respective nations by carrying out secretive and dangerous deeds of espionage and resistance during the war.

How was it possible for so many women to be so effective in this work? It is an enduring and, indeed, fundamentally accurate assumption about Civil War women spies that the degree of a particular woman's success was probably often directly related to her physical (and sexual) attractiveness to men, her ability to exploit her "feminine charms" in order to dupe men into betraying secrets or otherwise foolishly lowering their defenses. In his 1972 *Women Who Spied for the Blue and Gray*, Oscar Kinchen argued that for the Civil War woman spy, no tools in her arsenal were more potent than her very femaleness and her supposedly sex-specific powers of "feminine" deception, "feminine" persuasion, and, on occasion, seduction. A Civil War woman spy's advantage over her enemy increased substantially, he wrote, if she was "endowed with good looks or possessed with charming manners and a winsome personality." A plain woman, Kinchen implied, had a far tougher row to hoe if she hoped to succeed as a spy in her nation's service.[46]

Writing a few years earlier in her 1966 book *Bonnet Brigades*, historian Mary Elizabeth Massey likewise commented on Civil War women spies' manipulation of their "female charms" in the successful performance of their work. Massey pointed out, however, that although complex mid-century notions of gender laid the groundwork for a woman spy's exploitation of her powers of allure, persuasion, and deceit, at the same time those same notions guaranteed that her community would punish her in some fashion for taking advantage of those presumed powers. Civil War women spies, wrote Massey,

> made excellent newspaper copy and even those from prominent families received no mercy from the press. If not referred to outright as prostitutes, they were accused of having clandestine relations with specific officials, of being a "Cleopatra," "seductress," "courtesan," or insane. The respect ordinarily accorded upper- [and one could also add middle-] class women was cast aside when they were suspected, arrested, imprisoned, or banished.

Even if the case against her was flimsy, because she was assumed to have capitalized (as women were supposedly wont to do) on her physical attractions to men, a woman charged formally or informally with spying for the Union or the Confederacy faced the serious risk of losing stature in her community.[47]

Certainly the ways in which writers have consistently presented Belle Boyd, Rose Greenhow, and many other women like them reinforce the stereotype embraced by Kinchen and Massey. Southern women spies, wrote one Boyd biographer in 1928, "turned their attractions to good account. Skirmishes of restless eyes, ensnaring turbulence of lips, flirtatious forays and laughing retreats, ambuscades of virginal seduction—such wiles practiced by these women . . . more than once proved overwhelming when directed at officers and men from the North." And, he concluded, "Not the least of these wily daughters of the Confederacy was Belle Boyd."[48] Indeed, since her debut on the stage of public opinion, Boyd has appeared almost invariably as a temptress of quite dubious moral virtue. In May 1862 an article published in both the *Philadelphia Inquirer* and the *New York Herald* described Boyd as an "accomplished prostitute," a characterization to which Boyd herself responded with predictable outrage (she subsequently granted an exclusive interview to a *New York Tribune* correspondent who declared her innocent of all such charges, but who nevertheless noted that she was "certainly a provocator").[49] Most accounts of the period as well as more recent ones do not go to the extreme of calling Boyd a prostitute, but they uniformly emphasize her exploitation of her physical charms, her flirtatiousness, and her seductive powers in explaining her success.[50]

The image of Boyd that emerges from the various accounts of her wartime activities is not dissimilar to that of the older, widowed mother of four, Rose Greenhow. As early as 1861, in his description of the steps he had taken in response to Greenhow's activities, none other than Allan Pinkerton boldly stated his convictions about the means employed by this "very remarkable woman" of "almost superhuman power" in accomplishing her "unholy purposes." Among Greenhow's most dependable devices, Pinkerton wrote, were her "almost irresistible seductive powers," which she used to great effect on the soldiers and officers in blue, "not a few of whom she has robbed of patriotic hearts and transformed . . . into sympathizers with the enemies of the country. . . ." In Pinkerton's mind, Greenhow was still a woman whose forceful, compelling style and whose abiding attractiveness to men were the underpinnings of her success and made her an extremely dangerous enemy of the federal government.[51]

Similar remarks commonly appear in the accounts of other women spies on both sides of the struggle as well. "Antonia [Ford]," wrote Kinchen, "spent no small part of her time in primping before a large looking-glass in her room trying on one dress after another, arranging her beautiful dark blond hair and posing with her gorgeously colored fan. She is said to have culti-vated a voice so sweet and subdued as to add to her seductive appeal."[52] Pauline Cushman, wrote Harnett T. Kane in his 1954 *Spies for the Blue and Gray*, possessed the "rich dark coloring of her French mother and Spanish father, the heavy-lidded look of the professional temptress."[53] The model of the Civil War woman spy as beautiful charmer-deceiver-seductress is a dominant one in the literature on real women's activities—although the unmar-ried, middle-aged Elizabeth Van Lew seems to have been exempt from it. Van Lew, wrote one biographer pointedly, as if defending her reputation against assumptions to the contrary, was in fact "the opposite of a seductive lady," who "accomplished her ends without the help of charm or a lush figure or a coquette's air."[54] Van Lew serves as one of few exceptions to the rule, however. Like women spies in other wars, most Civil War women spies, according to tradition, depended on their feminine charms to accomplish their dastardly deeds.

Not only the accounts of real women who engaged in espi-onage and resistance during the Civil War but also at least some of the purely fictional contemporary literary representations of women engaged in such wartime work confirm this interpreta-tion. Certainly this is true of the central figures in the wartime writings of Northerner Charles Wesley Alexander: *Pauline of the Potomac* and *Maud of the Mississippi*, which revolve around the exploits of Pauline D'Estraye as she lends her brilliant skills as a spy to the Union cause; *General Sherman's Indian Spy*, the tale of Wenonah, a young "Indian maiden" who becomes instrumental in the success of General William T. Sherman's 1865 march from Atlanta to Raleigh; and *The Picket Slayer*, the story of Mary

Murdock, a young woman whose dealings with the occult lead her to become a dangerous agent of the Confederacy. Much like the historical women whose stories we have encountered, the three central figures in Alexander's tales are diverse in their backgrounds, but they share certain skills: they are all fine horse-women and expert sharpshooters, and possess some measure of athletic prowess. And like so many of their historical counter-parts, Pauline D'Estraye, Wenonah, and Mary Murdock also share a reputation for great physical appeal in the eyes of men. Men's good sense fades, Alexander tells us, in the face of the "dauntless, beautiful" Pauline D'Estraye, the "lovely and bewitch-ing" Wenonah, the "ravishing beauty and innocent purity" of Mary Murdock.[55]

The evidence clearly indicates that the stereotype of the Civil War woman spy as a beautiful and calculating (and preferably young) temptress of men has some resonance not just in litera-ture but in history. And indeed, it is only reasonable to assume that an individual woman's determination to elicit and transmit secret information and goods during wartime, and her desire to confound and thwart her enemy at every possible turn, would necessarily lead her to utilize all the weapons at her command. If, therefore, her culture's notions about gender and womanhood granted her certain sex-based advantages in performing such work—if, for example, men were expected to lose their capacity for good judgment in the face of a pretty young woman—that woman could only be considered remiss if she did not try to pro-mote her cause in the most opportunistic manner. Civil War women spies and resistance activists, who saw themselves as part of a deadly war effort, undoubtedly depended quite often on the advantages associated with their very femaleness: this is nei-ther a surprise nor a criticism. What must not be forgotten, how-ever, is the equally persuasive evidence that many women—not just Elizabeth Van Lew but also the great majority of the women who appear in such sources as the *Official Records* and whose

*Frontispiece from Charles Wesley Alexander's* Pauline of the Potomac *(1862), depicting the heroine in disguise besting a challenger.* Reprinted from the book.

looks and "feminine charms" received no formal notice whatsoever—clearly manifested abilities unrelated to their physical appeal in the eyes of men, among them physical vigor, shrewd intelligence, and a talent for masking their surreptitious activities over often protracted periods of time.

Chapter Three

# "Half-Soldier Heroines"[1]

※

*A Handful of Civil War Army Women
and Their Predecessors*

> Poor, self-sacrificing Annie, you, I hope, will get your reward
> in heaven when your campaigns and battles in this life are
> ended. For no one on this earth can recompense you for the
> good you have done in your four years' service for the boys
> in blue, in the heat of battle, on the wearied marches, and in
> the hospitals and camps.
>
> *Union soldier Daniel G. Crotty,* Four Years Campaigning
> in the Army of the Potomac, *1874*

Women who became activists engaged in espionage and
resistance were by no means the only women during the
Civil War to serve the armies of the Union and the
Confederacy in important, even militarily significant ways. One
recent scholar has pointed out that when London *Daily Telegraph*
correspondent George Augustus Sala reported from the United
States in 1863, he remarked specifically on the abundance of
women he encountered in a federal army camp at Brandy Station,
Virginia. Among these women Sala focused his attention on the
many who had come to join their husbands—primarily officers
but also enlisted men in the Union's Army of the Potomac—for
the winter. But soldiers' and officers' wives were not the only
women who accompanied the Civil War armies; nor was the peri-

od of winter quartering the only time when women were present. Army women also included soldiers' other female relations and friends, as well as laundresses, cooks, provisioners (also termed "sutlers" or "vivandières"), official and unofficial nurses, and of course those to whom the derogatory term "camp followers" has traditionally been applied: women who provided the men with sexual favors. Army women had all sorts of attachments to the military, some of them irregular, temporary, and brief, amounting to little more than visitation; others as permanent and formal as any soldier's. Some women traveled and lived with the Civil War armies for the purpose of fulfilling specific tasks—tasks that tended to multiply and diversify as time went on. Others set out from the start simply to do whatever they could to be helpful, not infrequently on the field of battle.[2]

Needless to say, by the time of the Civil War the presence of women in and around the army was hardly a pathbreaking development. In the European armies of at least the fourteenth through the eighteenth centuries, women were considered a regular part of the army's makeup, and they played specific, often essential roles that did not necessarily exclude combat. As European armies over the centuries gradually became more professional, more bureaucratic, and more masculine, and as war itself became more formalized, army women's numbers declined and became more strictly regulated. There is some evidence to suggest, however, that as their numbers declined and as their service became more regulated, those army women who remained with the troops may have experienced an increasing militarization of their status, reflected not least of all in their clothes. Historian H. Sinclair Mills describes a typical French army woman's garb in 1809: "A grey jacket, canvas shirt, high gaiters and hide belt. A knotted handkerchief held on an old felt hat." By the middle of the nineteenth century, Mills claims, French army women's uniforms had become significantly more sophisticated, resembling the uniform worn by the men in their units, modified

by a more elaborate hat or some other concession to conventional women's clothing such as a shortened skirt with long pants
underneath. Moreover, by the middle of the nineteenth century
French army women frequently carried a small sword and one or
more pistols, took part in marches and parades along with the
soldiers, and received formal pay for their service and formal dec-
orations for their bravery. It is true that by the time of the First
World War women's historical centrality to the military had been
all but forgotten. Nevertheless, for centuries European women
had effectively created a variety of positions for themselves—
some even paramilitary in nature—within the military system.[3]

That they had done so in America as well is made evident by
an 1802 act of Congress which attempted to *limit* women's numbers and to define more rigorously their formal place in the
national army. According to the act, the army's Subsistence
Department was bound to provide rations "to women who may
be allowed to any particular corps," but those women must not
number more than four per company (usually one hundred soldiers) in the corps.[4] This restriction, it appears, grew out of military conditions during the Revolutionary War, during which
George Washington's Continental army veritably teemed with
women, and indeed, "sustaining Washington's army in the field
or in garrison would have been next to impossible" without
them.[5] Continental army women—who usually numbered from
three to six per company—most commonly were the wives,
mothers, and daughters of men in the ranks. They received some
pay and drew rations for themselves and their children, and they
performed a substantial amount of traditional "women's work."
They were also held subject to military discipline, which meant
that they underwent courts-martial and endured punishment
when convicted of specific offenses. According to historian Linda
Grant De Pauw, the orderly book of a general encamped at Valley
Forge in the winter of 1778 notes that one Mary Johnson was
charged, along with a number of other men and women, with

plotting to desert the army. Found guilty, Johnson received a sentence of one hundred lashes and was subsequently "drummed out of the army by all the fifes and drums of the division." The court-martialing of women, De Pauw points out, "is perhaps the clearest evidence of their place in the military establishment." Within the military context, Continental army women typically did more than just "darn stockings and provide home cooked meals." Rather, their main duties most frequently fell with the medical corps and the artillery corps, where they served respectively as matrons and nurses (generally one matron and ten nurses per one hundred wounded in army hospitals), and as water carriers to the gun crews, who had to clean their cannons after each firing before it was safe to reload. In this latter capacity, at least some women moved from being water carriers to actually loading and firing army weapons themselves when the situation demanded it.[6]

Among Continental army women, the two about whom we have the most information are Margaret Cochran Corbin and Mary Ludwig Hays McCauley. Corbin was born in Franklin County, Pennsylvania, in 1751, and orphaned at the age of five when her father, Robert Cochran, was killed and her mother taken permanent hostage in an Indian raid.[7] After spending the rest of her childhood in the care of her mother's brother, in or around 1772 Margaret married Virginia native John Corbin. When John Corbin enlisted in Captain Francis Proctor's 1st Pennsylvania Artillery, Margaret accompanied him to the front. With her husband and his regiment, Corbin soon found herself under fire at the battle of Fort Washington in November 1776, where well-coordinated simultaneous attacks by the British forces compelled the surrender of what was a key strategic point in the Continental army's defenses. Corbin's husband was with the artillery in the thick of battle on the sixteenth of November, and when he fell, tradition has it that Corbin took over for him, loading and firing his cannon in his stead.

One reason why we know about Corbin's actions on the field at Fort Washington is because wounds from grapeshot that she received in the battle were serious enough to deprive her of the use of one of her arms. On June 29, 1779, in recognition of her courage and of the injury she had sustained while under fire, the Supreme Council of the State of Pennsylvania passed a bill in which it acknowledged that Corbin had become disabled while she "heroically filled the post of her husband, who was killed by her side serving a piece of artillery." The council allotted Corbin thirty dollars in immediate relief and also recommended her for consideration by the Continental Congress's Board of War for an increase in her rations. In response to the council's request, and again in recognition of her army service, the Continental Congress subsequently resolved that Corbin should receive, for the rest of her life, a monthly pension amounting to one half of a soldier's pay and, annually, a suit of clothes or its equivalent in money. In 1780 Congress also enrolled Corbin as the only woman in what was called the "Invalid Regiment," which had been created three years earlier and was then stationed at West Point essentially on guard duty. At West Point, Corbin remarried, to a man whose own disability apparently produced even more financial strain for the two as a couple than Corbin had known on her own as a struggling widow. Corbin subsequently petitioned for and received a further increase in her rations—from half to full, and to include the appropriate portion (257 gills per year, or approximately 3 quarts per month) of rum or whiskey, which had been withheld to that point on the grounds that she was a woman. She also received a retroactive allowance for the period during which her rations had stood at 50 percent.

For the rest of her life Corbin depended upon the mercy of the army and some private individuals to provide for her welfare. When the Invalid Regiment was disbanded in 1783, she stayed on in the West Point area, living at Highland Falls, New York, and drawing her supplies from the West Point commissary while also "requiring the ministrations of others for her bodily care."[8] Corbin's cantankerous personality added to her problems, transforming the work of caring for her into quite a chore for those willing to try. Wrote the West Point's Captain William Price to General Henry Knox in 1786: "I am at a loss what to do with Captain Molly. She is such an offensive person that people are unwilling to take her in charge."[9] By the time she died in about 1800, West Point officials and the area residents who had tended to her gratefully recalled Corbin's service to the Continental army at Fort Washington, but they probably also heaved a collective sigh of relief.

As for Mary Ludwig Hays McCauley, the details of her early life are hazy.[10] She seems to have been the daughter of German immigrants to the American colonies who settled either near Trenton, New Jersey, or in Lancaster County, Pennsylvania. Probably born in 1744, Mary was a domestic servant at the home of a Carlisle, Pennsylvania, doctor when she became acquainted with John Hays, a young barber who had a shop nearby. The two married in 1769.

On December 1, 1775, John Hays—like John Corbin—enlisted as a gunner in Proctor's 1st Pennsylvania Artillery. When his initial term of service expired, Hays enlisted in the 7th Pennsylvania Regiment, and so found himself at Monmouth, New Jersey, in June 1778, where the Continentals engaged a British force commanded by Lord Cornwallis in temperatures that exceeded 100 degrees. At some point during the battle, when her husband was wounded in action, Mary Hays took his place at his weapon and "performed some act of unusual heroism," probably functioning—like Corbin—as an emergency gunner herself.[11]

Mary Hays so effectively fulfilled the role of army woman at Monmouth that more than forty years after the battle, the legislature of Pennsylvania responded to her petition for funds with an immediate lump sum of forty dollars as well as a lifetime pension of forty dollars per year. In doing so, the legislators recognized McCauley not as a deserving soldier's widow but as an individual who had performed her own meritorious services during the war. Despite her pension, however, evidence suggests that after her second husband died, Mary Hays McCauley, like Margaret Corbin, struggled to support herself. According to historian Edward Biddle, an old book he found in the Cumberland County, Pennsylvania, Commissioner's office in the 1920s contained a number of entries relating to the daily payments McCauley received from that office for custodial work. An entry dated March 29, 1811 read: "Molly McCalley, for washing and scrubbing the court house, in part—$15.00"; and another from August 15, 1813, noted her payment for "cleaning, washing and whitewashing the public buildings." "These items," Biddle concluded, "furnish authentic information concerning her manner of obtaining a livelihood at that period of her life." Although McCauley spent the last decades of her life doing menial labor, when she died in 1832, obituaries respectfully focused on her contributions to the patriots' cause. "The history of this woman is somewhat remarkable," commented the Carlisle, Pennsylvania, *Herald* on January 26, 1832. McCauley, the article continued, had "acted so much the part of a heroine as to attract the notice of the [Continental army's] officers. Some estimate may be formed of the value of the service by her, when the fact is stated that she drew a pension from the government during the latter years of her life."[12]

Mary Ludwig Hays McCauley and Margaret Cochran Corbin were two among perhaps thousands of army women who served with the Continental army during the American Revolution,[13] and as such were the direct predecessors of the women who traveled with the Union and Confederate armies during the Civil War. Although the term does not seem to have existed during the Revolution, a number of Civil War army women earned the designation "daughter of the regiment" for taking on the manifold and at the same time only vaguely defined responsibilities that fell to army women generally. Most regiments that had a designated "daughter" initially may have conceived of her primarily as a kind of mascot or "guardian angel" and nurse, but as the regiment faced the reality of war, the daughter's role typically expanded to include more concrete tasks, including rallying the soldiers to fight, bearing the regimental colors on the march and sometimes on the field, and even participating in battle herself— for as the stories of Corbin and McCauley demonstrate, the battlefield was indeed a place where individual roles and tasks became less distinct, and all available personnel, regardless of sex, were known to take up arms on occasion.

As in the case of the women who became active in Civil War espionage and resistance, a handful of army women—in this case all from the North—captured an unusual amount of attention both during and immediately after the war for their remarkable courage in the face of battle, their endurance in the face of the hard conditions of the soldier's life, and their tenderness in the face of the war's brutality. These women—the most famous of whom was Annie Etheridge—left behind a cache of evidence about their lives and their work sufficient to reconstruct their stories in considerable detail.

Annie Etheridge was born Lorinda Anna Blair in Detroit, Michigan, in approximately 1840.[14] According to more than one source, Etheridge spent much of her early childhood in comfort and privilege—in Michigan and perhaps also in Wisconsin and Minnesota—until her father either lost or squandered most of the family's resources, plunging them into poverty at about the time Annie reached the age of twelve. In 1860 Annie married James Etheridge and at the outbreak of the Civil War, when James enlisted in the 2nd Michigan Infantry Regiment, Annie followed him.[15] James apparently deserted the army very quickly, but his action did not distract his young wife—described by one contemporary as "about five feet three inches in height, fair complexion . . . brown hair, vigorous constitution, and decidedly good looking"[16]—from

her goal of serving with the Union army. Annie Etheridge promptly transferred to the 3rd Michigan, in which she apparently knew
many of the soldiers, and served as that regiment's "daughter"
until it disbanded three years later. She subsequently reenlisted
with many of the 3rd's veterans in the 5th Michigan, remaining
with this regiment for the duration of the war.

By the end of Annie Etheridge's four years with the Union
army, she was a veteran of a number of the war's most gruesome
engagements and campaigns. Etheridge's devotion to the Union
cause first took her onto the field at Blackburn's Ford, the site of
a vigorous skirmish on July 18, 1861, near Centreville, Virginia,
that preceded the armies' first real contest at Bull Run. Three
days later Etheridge stood with the 3rd Michigan's still-green
troops at the rear of the Union army while other regiments at the
front engaged General P. G. T. Beauregard's and Joseph E.
Johnston's equally green Confederates at Bull Run, and tradition
has it that she was among the first to encounter the badly beaten
men in blue as they retreated in confusion. Sources also locate
Etheridge on the field with her regiment at the battle of
Williamsburg, Virginia, a costly Confederate defeat in May 1862
in which some gray regiments lost half their numbers and the
Union army lost over 2,000 soldiers; at the second battle of Bull
Run in August 1862, a far more severe defeat for Union General
John Pope's Army of Virginia, which was attempting to carry out
General McClellan's advance on Richmond but was instead
forced to retreat after suffering 16,000 casualties (in contrast
with the Confederate army's loss of 9,200); at the crucial battle
of Antietam in September 1862, famous for being not only the
first major turning point of the war but also the war's single
bloodiest day; at Fredericksburg in December 1862, where over
12,000 Union soldiers were wounded or killed in a misguided
assault on a seven-mile-long Confederate line perched on the
heights just outside of town; at Chancellorsville in May and at
Gettysburg in July 1863, in which two battles the combined loss-

es for the Union and Confederate armies numbered close to 80,000; and at Spotsylvania in May 1864, the site of some twenty hours of fighting considered among the most vicious in the entire war.

Through all these mercilessly bloody engagements Etheridge maintained a reputation for bravery, stamina, modesty, patriotism, and kindness. A Maine recruit who described in his journal his first encounter with Etheridge—at Chancellorsville—used language that was echoed by others in their comments about her, and in their comments about other army women as well. "Commenced to rise about daylight," he wrote on May 2, 1863,

> and the first thing that greeted our optics was a female rising up from the ground. It was none other than that heroine of the War, Annie Etheredge [*sic*], and a braver soul cannot be found. She is always on hand and ready to bear the same privations as the men. When danger threatens, she never cringes. At the battle of Fredericksburg she was binding the wounds of a man when a shell exploded nearby, tearing him terribly, and removing a large portion of the skirt of her dress. This morning she was surrounded by soldiers on every side, laying outside with no covering but her blanket, but such lodgings must have been selected voluntarily, for there isn't a man at any of the headquarters who wouldn't gladly surrender his bed and tent to her.[17]

A week later another soldier in the 17th Maine wrote home to his mother from Virginia:

> I saw one young lady in the very front of the battle dressing wounds and aiding the suffering where few Surgeons dared show themselves. That girl is Anna Etheridge, a second—a more than—Florence Nightingale. You may have read of her. She is always to be seen riding her pony at the head of our

Brigade on the march or in the fight. Genl. Berry used to say she had been under as heavy fire as himself.[18]

In addition to serving with her regiment on the field of battle, Etheridge also spent time as a nurse in a Union army hospital and on board a federal hospital transport ship in the winter of 1861–62, and at a City Point, Virginia, army hospital in the fall of 1864. On these stints away from the regiment she met a number of regular army nurses who universally praised her abilities as a caretaker as well as her indomitable, if reserved, temperament. At City Point, Etheridge met Mary Morris Husband, who later described her as "very reticent, with a reserve & apparent pride of manner, toward strangers."[19] Etheridge also encountered Cornelia Hancock, a nurse from New Jersey who wrote home to her family that the by then quite well-known Etheridge was "very bare of clothes. She wants thee to buy her a skirt exactly like mine and two pair of stockings like my old brown ones."[20] Clearly Annie Etheridge had come to the army to work, not to serve as an ornament for the soldiers' visual enjoyment.

According to one source, Etheridge never carried a musket, but like many Civil War daughters of the regiment and army women, she traveled armed, in her case with a pair of pistols that she may or may not have found occasion to use. Etheridge's other equipment included a horse, a sidesaddle and saddlebags filled with lint and bandages for tending the wounded, and a blanket in which she nightly wrapped herself as she made her bed on the hard ground like a soldier. In addition to nursing in the field, apparently with complete disregard for her own safety, during encampments Etheridge did some cooking for the regiment and performed other chores. In further fulfillment of her mission as daughter of the regiment, Etheridge provided encouragement to the soldiers when their energy and their daring waned in battle, riding past trenches and calling on the men within to rise up and beat the rebels, shaming those in retreat into returning to the fray by insisting that if necessary, she herself would lead them back into battle. Of Etheridge's bravery under fire there is little question, as the story told by one of the men who served with her in both the 3rd and the 5th Michigan regiments reveals. "Anna," wrote Daniel G. Crotty, describing an incident during the battle of Deep Bottom, Virginia, in the summer of 1864,

> has remained with the colors, but this time we are up too close to the front line, and unless we get back we may be captured. So we have to do some tall walking to get out of the swamp we have got into. Anna falls back with us in *good order*, but her dress is a little torn by the brush. One of our boys is borne back wounded, our heroine does up his wound. The balls fall thick and fast around her, but she fears them not, and performs her task as cooly as if she was in camp and out of danger.

"I need not mention this one instance," Crotty continued; "hundreds of the same kind could be related of her. She is still with us through thick and thin for the last three years."[21] Indeed, by May 1863, in recognition of her service up to that point, "Gentle Annie" had already received the Kearny Cross, given in memory of General Philip Kearny, killed at the battle of Chantilly, Virginia, in September 1862, to "meritorious and distinguished non-commissioned officers and privates" in his division who consistently held to Kearny's own "high standard of a true and brave soldier."[22] Etheridge may have been wounded once by a bullet grazing her hand; her clothes apparently bore holes from countless shots and bits of shell.

Postwar writers celebrated Etheridge's fine character, her hard work on behalf of the Union army, and her insistence on sharing the same conditions of camp life—hard ground, poor food, inadequate sanitation, and an utter lack of privacy—as the soldiers with whom she served. They consistently recalled the respect she had earned not only among members of her own regiment but among all who knew her. Indeed, in July and again in September 1864, when General Grant attempted to streamline the Union army in Virginia by ordering the removal of all women from military camps in the area, a host of officers ranging as far up as the corps commander signed a petition asking that Grant make an exception in Etheridge's case. "Mrs. Annie Ethridge [*sic*]," wrote G. W. Holmes, captain and provost marshal of the 3rd Division, 2nd Corps, on July 3, "has been with the 3rd Michigan vols. since its organization. This lady has been of great service to the regiment in time of action, in consequence of which the officers and men of the regiment have become extremely attached to her."[23] The petition was ultimately unsuccessful, however, and Grant's order led to Etheridge's temporary sojourn as a nurse at City Point. The petition nevertheless testified vividly to the widely held perception of Etheridge's value to the army, as a caretaker, comrade, and inspiration to the men in the ranks. Wrote one memorialist in 1866: "Were our government to order a gold medal to be given to the woman who has most distinguished herself by heroic courage on the field . . . there can be little doubt that the united voices of the soldiers and of all the army nurses would assign the honor to Anna Etheridge, of Michigan."[24]

Civil War nurse and sanitary-aid activist Mary A. Livermore also remembered Etheridge kindly and with deep respect, recalling that throughout her four years of service Etheridge had fearlessly positioned herself in the thick of battle to inspire her men to deeds of valor; and at least one poet composed a tribute in verse entitled "To Miss Anna Etheridge, the Heroine of the War." In his 1874 memoir, Crotty, who as the 3rd Michigan's color-bearer had carried the regiment's flag into battle, commented on Etheridge's seemingly unparalleled devotion to the regiment, and he conjectured that there were few women who could measure up to the standard she had set for kindness and care, and her willingness to leave home life behind and boldly "cast her lot with the soldiers in the field." In 1899 A. Mulholland St. Clair, who had

*Etching of Annie Etheridge surrounded by grateful Union soldiers.* Reprinted from Linus P. Brockett and Mary C. Vaughan, *Woman's Work in the Civil War* (1867).

*Annie Etheridge after the war, wearing her Kearny Cross.* Courtesy of the Michigan Historical Center, State Archives of Michigan.

served with the 116th Pennsylvania, recalled his own encounter with the "cool and self-possessed" Etheridge at Gettysburg as she "galloped back from the line of battle" on her horse in order to get some information before returning to the front, without seeming to mind the blast of shot and shell. To those who knew her, Etheridge was the embodiment of what a daughter of the regiment should be: brave, constant, tender, possessing nerves of steel, and willing to join the fight as necessary, encourage the men to greater valor, or remain in the rear treating wounds. No tribute, it seemed, was too great for this army woman; no compliment was too grand to signify her true worth.[25]

Etheridge was still with the regiment when the 5th Michigan mustered out on July 17, 1865. Wrote Crotty: "Noble Anna is with us to the last, and her brave womanly spirit brakes [sic] down, and scalding tears trickle down her beautiful bronze face as each of the boys and comrades bid[s] her good-bye."[26] After the war, Etheridge seems to have planned to write an account of her wartime service, which she hoped to sell. Instead, she was kept busy earning her living as a clerk in the United States Pension Office and fulfilling the role of wife to her new husband, Charles E. Hooks, a veteran of the 7th Connecticut Infantry, whom she married in March 1870.[27] In 1886 United States Senator Thomas Palmer oversaw the passage of a bill granting Etheridge—who in 1878 had been removed from her civil service job in the wake of the "petty intrigues" of those who considered others to be needier—a pension of twenty-five dollars per month for her wartime service as the 3rd and then the 5th Michigan's daughter of the regiment. Twenty-five years later, in "very straightened circumstances," Etheridge applied as well for the pension due to her husband, who had died in 1910. Annie Etheridge died in 1913 and was buried in Arlington National Cemetery, an exceptional, and perhaps unprecedented, honor.[28]

In her own time and after, Annie Etheridge was undoubtedly the most famous Civil War army woman. The name of Kady

Brownell, however, also became familiar both to a large number of soldiers and to a popular audience in the years during and after the war.[29] Born in 1842 in a military barracks in Africa, Kady Southwell was the daughter of a Scottish soldier-father and a French mother. Following the early death of her mother, Kady was sent as a child to live with Scottish family friends, the McKinzies, in the United States. As a young woman of eighteen or nineteen, then a weaver living near Providence, Rhode Island, Kady married a millwright named Robert S. Brownell in March 1861, and at the war's outbreak a month later followed him into the sharpshooter division of the 1st Rhode Island Infantry Volunteers, known as the "Mechanics Rifles." When the company reached Washington and Kady Brownell revealed her intention to remain with her husband, none other than Ambrose E. Burnside—then a colonel and the regiment's commander—turned her back. Unrelenting, Kady Brownell appealed to Rhode Island Governor William Sprague for his support. Receiving it, she returned to Washington and rejoined her husband, who, along with Burnside, subsequently gave up all efforts to persuade her to remain in Providence. "From that moment on," writes one source, "she was accepted by every one as a bona fide soldier."[30] Within short order, the 1st Rhode Island named Kady Brownell its daughter of the regiment.

Unlike Annie Etheridge, who seems to have worn a simplified version of standard female dress for the period, Brownell in her capacity as daughter of the regiment and sometimes color-bearer (early on in the war a position typically reserved for men whose courage had identified them as inspirational figures)[31] dressed in a modified military uniform: a light-colored blouse, a knee-length dark-colored full skirt with tasseled sash, trousers and boots. Whereas Etheridge carried two pistols, Brownell carried a sword and a rifle on her belt, and she made a point of learning how to use her weapons, practicing daily with both until she became completely comfortable with them. According to one source, when Brownell's turn came during regular target practice, her comrades were so impressed with her steady hand and attitude that they let her fire as often as she wanted. As for her use of the sword, over time Brownell made certain that "no soldier in the regiment was her equal at a slashing sabre stroke."[32] A hearty woman "of good sound physical health"[33]—described as about five feet tall, with a dark complexion, dark hair, and blue eyes—Brownell, like Etheridge, approached army life with good cheer, expecting no special favors in deference to her sex, living and marching with the men and facing the enemy's fire without complaint.

Brownell's first combat experience came quickly. Like Etheridge, she was present with her regiment when the Union and Confederate armies engaged one another for the first time in the chaotic first battle of Bull Run. From the start, Brownell made it clear that she did not intend to be a "mere water-carrier, nor an ornamental appendange,"[34] and instead marched side by side with her husband as the troops moved south from Washington through the blistering July heat into Virginia. According to tradition, when the battle commenced at mid-morning on the twenty-first of July, Brownell positioned herself as guard over the regimental flag so as to provide a rallying point for her men, remaining there throughout the day as the two equally disorganized armies struggled for advantage. Brownell held her position even during the late-afternoon collapse of the Union troops into a confused retreat, when the frantic boys in blue stumbled over a number of civilian spectators in their rush back to Washington. It took a soldier from a Pennsylvania regiment more cool-headed than those on the run to drag her to safety, whereupon she began a search for her husband, whom she found unharmed.

Not long after Bull Run, in August 1861 the 1st Rhode Island disbanded and Kady and Robert Brownell returned with the regiment to Providence, where each received a regular army discharge. Undaunted by the Union rout they had witnessed, however, the two decided to reenlist in the reorganized 5th Rhode

*Kady Brownell, dressed and armed as she would have been when she traveled with the 1st and 5th Rhode Island Infantries.* Reprinted from Frank Moore, *Women of the War* (1866).

Island Infantry in October. With this regiment they went on to participate in Burnside's capture of the island of Roanoke, Virginia, in February 1862, and also in his campaign to occupy New Bern, North Carolina, a month later. Having marched with the troops to New Bern through many miles of mud, and undoubtedly believing that she had proven her mettle at Bull Run, Brownell hoped that she might be allowed to serve formally as the regiment's color-bearer during the anticipated battle there. As it turns out, she seems to have received permission to carry the flag in front of the troops only up to the point in time when the soldiers received their orders to charge the enemy.

Although bearing the colors was a great honor, Brownell's more important service to her regiment at New Bern seems to have been an act that witnesses later claimed saved the lives of a great number of her comrades. According to one account, just as a number of Union regiments were getting into their battle positions on the morning of March 14, members of the 5th Rhode Island came out of a clump of woods from an unexpected direction, giving the appearance that they might be a disguised rebel force preparing to attack. Realizing that a misunderstanding might lead the regiments already in line to open fire, and with no fear for her own safety, tradition has it that Brownell—who had moved to the rear as ordered—ran forward into clear view of those already in place, carrying her regiment's flag and waving it wildly until the 5th Rhode Island soldiers' identity became clear to the surrounding regiments. Minutes later, with her comrades momentarily safe from friendly fire at least, Brownell returned to the rear and took up the work of caring for the wounded. Years later a *New York Times* reporter interviewed Brownell about the events at New Bern. "That fight was short, sharp, and sweet," the reporter quoted Brownell as saying.

> Whew!—it was hot while it lasted. I was in it from beginning
> to end until my husband got the rifle ball which crippled him

for life. I was in an exposed position. It was necessary, you see, to inspire the men. Whenever they saw me they rallied around me. I felt that the sight of a woman might inspire them, and I think it did.[35]

At least one contemporary account indicates that Brownell actually failed to abide by the order at New Bern that she remain in the rear. Rather, wrote the author of an August 1862 article in the feminist reform journal *The Sibyl*, in addition to being "on the field during the whole of the engagement, attending to the wounded, and giving encouragement by her fortitude and presence to the soldiers," Brownell also seized the flag of another Union regiment when its color-bearer fell in battle, carrying it across the field and herself possibly being wounded in the effort.[36]

It bears note that, unlike in the case of Etheridge, the precise nature and the significance of Brownell's service to her regiment and her army at the battle of New Bern became the subject of some dispute after the war. Early in 1866 a former officer of another Rhode Island regiment who had been present at New Bern responded to a query about Brownell with the claim that he was unaware that she had done anything particularly brave there, though he admitted having seen her attending to the wounded with great care. Another, formerly a captain of a 5th Rhode Island company, similarly asserted that from what he himself had seen he did not think that Brownell had done anything special during the battle, though he agreed that he had heard many stories to that effect. A third, also a former captain in the 5th Rhode Island, challenged the account that had been published in a number of newspapers describing Brownell's exceptional bravery on the field at New Bern, though he too admitted that she deserved high praise for her care of the sick and wounded; that she would certainly have distinguished herself in battle had she been allowed to; and that when he had ordered her to the rear following her several requests to be allowed to carry the flag at the head of the regiment even into the heat of the battle, she had only reluctantly complied.[37]

If these former comrades-in-arms were purposely downplaying the martial quality of Brownell's service at New Bern, their reasons for doing so are not clear. Perhaps they were simply honorably seeking to limit any postwar romanticization of the events at New Bern in which Brownell had participated. Perhaps they had become so accustomed to army women's diverse acts of bravery in the field that they saw no reason to single Brownell out, or perhaps they felt that Brownell's extreme courage in the field somehow left their own courage in doubt. In any case, stories of her soldierlike actions at New Bern and elsewhere persisted determinedly alongside such challenges. As in the case of Annie Etheridge, postwar writers liberally praised Kady Brownell for her devoted service to the Union and her courage under fire, and like Etheridge, Brownell inspired at least one poem which memorialized her many contributions to the Union cause, including her quick-witted and lifesaving action at New Bern.[38] Stories of Brownell's paramilitary accomplishments were in fact instrumental in earning her a government pension: J. M. Wheeler, who himself had challenged Brownell's reputation in 1866, twenty years later came to her defense in connection with her pension application, asserting that Brownell had indeed carried the flag at the head of the regiment at New Bern, and that she had also saved the lives of many Union soldiers in much the same manner she was reputed to have done: rushing forward to identify them as Yankees just when it appeared that they might be attacked by friendly fire. Whatever the precise details of her actions at the battle of New Bern, even this former skeptic acknowledged that Brownell's behavior there, in her capacity as daughter of the regiment, had earned her special recognition in the form of a government pension.[39]

Robert's wound at New Bern brought both of the Brownells' military careers to an end. Once Robert was able to travel, the couple received a transfer, first to Rhode Island and then to New

York, where Robert convalesced for several months at the Soldier's Relief Hospital, during which time his wife tended to him personally. Early in 1863, when it became clear that Robert would not fight again, both Brownells received their discharges from the army. Writing in 1889, Mary Livermore claimed that Kady Brownell then retired with her husband "to private life and domestic duty."[40] In fact, despite Robert's invalid pension from the army and his jobs first at the New York Steam Engine Works Factory, then as manager of an estate on East Seventy-sixth Street, and then as a patrolman for the Department of Public Works, Kady and her husband found it difficult to make ends meet, moving from one residence to another and pouring a substantial portion of their money into the payment of medical bills.

By 1884, after several years of teetering on the edge of impoverishment, Kady Brownell determined to apply for a small government pension of eight dollars per month in her own name, which she received. Still the Brownells struggled financially, and in 1895, recognizing that their survival increasingly depended on her labor, Kady Brownell took a civil service examination that qualified her for a job as a matron at the New York City Park Department's headquarters. She continued at the Park Department for ten years, and then in 1905 accepted the job of custodian at the formerly plush Jumel mansion in Washington Heights. Kady and Robert moved into an apartment on the top floor of the mansion, and it was there in 1913 that she received a *New York Times* reporter who had taken an interest in her story. This reporter went on to publish a moving account of the Brownells' situation, in which he described Kady Brownell's careful preservation of her war souvenirs, notably the "togs which she had worn on long marches and in murderous battles," a "tarnished and torn" bit of the bullet-ridden flag she had carried, and a framed letter from General Burnside, dated 1868, in which he attested to her "devotion to the cause of the Union," her instrumentality in saving "many worthy officers and soldiers from death," and the full "gratitude and respect" accorded to her by "all of the officers under whose command she was placed."[41] Two years after this article appeared, on January 5, 1915, Kady Brownell died at a Woman's Relief Corps Home in Oxford, New York, at the age of seventy-two. Robert carried on without her for several months, applying in vain for a reimbursement from the government for the expenses he had incurred during Kady's last sickness and burial, and for an increase in his own twenty-four-dollar-per month veteran's pension. He died in September.

We know a reasonable amount about the lives of Annie Etheridge and Kady Brownell both before and after the war. Unfortunately, the same is not the case for another well-known daughter of the regiment, the 1st Michigan Cavalry's Bridget Divers (alternately "Deavers," "Devens," and "Devins").[42] In fact, we know virtually nothing about Divers before the war except that she was an Irish immigrant of modest social origins who in her early twenties joined the recently organized cavalry regiment, probably with her husband and possibly also with a child. Once the war began to be fought in earnest, however, Divers's name became widely known in her regiment and in the brigade to which the regiment belonged. In addition, her activities on behalf of those with whom she served brought her to the attention of numerous others within and outside the military.

Familiarly dubbed "Irish Biddy" or "Michigan Bridget" by those who knew her best, daughter of the regiment Divers, like Brownell and Etheridge, became famous for her exceptionally high level of concern for the soldiers she identified as being under her care. Various accounts exist of a particular incident towards the end of the war in which Divers revealed her dedication and loyalty to her men. The occasion was a raid in which the 1st Michigan Cavalry participated under General Philip Sheridan's command, and during which the regiment's colonel was wounded and its captain killed. After the raid was over, despite the fact that she herself had gone virtually without sleep for several days, Divers tended as best she could to the wounds of the colonel before accompanying him by train to a hospital at City Point. Divers then rested briefly at City Point before returning to the front, only to discover that the body of the regiment's dead captain had been left on the field. Enlisting the help of an orderly, Divers took her horse fifteen miles into rebel territory to rescue the captain's body, which she then slung over the back of her horse and brought back to City Point. There, she obtained a coffin and saw to the body's shipment home to Michigan. Rebecca Usher, a nurse from Maine who met Divers at City Point, wrote home to her sister about the events that had brought Divers there. "I saw a few days since Bridget Devins," wrote Usher,

> who has been with the 1st Mich. Cav. ever since they came out. She had just come in with the body of a Cpt. She had the body bound to her horse & took him 15 miles on horse back & then came with him in the cars[,] procured a coffin & sent him home. She says it is the hardest battle they have had & the ground was covered with the wounded & no one to take care of them. She had not slept for 48 hours, having worked incessantly dressing wounds.[43]

Usher was not the only Civil War nurse to encounter Divers at City Point. There, she met Mary Morris Husband and Cornelia Hancock (both of whom also met Annie Etheridge), and Charlotte E. McKay. All three nurses reported favorably on the experience, but McKay's comments were particularly respectful. Divers, she wrote after their meeting,

> has probably seen more of the danger and hardship than any other woman during the war. She has been riding with the cavalry all the time, going out with them on their cavalry raids— always ready to succor the wounded on the field—often getting men off who, but for her, would be left to die, and fearless of shell or bullet among the last to leave. Protected by officers and respected by privates . . . she makes her home in the sad-

dle or the shelter tent; often sleeping in the open without a tent, and by her courage and devotion, "winning golden opinions from all sorts of people."[44]

Bridget Divers became widely known for her valiant efforts on behalf of the wounded, for her courage under fire in battle, and—like Etheridge and Brownell—for her willingness to position herself in such a way as to generate among the men in the ranks the greatest enthusiasm that they could muster for the fight. One former comrade-in-arms described an incident at the June 1862 battle of Fair Oaks, Virginia, a tactical victory for the Union, but one whose substantial casualties—five thousand for the Union and over six thousand for the Confederacy—are said to have been instrumental in further unnerving the already tentative McClellan. That day, wrote G. Foster White a year after the war, Union soldiers were busy eating their lunch when rebels let loose their first volley, following it with a heavy barrage of fire. Surprised by this sudden attack, many of the soldiers in blue nevertheless sprang to arms, but a number of them became panic-stricken and apparently resistant to all attempts to rally them. When the order to advance came, it was met with an unenthusiastic response—until Divers came into view. Taking her soldier's cap in her hand, Divers

swang it in the air and shouted "Arrah." Go in Boys and bate [beat] Hell out of them. and rivinge me Husband [who had apparently died in battle] God be wid ye, which pluck brought a laugh and shots. which cheered us up, and with 3 Cheers for "Irish Biddy" and the 7th [Massachusetts] we went forward and with the 10th Mass and other Troops drove the enemys center back and held them for sometime.

On this occasion as on many others, Divers's "enthusiasm and pluck," White noted, "cheered us up and sent us fo[r]ward with a hearty good will." [45]

Descriptions of Divers portray her as a modest, unaffected, and

*Etching depicting Bridget Divers, bearing the colors in the thick of battle.*
Reprinted from Mary Livermore, *My Story of the War* (1889).

robust woman of unsurpassed fortitude, enthusiasm, kindness, and courage, who reportedly dressed in a "plain cassock" and a soldier's cap while traveling with the army, and who over time developed the athletic body and tanned complexion of a veteran soldier. In addition to her contributions as a nurse, her inspirational acts on behalf of her regiment, and her services as essentially a substitute soldier when the need arose (Divers earned a reputation as an expert equestrienne who had had more than one horse shot out from under her), those who knew her claimed that she also performed a special function for her regiment—as well as for the division to which the regiment belonged—as a "living directory" of soldiers' names, needs, and military records. According to J. R. Miller, formerly a field agent for the soldiers' aid organization the United States Christian Commission, when inquiries about men in her regiment or division came to the various wartime relief commissions, Divers was always the first to be contacted, for she could "give all the desired information" as her "memory of names and places was truly wonderful." And, he added, "Her whole soul was in her work. No day was too stormy or too cold for her. She encountered all obstacles, and battled successfully every discouragement in the prosecution of her duties." According to Miller, on occasion Divers even fancied herself an acting chaplain for the regiment. She seemed, he wrote, "to take a very deep interest in the spiritual condition of the men, and to understand her work in this line even better than many chaplains, and certainly had more zeal than too many of them."[46]

Given the degree to which Divers's name was known during the war, it is especially surprising that we know so little of what became of her in its aftermath. Accounts agree, however, that Divers had grown accustomed to army life and thus chose to remain with the military in a detachment that traveled west after the war to advance and defend the frontier. Beyond this, however, we know nothing, although it is safe to conclude that Divers's postwar life was one of hard work and hard military service. However much she enjoyed army life with all its adventures, as was true for Etheridge and Brownell, Divers's postwar years were not likely years of leisure.

Two other Civil War army women have left sufficient records to permit a reasonable retelling of their stories. The first of these is Arabella ("Belle") Reynolds, the wife of an enlisted man who eventually rose to the rank of colonel. As with Etheridge, Brownell, and Divers, postwar writers universally extolled Reynolds's contributions to the Union army's (and her particular regiment's) welfare. Although we have no record of Reynolds engaging in any military or paramilitary activities per se, nevertheless, as with the others, her eager assumption of the unofficial role of nurse to her regiment, and her untiring execution of other self-imposed duties, made her a source of inspiration to the men whom she tended. As a result, about a year into the war, various officials decided to express their gratitude by distinguishing Reynolds officially as the 17th Illinois Infantry's daughter of the regiment.[47]

Arabella Macomber was born in Shelburne Falls, Massachusetts, in 1843. When she was fourteen years old, she moved with her family to unsettled Iowa, from whence she returned briefly to Massachusetts in order to complete her education before becoming a schoolteacher in Iowa's Cass County. In 1860 Belle Macomber married John G. Reynolds, with whom she moved to Peoria, Illinois. When the war broke out, John enlisted immediately in the 17th Illinois and his wife decided to go with him. She was then eighteen years old, and according to one source, numerous friends and relatives sought to convince her of the folly of her undertaking, but to no avail. Reynolds arrived in the camp of the 17th Illinois on August 11, 1861, and three days later—after overcoming (as Kady Brownell had done) some resistance from the regiment's colonel—headed with them to the front.

Described in one source as "tall, handsome, and vivacious,"[48] Reynolds seems to have won the hearts of the soldiers of the 17th very quickly, though her own initial impression of army life was rather grim. After the war, Reynolds composed a sketch of her wartime experiences which included a reminiscence of her first taste of camp life, and which appeared—undoubtedly somewhat revised by the volume's editor, Frank Moore—in an 1866 compilation of stories about Union women's involvement in the war. Reynolds's account reminds readers that the life of an army woman during the Civil War was not exclusively one of excitement and rewarding adventure. "How could I stay in such a cheerless place?" she asked herself while bivouacked with the 17th Illinois at Bird's Point, Missouri. "No floors, no chairs, the narrow cot my seat, my feet imbedded in the hot sand, the confusion of camp close around me, with but the thickness of cloth between me and the eyes of all, the scorching August sun streaming through the low-roofed covering,—it seemed almost too much to endure; but I resolved to make the trial."[49]

And make the trial she did, despite her initial uncertainty. As she settled into army life, Reynolds readily took up the work of

*Belle Reynolds.* Reprinted from Frank Moore, *Women of the War* (1866).

caring for the regiment's sick and wounded, sewing for them, and sending letters to newspapers on the home front informing readers of ways in which they might contribute to the health and well-being of the men in the field. When the regiment moved, Reynolds moved with them, sometimes riding in an army wagon, ambulance, or on the back of a mule, sometimes marching beside the troops carrying a musket. Reynolds followed the 17th Illinois into garrison duty and into battle: as with Etheridge and the others, sources identify Reynolds with a number of important battles and campaigns. With her regiment she traveled the Mississippi River in connection with General Grant's successful campaigns against Forts Henry and Donelson in early 1862. From there she and her regiment moved on to the great battle of Shiloh, Tennessee, in April, where the vicious fighting that took place over the course of two days produced by far the worst casualty figures in the war up to that point (thirteen thousand for the

Union and over ten thousand for the Confederacy) and forced both the North and the South into a realization of the cost that the Civil War would ultimately exact. In the spring and early summer of 1863, Reynolds's regiment participated in the Union forces' steady bombardment of the Confederate garrison at Vicksburg, Mississippi, which was desperately—and unsuccessfully—defended by General John C. Pemberton and twenty thousand troops seriously debilitated by hunger and disease. Throughout her tenure with the 17th, which lasted until the fall of 1864, Reynolds—like Etheridge and the others—refused any privileges, eating the same food as the soldiers, sleeping on the ground, drinking water from pools and brooks along the way, and never complaining, even on marches forty or fifty miles in length. By the spring of 1862, one source notes, Reynolds was already "almost a veteran, used to tent life and hardened to long days on the march."[50]

Historical memory of Reynolds's wartime service is dominated by her experiences on board the hospital ship the *Emerald*, which docked at Pittsburg Landing on the Tennessee River after the battle of Shiloh in order to transport farther to the north the Union soldiers who were most in need of medical care. "Soon the wounded came pouring in upon us," she wrote, "and for thirty-six hours we found no rest." Not only did Reynolds exhaust herself in tending to hundreds of soldiers in the wake of the great battle, but she claimed also to have found herself in the unwelcome position of trying to prevent retreating soldiers from storming the *Emerald* in a frantic attempt to escape the field of slaughter. Under orders from an army captain, Reynolds stationed herself on the ship's "hurricane deck" with a revolver in hand, turning back hordes of desperate men who were bent on boarding the *Emerald* no matter what. Fortunately, additional gunboats and fresh troops arrived in time to bring some relief. Still, the scene at Pittsburg Landing was one of chaos. When night fell, Reynolds recalled, none were "calm, and free from distracting anxiety and pain, save the long ranks of dead,"[51] and morning found Reynolds still hard at work nursing the wounded who continued to be brought in from the field. Hours later she was relieved to meet up with her husband, of whose fate in the battle she had heard nothing.

It was in response to Reynolds's service with the 17th Illinois at Shiloh that officials chose to commemorate her devotion to the regiment. On April 16, 1862, just over a week after the battle, Governor of Illinois Richard Yates signed a document formally identifying Reynolds as the 17th's daughter of the regiment and recognizing that her "meritorious conduct in camp and on the bloody field of Pittsburg Landing" had earned her an honorary commission as a "major."[52] As it was written, the commission brought with it both responsibilities and rights. Reynolds, wrote Yates, must continue to perform the duties associated with the office of regimental daughter and obey all orders received from her superior officers; at the same time, she should expect the obedience of "all officers and soldiers under her command." Notably, the commission left the details of Reynolds's future service vague, in line with the typically open-ended nature of the role of an army woman. As in the case of spies Antonia Ford and Pauline Cushman, Reynolds's commission as a major was essentially honorary and did not alter her place in the official chain of army command. Still, it acknowledged in an important and rewarding way the value of her services to the army and the Union cause, and it can only have made its subject proud.

When Yates confirmed Reynolds's status as the 17th Illinois's daughter of the regiment, he meant to commend in a formal way her courageous service as a nurse and as a source of inspiration and motivation to the soldiers of her own regiment and others. He did not, however, cast her in the paramilitary light we associate with other Civil War army women and daughters of the regiment. Indeed, the evidence strongly suggests that Reynolds was not particularly comfortable performing duties that had a more soldierlike quality to them, though she clearly held her own in the defense of the *Emerald*. We have no accounts of her carrying the regiment's colors on the march or in battle, or rallying the troops in the field when their own courage ebbed. In contrast, a story has persisted which suggests that although Reynolds was not in the least bit cowardly, she was also not battlewise in the way we understand Etheridge, Brownell, and Divers to have been. According to Reynolds's own sketch of her wartime service, after her husband departed for the battlefield at Shiloh, she and another army woman, identified only as "Mrs. N," but presumably also the wife of a soldier, took their time packing their trunks in preparation for leaving camp, despite the fact that the enemy had clearly drawn very near. Eventually a wagon master came upon the women and urged them to run for cover, which they did, briefly taking refuge—or so they thought—in a deserted tent they believed to be at a safe distance from the action. In fact, it was not: soon the regiment's quartermaster found Reynolds and Mrs. N. and insisted that they evacuate. When the women finally made it to the *Emerald*, they took up the task of caring for the wounded.

Although Reynolds may not have been drawn to perform acts of military valor on the battlefield, the soldiers with whom she served remembered her courage nonetheless. "Hundreds of soldiers," wrote General Grant's adjutant, John Rawlins, to Governor Yates after Shiloh, "will never forget the work of charity and bravery that Mrs. Reynolds is doing, single-handed, these days. I know of no woman who is helping the sick and melancholy soldier boys like this brave young woman—scarcely more than a schoolgirl."[53] Years later General Lewis Wallace, who had commanded a division at Shiloh, wrote that "the Union troops . . . blessed the day that the wife of Col. John G. Reynolds came among them."[54]

Reynolds remained with her husband and her regiment until the fall of 1864, with perhaps only one short break following Shiloh when she traveled home to Peoria to rest. The 1863 Vicksburg campaign was the last one in which Reynolds saw active service. Sometime after Vicksburg fell to the federal forces, John Reynolds's enlistment expired and the two retired from military life. At some point in the next two decades, they moved to California, for by 1891 Belle Reynolds (her husband's fate is unknown) was living in Santa Barbara and was a familiar face among veterans living in the West, in consequence of having attended a number of veterans' reunions and encampments all across the region for several years. According to an 1898 article in the *Washington Post*, when President Benjamin Harrison visited Santa Barbara, California, in 1891, he "paid more attention to Major Belle Reynolds than to any of the hundreds of political leaders and rich men of California who gathered around him."[55] Clearly Reynolds did not consider her years of military service insignificant; neither did those to whom her name and her wartime contributions to the Union were familiar.

Army woman Belle Reynolds's designation as daughter of the regiment for the 17th Illinois came a year after her service to the Union army began. As for the last of the five best-known army women of the Civil War—the Russian émigré Nadine Turchin—she never received a formal designation as daughter of the regiment at all, though her valiant service on her regiment's behalf is well documented.[56] Like Kady Brownell, the former Nedezhda Lvova was born into military life. The daughter of a Russian army officer, Nadine was raised in military camps in Europe. Her husband, John B. Turchin (born Ivan Vasilevitch Turcheninov), was also of Russian extraction and may have been a subordinate officer in her father's army when Nadine met him. Nadine and John married in what was then Cracow, Russia, in May 1856, soon thereafter immigrating to the United States, where they settled in Illinois. By 1858 the Turchins were living in the town of

Mattoon and John was working for the Illinois Central Railroad as an engineer. It was in connection with his job at the Illinois Central that John met George McClellan—then a vice president of the railroad company—who may have seen to John's June 1861 appointment as colonel in command of the 19th Illinois Infantry.[57] In any case, in the wake of her husband's appointment, Nadine Turchin decided to follow John into the field.

The precise nature of Nadine Turchin's contributions to the Union war effort is difficult to tease out, at least until May 1863, when she began to keep a regular diary. We know that at the time Nadine Turchin joined the 19th Illinois with her husband she was already thirty-five years old, making her considerably older than Etheridge, Brownell, Divers, or Reynolds. Indeed, it is likely that Nadine Turchin's maturity allowed her to serve more effectively as the regiment's figurehead "mother," its compassionate maternal representative, than as its inspirational, battle-ready "daughter." How much of an active motherly role Nadine Turchin assumed in relation to the troops under her husband's command is also not certain, although there is strong evidence to suggest that in the first years of the war she spent a good deal of her time as a caretaker for the sick and wounded, and towards the middle of the war she belatedly received a formal designation as a regimental nurse. Certainly the soldiers in the 19th Illinois felt deeply grateful to her for her services on this score: "Dear Madame Turchin!" recalled one former member of the regiment years later; "how we all respected, believed in, and came to love her for her bravery, gentleness and constant care of the sick and wounded in the Regiment."[58]

From mid-1863 on, however, although she continued to devote a measure of her time and energy to the common soldiers, Nadine Turchin increasingly focused her attention on her own husband's physical and emotional needs as he rose through the ranks, serving above all as his personal mainstay and companion in camp and on the march. Perhaps surprisingly, this shift in her concentration did not decrease the respect of the men who surrounded her. Wrote then Senator J. B. Foraker, who had served with Turchin, in 1901:

> Mrs. Turchin . . . accompanied Gen. Turchin on his campaigns. I knew her as his wife, and every man who belonged to his brigade admired her as much as they admired the General. She was with him constantly in the field, shared with him all the privations of the camp and all the dangers of the battle. She ought to have a pension for her personal services. . . .[59]

In his 1902 petition for a pension for Nadine Turchin, a former captain of the 61st Illinois named S. T. Carrico similarly emphasized her loyalty to her husband, insisting that such loyalty "deserves at least the recognition that . . . [they] get who never saw a live or dead rebel, or fired a gun who draw $12.00 per month for 'Inability to Perform Manual Labor,' which in many cases is an infernal lie."[60]

In addition to the evidence of her ongoing work as a nurse and of her late-war focus on her husband's physical welfare, there are a number of stories, however, that gained common currency both during and after the war regarding Nadine Turchin's displays of military acumen and valor, particularly early on in the conflict. The most famous of these stories claims that in the spring of 1862 when the 19th Illinois was on the march into Tennessee, John Turchin became very ill and for several days had to travel by ambulance. While her husband was incapacitated, the story goes, Nadine Turchin took his place as regimental commander and, "while ministering kindly and tenderly to her husband," provided leadership to his men that was "so judicious that no complaint or mutiny was manifested, and her commands were obeyed with the utmost promptness."[61] Writing of the same incident, another source insisted that Nadine Turchin was "not one whit behind her husband in courage or military skill"; that she was "utterly devoid of fear" on the battlefield; and that on at least one occasion, "manifesting perfect indifference to shot or shell, or minie-balls, even when they fell thickly around her, she led the troops into action, facing the hottest fire, and fought bravely at their head." Only when John Turchin was sufficiently recovered so as to resume command of the regiment, the account continued, did Nadine return to the care of the sick and the wounded.[62]

Despite the loyalty of the troops to the wife of their commander and their likely respect for her lifelong association with the military, it seems quite improbable that Nadine Turchin would have been permitted (even informally) to assume full command of her husband's regiment in battle. It is important to note, however, that as with Etheridge and the others, tales of Nadine Turchin's military savvy, daring, and occasional assertion of authority circulated for years after the war. "It is a matter of record," wrote the author of a 1902 newspaper article about her, "that Mrs. Turchin, in Paint Rock valley, between Winchester, Tenn., and Larkinsville, Ala., went back and brought up a section of artillery, and directed the fire on the bushwhackers, who were mercilessly peppering the federals from the rocks of the mountainside." At another time, the writer continued,

> when there was a threatened stampede of the wagon train bearing the ammunition of the Union forces, Mrs. Turchin drew a revolver, stood in the road, and commanded the teamster at the head of the train to throw his wagon across the road to blockade the train, so as to hold the ammunition.[63]

Such stories persisted, like the accounts of Brownell's paramilitary actions at New Bern, suggesting that at least during the early months of her association with the 19th Illinois, Nadine Turchin, too, had demonstrated her willingness to assume the role of a soldier when the need arose. In contrast, her diary attests to the fact that from May 1863 on, although she remained as close as she could to her husband in all of his movements, Nadine Turchin kept well behind the lines of battle and was even concerned that she should keep a discreet distance from the troops. Describing the grisly two-day battle at Chickamauga in Tennessee in September 1863 she noted: "I left my husband, as I never stay among the troops except when it is impossible to do otherwise, I remained with the train. . . ." And after Union General Joseph ("Fighting Joe") Hooker's foggy "Battle Above the Clouds" at Lookout Mountain, Tennessee, two months later she wrote pointedly: "I remained at general headquarters, having no contact with the troops, except when absolutely necessary."[64]

What seems most likely from all this is that in the first months of the war Nadine Turchin took a more active and perhaps even occasionally military or paramilitary role with her regiment, and that, like Brownell at New Bern, she only retreated to the rear when she was finally ordered to do so in no uncertain terms. To answer the question of why her behavior might have changed midway through the war, however, requires familiarity with her husband's war record. As it turns out, although he would later be remembered as "one of the grandest men of Illinois" and "one of the most active officers in the service,"[65] during the summer of 1862 John Turchin's reputation and his future as an army officer were in doubt. In July he faced a court-martial to determine the validity of a series of charges that included neglect of duty in maintaining military discipline, conduct unbecoming an army officer and gentleman, and disobedience of orders. The primary focus of the court-martial was Turchin's apparent failure to maintain control over his troops, resulting in their trespassing of army regulations forbidding foraging, plundering, and pillaging while they were in Athens, Alabama, some weeks earlier. But the charge of disobeying orders also included a direct reference to Nadine: specification 4 of the third charge noted that Turchin had violated general orders that had been issued that spring for the army's Department of the

Ohio (which at that point included Ohio, Indiana, Illinois, Michigan, Wisconsin, the Cumberland Gap, and much of Kentucky) forbidding military wives to follow their men—soldiers or officers—into the field. Although he pleaded not guilty to everything else, Turchin could not deny this charge. The court subsequently found him guilty on all counts except that of conduct unbecoming a gentleman, and sentenced him to dismissal from the service.[66] Within short order, however, President Lincoln overruled the court's decision and simultaneously promoted John Turchin to the rank of brigadier general.[67] Still, it represents no great leap of logic to deduce that her husband's close call with an embarrassing dismissal from the army probably inclined Nadine Turchin thenceforth to take shelter at the rear of her regiment from prying political eyes, especially if she had been too active in the front early on, and to downplay any of her previous activities in the field.[68]

By the time he left the army in the fall of 1864, John Turchin had served not only as commander of the 19th Illinois but also as commander of the Army of Ohio's 8th Brigade of Infantry, and the Army of the Cumberland's 2nd Brigade of Cavalry, 1st Brigade of Infantry, and 3rd Brigade of Infantry.[69] Through it all, Nadine Turchin was there, and her diary reveals that despite (or perhaps because of) her long-standing familiarity with and affinity for army life, the frequent changes in her husband's assignments thoroughly annoyed her. She was, for example, entirely unimpressed with the quality of the cavalry division put under General Turchin's command in the spring of 1863, and confided in her journal that the division was "in deplorable shape—injured horses, half of the regiments ignorant of training rules or tactics"—requiring her husband to spend at least three months getting them ready for action. Later, when John Turchin was returned to an infantry command, his wife expressed anger that he had accepted the assignment "with perfect equanimity" despite what appeared to be a demotion.[70]

Perhaps more important than her predictable disgruntlement about what seemed to be a disrespect for her husband's abilities as a commander and a soldier, was Nadine Turchin's total boredom with her own life during this period. Reading her diary, it becomes vividly clear that Nadine Turchin was a woman who liked and was accustomed to action. Indeed, she complained regularly about her "monotonous and boring daily routine," which provoked "the same moral exhaustion that overwhelms you when you are tied up irrevocably to an unsympathetic milieu." The controversy that had threatened the military career of her husband left her tired, "broken and exhausted," but the dullness of her daily existence was absolutely crushing. While in camp she occasionally did needlework, read newspapers, took horseback rides, and chatted with the men around her, but she was struck by the fact that such seemingly unimportant pastimes amounted to little more than "an insignificant use of a woman's day." "I begin to long for one thing alone," she wrote on one occasion: "rest, oblivion, peace of daily life—welcome forerunner to the eternal rest of death"—although "God knows," she added, "that such an attitude is not in my nature, for I would rather live a few years of life exuberant, full, brilliant, than a long existence of dull inertia." Nadine Turchin yearned for more purposeful labor. "My life here is idle and useless," she wrote. "This life is rude, noisy, filled with din and violent sensations, and yet it is empty and purposeless. For, all in all, I do not see any clear goal before me." Nadine was glad of the opportunity to provide for her husband in a variety of ways: "I can watch over his needs every day," she wrote in September 1863 while encamped near Chattanooga, Tennessee, "and I am there to take care of him in case he should be wounded." Above all, however, she yearned to follow the troops. "Yesterday I went along with the infantry for the first time this year," she wrote happily on August 2, 1863. When she was able, Nadine Turchin got as close to the battlefield as she considered both physically and politically safe. During the battle of Chickamauga, she at one point rode her horse to within visual range of the fight, then climbed up into some trees to watch until she was discovered and told to get farther to the rear. Most of the time, however, she remained on the periphery of the battles in which her husband and his troops were engaged.[71]

Fortunately for posterity, however, Nadine's boredom led her to spend a good chunk of her time writing in her diary, and her entries—many of them lengthy—display considerable thought. Although it is clearly unreasonable to extrapolate too freely from one woman's words the mentality of other women who similarly traveled with the Civil War armies, Nadine Turchin's diary does provide insights into her state of mind over the course of an extended association with the Civil War military. We know, for example, that she fretted about her own moments of inaction no more than she did about those of the army she and her husband served. In May 1863 she wrote, "It is inconceivable that the army does not march. What are they doing?" In early June she expressed irritation with the army's continuing indolence: "The same dull inaction," she wrote, "the same stagnation in spite of the most formidable situation, the same scattering of troops." A few days later she grumbled that the "great Army of the Potomac and its heroic chief [at that point Joseph Hooker] are lying quiet, as if they could do nothing else for the country but live in tents and do some training." When General Robert E. Lee's Confederate Army of Northern Virginia invaded Pennsylvania in June 1863, Nadine Turchin wrote with irony: "Hurrah for our friends, the enemies! A few more strikes of this kind, and perhaps you shall succeed in waking us up."[72]

Of course, John Turchin's troops did see battle, and Nadine was powerfully moved by the experience. Of one confrontation she wrote, "It was a thrilling spectacle. . . . It was great, it was beautiful. From this scene one could understand the somber and terrifying poetry of combat." She also revealed herself to be an eager student of military tactics and strategy. "I am most anxious to see the army of the Republic in action," she wrote while stationed at Murfreesboro, Tennessee, in June 1863.

> Yet, I say again and again: if Burnside withdraws [from southern Kentucky] in order to join forces with Grant, the army of [General William S.] Rosecrans should not advance. For as soon as he [General Ambrose Burnside] is far enough away, the Rebel forces will occupy Kentucky and Tennessee—first those that are ranging in East Tennessee, then the ones that will be sent from Virginia—and will overwhelm the detachments scattered here and there to guard bridges and railroads. . . .

"Really," she boasted later, "I think that the commanding general should take me as his chief of staff or at least as his personal advisor. I have the power of reading the future of their operations."[73]

Although she was a general's wife, like other army women Nadine Turchin was by no means spared the typically harsh conditions of camp life. With some of the same gritting of teeth to which Belle Reynolds confessed in her reminiscence of Bird's Point, Missouri, Turchin wrote of the challenges of settling into camp near Winchester, Tennessee, in July 1863. "I pitched my tent under the open sky near the town," she wrote, "which is no more than a miserable hamlet built in the miserable region that surrounds it. . . . I slept in a miserable military tent, called [a] 'pup tent,' which was carried under the saddle by one of our colored domestics. This shelter was sufficient for me, but I had nothing to eat." Some weeks later she wrote, while at Chattanooga: "The camp in which I have been living is that of the trains stationed on the right bank; it is noisy, dirty, exposed to the sun, and filled with beasts of burden and all of the rough individuals servicing the troops." Nor was she spared the grueling marches that provided a kind of grim punctuation to the tedium of army life. "I shall never forget the march that night!" she wrote in September 1863 during the battle of Chickamauga, which was fought in such dense woods that soldiers could rarely see the enemy and their random gunfire set the trees alight. "It was an appropiate foretaste of the horrors of the two following days. . . . One had to stop every so often and wait for half an hour before moving some hundred-odd steps and stop again. It must have been about eight o'clock in the morning, when exhausted by fatigue, eyes burning from smoke, I reached the troop camp and rejoined my husband."[74]

In the midst of her frustrations, Turchin did find time to consider a few positive aspects of the Union army experience, among them the simple nobility of the common American soldier. "A citizen-soldier," she wrote in November 1863, "who feels free by his birthright endures all things because he does not feel obliged to endure them. He has volunteered to serve for the love of liberty." She also occasionally pondered the beauty and the curiosities of the land that surrounded her. But unlike Etheridge and the others, as far as we can tell, for Turchin the frustrations of her life with the Union army—at least in the second half of the war—far outweighed the satisfactions. Not least among those frustrations was her certainty that various native-born army officers consistently failed to appreciate her husband's superior military training and, indeed, her conviction that women's abilities suffered from a general lack of respect. "Eternal slaves of fatal destiny!" she wrote bitterly in June 1863. "Shall we ever see the day when mankind is civilized enough to consider seriously our position in the society where they allow us to be everything but intelligent beings authorized to enjoy the rights guaranteed to *All!* by the American constitution: freedom, equality, and the pursuit of happiness." Nadine Turchin was unstinting in her praise of women like herself who had proven their devotion to the Union cause through deeds and endurance. "In this great conflict I do not see any great men," she wrote, her husband undoubtedly excepted. "Only the women are great, the majority because of their suffering, some for showing their great and high moral virtues."[75]

John and Nadine Turchin left the Union army in the fall of 1864. How they spent the period immediately following their departure from the army is not known, but it is clear that as they approached their twilight years in Radom, Illinois, the Turchins were mired in poverty. Beginning in 1900, ten years after he initially applied for one, John Turchin finally received a government pension of fifty dollars per month (his earlier claim had been denied due to a misunderstanding concerning the final outcome of his court-martial). When John died in 1901, Nadine applied for a pension of thirty dollars per month, notably as his widow, not as an army woman herself. The pension came through in 1902, and it served as her primary financial support for two years, until she died in 1904.[76]

Chapter Four

# "As Brave As a Lion and As Pretty As a Lamb"[1]

❋

*More Civil War Army Women, Real and Fictional*

Molly Pitcher is one of the most revered symbols of our national patriotism. Her image looms throughout the land . . . reinforced through books, paintings, and illustrations. . . . Molly seems to be a cultural personification of liberty. . . .

*Carol Klaver, "An Introduction to the Legend of Molly Pitcher," 1994*

We know enough about Annie Etheridge, Kady Brownell, Bridget Divers, Belle Reynolds, and Nadine Turchin to be able to narrate their stories in some detail. About a great many more Civil War army women we know far less than we would like. We are aware of some only because they received a degree of public notice at the point when their respective regiments mustered in, when elaborate ceremonies and parades drew popular attention to their presence with the troops, especially if, like Kady Brownell, they dressed in colorful and unusual outfits. In December 1861 *Frank Leslie's Illustrated Newspaper* reported that a woman teacher from a Pittsfield, New York, girls' seminary had joined the Morrison Cavalry as its daughter of the regiment. This unnamed woman was, the article noted, at once a "daring horsewoman" and a "thorough lady," an individual "in whom the cavaliers have a charge worthy of their zeal." Around the same time, another newspaper reported schoolteacher Hannah Ewbank's attachment as daughter of the regiment to the 7th Wisconsin Infantry—probably in September 1861, when the regiment was mustered in. Ewbank's uniform, the paper noted, consisted of a blue jacket trimmed with gold lace and sporting military buttons; a scarlet skirt trimmed with gold and blue lace; white pants and a white vest; boots and white kid gloves; and a blue velvet hat decorated with lace and yellow feathers. "A more jaunty or bewitching little Daughter of the Regiment," the article commented lightheartedly, "never handled the canteen."[2]

The 6th Massachusetts Infantry might have challenged such claims with boasts about their own daughter of the regiment, Lizzie Clawson Jones, who dressed in a "costly and beautiful" uniform that the regiment had presented to her in July 1861. Jones's uniform included a hat decorated with red, white, and blue feathers on one side and a gilt wreath with the numeral 6 at its center on the other. Among the equipment Jones carried was an embossed silver canteen. And then there was the 39th New York, also known as the Garibaldi Guard, which traveled with several women—no fewer than six, according to the *New York Herald* of May 29, 1861—who donned blue dresses trimmed with gold lace, red jackets, and hats or caps decorated with feathers. The 25th Pennsylvania under the command of Colonel Max Einstein also took with it five women dressed in "short blue skirts" (undoubtedly with long pants or pantalettes underneath). Other army women in the early days of the war attracted attention more for their equipment than for their clothing: Sarah Taylor, daughter of the regiment for the 1st Tennessee, appears in the records not just on account of her "neat blue chapeau" but also because of the weapons she bore, which included a sword and more than one silver mounted pistol attached to her belt.[3]

At least one Southern daughter of the regiment drew notice

*Purportedly Belle Boyd. This picture reflects the sort of clothing Civil War army women typically wore. Boyd would not have dressed this way as a spy, but she might have dressed in such garb for her stage performances after the war.* Courtesy of the Chicago Historical Society.

not because of her looks but because her behavior earned her the disrespect of a private in the ranks of her Georgia regiment. He had seen her acting altogether "too free and easy," he wrote, as if she were drunk. "A drunken man," he grumbled, "is bad enough, but a drunken woman is an awful sight."[4] Most army women did better, however. In 1894 the citizens of Fredericksburg, Virginia, gathered to dedicate a monument to Lucy Ann Cox, who had served as daughter of the regiment for the 13th Virginia. According to the Richmond *Star* (July 21, 1894), Cox—like many army women—had followed her husband into the military. Throughout her service she had repeatedly demonstrated her willingness to suffer as the men suffered, to march as they marched (usually refusing offers to ride in the regiment's ambulances or wagon trains), and to respond with "untiring solicitude" and good cheer to every request for assistance from every Confederate soldier she encountered, though she reserved her most devoted attention for her own company, the 13th Virginia's Company A. "No march was too long or weather too inclement," wrote one memorialist, "to deter this patriotic woman from doing what she considered her duty." Cox remained with the 13th until Appomattox.[5]

Snippets of information also appear regarding women who were not specifically designated daughters of the regiment but who nevertheless performed similarly wide-ranging roles as army women of the North and the South. More than one source mentions a laundress attached to the "Irish Brigade" (which consisted of New York's 63rd, 69th, and 88th Infantry regiments) who stood with the troops at bloody Antietam in September 1862 and drew attention there for her vigorous efforts to cheer the men on to fight. Similarly, we read that Elizabeth Finnan, who joined the 81st Ohio Infantry as a laundress, over the course of three years of fighting not only came to perform nursing services but also marched in the ranks carrying a musket, slept, soldierlike, in her own tent, and contributed her energy to the work of providing intelligence to the

Union command, possibly influencing in some measure the out-come of the November 1863 battle of Lookout Mountain, which gave an important advantage to the Union army in hotly contested Tennessee and helped to lay the groundwork for General William T. Sherman's campaign against Atlanta in 1864. We read of Rose Quinn Rooney, a matronly Irish woman who served with Company K of the Confederacy's 15th Louisiana from June 1861 until the end of the war, and who first saw battle at First Bull Run, where she reportedly "signalized her courage and devotion by bravely pulling down a fence in the midst of bursting shells to let the Battery of the Washington Artillery pass through." Rooney was also present at Gettysburg, where her regiment was among those who attacked Culp's Hill on July 2. According to Confederate nurse Fannie Beers, Rooney was indefatigable, and made herself useful to her company and regiment in every way she could imagine, even in the heat of combat. Rooney, wrote Beers, "served with the undaunted bravery which led her to risk the dangers of every bat-tle-field where the regiment was engaged, unheeding the zip of the miniés, the shock of shells, or the horrible havoc made by the solid shot, so that she might give timely succor to the wounded or com-fort the dying." As the story goes, Rooney's devotion to her regi-ment was matched by her antagonism towards the Yankees: when Union soldiers took a number of the more defiant men in her regi-ment prisoner at Appomattox, she demanded that they take her, too. For two weeks she was stationed as a nurse in a hospital in Burkesville, Virginia, which housed soldiers from both armies; she then spent time in an all-Yankee hospital in Petersburg, from which she made her way home to New Orleans, where she became matron of the local soldiers' home. There, she tended to Confed-erate veterans and became a member of a Louisiana veterans asso-ciation. She died in 1895.[6]

At least one other Irish woman, Betty Sullivan, also traveled with a Louisiana regiment and became well known for sleeping on the ground with a simple blanket for a covering and a knapsack for a pillow. According to one source, Sullivan so dedicated herself to the care of the soldiers in her regiment that they honored her with the nickname "Mother" and one after another swore their willingness to die on her behalf. Other sources mention an army woman of German birth, the wife of a soldier named John Bahr who served as a hospital steward for her husband's regiment—the same Washington Artillery of New Orleans for which Rose Rooney had cleared the way at First Bull Run, and one of the best-respected artillery units in the Confederate army—and who went on to prove herself "as true as steel" by tolerating without complaint all the demands of army life. Long, weary marches, the tedium of camp life, the strain of battle, and the horror of battlefield carnage also failed to deter the Union's Ellen Goodridge, who like so many other army women North and South proved herself worthy. A native of Wisconsin, Goodridge followed her beloved, one James Hendrick, into the army and remained with him and his regiment for four years until Hendrick died shortly after General Lee's surrender in April 1865. Having signed on as an army cook, Goodridge also tagged along on skirmishes and raids, performing whatever tasks she could to help the men in uniform and on one occasion receiving a bullet wound in her arm, presumably while she was on the field binding the wounds of others. A small amount of information has come down to us about an army woman known only as "Dutch Mary." According to John Haley of the 17th Maine Infantry regiment, Dutch Mary cooked and did laundry for the regiment, but she also tended the wounded, even on the battlefront. Haley also noted that Dutch Mary wore a Zouave-style uniform that made her look rather manly, and in camp she did not hesitate to drill with the soldiers, performing more than adequately on this score. "The way her legs fly when executing a wheeling operation," Haley noted, "reminds me of some swift-moving insect."[7]

Of some Civil War army women, such as Confederate Jane

Claudia Johnson, we can learn a bit more. The daughter of a distinguished North Carolina family, at the time of the war's outbreak Johnson lived with her husband Bradley in Maryland. Her relationship with the Confederate army began when Bradley decided to raise a company of Maryland troops to serve the Southern cause. Other Maryland men did the same, and in late May 1861 when the new enlistees all gathered at Harpers Ferry in what was then Virginia, it became evident that the several officers must find a means of clothing and arming their eager recruits. At the time, President Lincoln's determination to hold Maryland in the Union proved a serious obstacle to soliciting the home-state government for assistance. Recognizing this, Johnson—who wanted to see her husband's company succeed—volunteered to appeal directly to the people of her native state instead. Imploring the North Carolina state government to come to the aid of the secessionist Marylanders, Johnson received a grant of five hundred rifles and other necessary equipment, along with a sum of money she could use to purchase supplies such as blankets, clothing, cooking utensils, and tents. With these goods Johnson returned to Harpers Ferry and helped to transform a ragtag group of recruits into the Confederacy's 1st Maryland Regiment.

Johnson then went on to accompany her husband and his company of troops for the better part of a year. She remained with the company until they left Harpers Ferry in June 1861, then rejoined them a month later, traveling with them and primarily nursing the sick and wounded until the regiment was disbanded in 1862. When the troops mustered out, they presented her with the regimental flag and a letter in which they celebrated her contributions to their welfare. In her response to this tribute, Johnson honored the soldiers' devotion with a promise: "As I have been with you in the trials you have undergone in the south, so will I ever be, and no member of the First Maryland Regiment will ever want a friend while I live." Later in the war, when her husband assumed command of a reorganized Maryland

Line, Johnson spent another winter with the army. During that time, according to a letter of appreciation presented to her in 1894 by Maryland Line veterans, Johnson not only cared for the soldiers' health but also put together a collection of books for their use and encouraged the construction of an ecumenical chapel for their edification.[8]

As in the case of Jane Claudia Johnson, we have access to a reasonable amount of information on Marie Tepe (alternately "Tebe"), a Frenchwoman who in 1849, at approximately the age of fifteen, immigrated to the United States, where she married a Philadelphia tailor named Bernardo Tepe the following year. Eleven years later, in April 1861, Marie Tepe (who came to be known as "French Mary") followed her husband into Company I of the 27th Pennsylvania Infantry, probably against his wishes. Writes one source: "Tebe wanted to leave his wife at home to manage the small tailor shop, but she refused to stay and went out with the regiment. . . ." Marie Tepe did not remain with her husband or the 27th, however: sometime before the end of 1862—apparently because of an incident in which Bernardo, along with some other soldiers, stole a sizable portion of the money she had earned as a sutler—Marie Tepe transferred to the 114th Pennsylvania (Clarence H. T. Collis's "Zouaves d'Afrique"). With both the 27th and the 114th Tepe served as a sutler, providing tobacco, whiskey, and foodstuffs to the soldiers. She also cooked, washed, and mended for the men in the ranks. In addition, she was a constant companion to the soldiers on the battlefield, coming under fire, by one account, some thirteen times. Like Etheridge's 3rd and 5th Michigan Infantry regiments, Tepe's fighting 114th Pennsylvania was engaged at the first battle of Bull Run, as well as at the battles of Fair Oaks, Fredericksburg, Chancellorsville, Gettysburg, and Spotsylvania—where a soldier from a different unit described her as appearing to be "about 25 years of age, square featured and sunburnt. . . ." Tepe received a bullet in her left ankle at Fredericksburg while tending to the wounded, and this, along with her particularly courageous behavior at Chancellorsville five months later, where she endured the hazards of combat in order to bring water to her weary troops, resulted in her being honored—like Etheridge—with the Kearny Cross for bravery in the spring of 1863. "She was a courageous woman," wrote the 114th Pennsylvania's Frank Rauscher in his memoir of his Civil War military service, "and often got within range of the enemy's fire whilst parting with the contents of her canteen among our wounded men. Her skirts were riddled by bullets. . . ." Tepe mustered out of the Union army with the rest of the 114th Pennsylvania in May 1865 and went to live near Pittsburgh with her second husband (Bernardo died at Gettysburg), Richard Leonard, who had served as an orderly with the 114th. Her final years seem to have been unhappy ones, characterized by indigence and physical suffering—the bullet she took at Fredericksburg was never removed. In 1901 Tepe committed suicide.[9]

A number of sources mention a twenty-year-old army woman from Menominie, Wisconsin, named Eliza Wilson, who first came to the attention of a correspondent for the popular *Frank Leslie's Illustrated Newspaper* in August 1861. "A Young Heiress Goes to the Wars with the Fifth Wisconsin Regiment" read the headline, which was followed by a discussion of the conditions surrounding Eliza Wilson's decision to serve. It seems that Wilson's father, William Wilson, was an extremely wealthy mill owner who had fashioned a company of soldiers—Company K, also known as the Dunn County Pinery Rifles—from the men in his employ, many of whom had been with him since they were boys. Having encouraged and been active herself in the formation of Company K, and being an avid supporter of the Union cause, Eliza Wilson decided that she would join her father's company as they mustered into the 5th Wisconsin.

If observers expected this child of privilege—"a young lady of rare beauty and accomplishments"—to abandon the regiment in short order, they were mistaken. Eliza Wilson eagerly assumed the tasks associated with a daughter of the regiment, both ceremonial (heading the regiment when it was on parade or on the march) and grueling (tending to the sick, wounded, and dying on the battlefield). Taking her charge seriously, Wilson made herself useful and soon earned the gratitude and the blessings of those she served. Moreover, despite her privileged background and the presence of a servant to assist her, Wilson proved herself hearty. She was still with the regiment in June 1862 when one soldier praised her in a letter home. "We have not seen a woman for a fortnight," he wrote,

> with the exception of the Daughter of the Regiment who is
> with us in storm and sunshine. It would do you good to see
> her trudging along, with or after the regiment, her dark brown
> frock buttoned tightly around her waist, her what-you-call-ems
> [pants] tucked into her well fitting gaiters, her hat and feather
> set jauntily on one side, her step firm and assured, for she
> knows that every arm in our ranks would protect her. Never
> pouting or passionate, with a kind word for every one, and
> every one a kind word for her.

Tellingly he added: "Were it not for her, when a woman would appear, we would be running after her, as children do after an organ and a monkey."[10]

As slaves escaped en masse to relative safety behind the Union lines, and as the Union army began forming regiments of African-American soldiers, undoubtedly a large number of African-American women also found their way into official or unofficial service to the Yankee military. Unfortunately, we know the details of only one black army woman's Civil War service, because she left behind a unique memoir.[11] Born a slave in Georgia in 1848, Susie Baker (who later became Susie King Taylor) gained her freedom in April 1862 at the age of fourteen when her uncle dragged her along with his own family onto a federal gunboat passing near Georgia's Fort Pulaski, captured that same month by Union forces. As contraband of war, Susie Baker and a number of her family members soon found themselves enlisted in a newly formed regiment of black soldiers which the commander of the Union's Department of the South, Major General David Hunter, had organized at Port Royal Island off the South Carolina coast. Susie Baker was initially appointed laundress of the 33rd U.S. Colored Troops (initially the 1st South Carolina Volunteers), but before long her responsibilities with the regiment began to multiply, thanks to her obvious skills as a nurse and her unusual ability to read and write—her grandmother had secretly sent her to a friend's school for lessons when she was a small child. In addition to doing the men's washing and some cooking, Susie Baker tended to them when they were sick or wounded and also taught them how to read and write. At the same time, by her own account, she learned to clean, load, and fire a musket, which she described as "great fun."[12] Baker's devotion to her regiment earned her the gratitude of the men with whom she served; it also attracted the particular attention of at least one soldier, Edward King, a sergeant whom she married before the end of her first year of freedom. Along with her husband, Susie Baker King remained with the regiment until they were mustered out on February 9, 1866. Years later her connections with the regiment were still strong, and she helped to organize a branch of the Woman's Relief Corps. "My hands have never left undone anything they could do," she later wrote, "toward [the] aid and comfort" of the soldiers of the Union army, black or white, "in the twilight of their years."[13]

Plumbing the rich stories of the army women for whom we have detailed records, and pondering the bits and pieces of information we have about the others, it is worth noting that although the Civil War army women who appear most readily in the historical record came from a variety of backgrounds, a sizable proportion were foreign-born immigrants, and only a very few seem to have abandoned lives of significant material comfort for the front. Rather, most seem to have readily undertaken the challenges of military life: to them, hard labor was no stranger, and they would return to lives of labor after the war was over. As such, army women were generally unlike so many of the middle-class and elite, mostly native-born women who chose to go to war as hospital nurses and who later wrote, among other things, of the overwhelming and disconcerting experience of adjusting to such arduous work.[14] Army women were generally more like the women who made up the bulk of the wartime female hospital staff: working-class and black women for whom hospital service represented another form of hard labor—albeit one that was a potential source of unusual excitement and adventure—in lives in which such labor was a familiar necessity.[15] Civil War army women for the most part had deep wells of both physical and psychological hardiness on which they could draw once they embarked on life in the military, and of which middle-class observers took careful note. Wrote memorialist Frank Moore at the beginning of his chapter on Bridget Divers, "The Heroines of the Great War for the Union, like its heroes, have come from every class of society, and represent every grade in our social scale." He then proceeded with relative accuracy to divide those "heroines" into lines of service: "Ladies of the highest refinement and social polish" who "left homes of luxury and devoted themselves, week after week, and month after month, to daily labor and nightly vigils in the wards of great hospitals" as nurses; and other women, such as Divers, "no less praiseworthy and admirable," who, though "born in less favored circles . . . brought" to their war work, "if not the elegance of the boudoir, the hearty good will, the vigorous sense, and the unwearied industry of the laboring class."[16]

When Moore and other postwar interpreters of Civil War army women's experience noted the hardscrabble roots of women like Divers, they sometimes gave voice to popular Victorian assumptions about working-class women's supposedly questionable morality. In 1867 historians Linus Brockett and Mary Vaughan wrote of army women generally: "There were very, probably, many others of this class of heroines who deserve a place in our record; but . . . in some cases they failed to maintain that unsullied reputation without which courage and daring are of little worth."[17] However, among the individual army women these writers chose to celebrate, there was not one in whom they detected (or suspected) such flaws. The only women to earn a spot in the commemoratives were those whom postwar historians considered—in some cases explicitly—worthy of inheriting the noble mantle of a legendary army woman of the nation's first great war, a woman popularly known as "Molly Pitcher."

Who was this Molly Pitcher? Down into the twentieth century, the name "Molly Pitcher" has been intertwined most intimately and most consistently with the historical individuals Mary Ludwig Hays McCauley and Margaret Cochran Corbin. The Molly Pitcher story has several versions, some of which replicate more closely than others the details of one or the other woman's Continental army career, but all versions involve an army woman of working class and perhaps also immigrant roots who takes up the task of loading and firing her husband's artillery piece when he falls in battle. In the case of both McCauley and Corbin, there have arisen devoted followings of individuals determined to see that their chosen heroine is recognized and celebrated appropriately as the "true Molly Pitcher." Evidence clearly indicates, however, that even by the time of the Civil War the name "Molly Pitcher" had begun to emerge in the popular American consciousness not as standing for a historical figure but rather as the name associated with a mythical substitute for McCauley, for Corbin, and indeed for Continental army women generally. At the hands of various storytellers and mythmakers after the Revolution—and subsequently throughout and well beyond the Civil War—the name and imagery of "Molly Pitcher" offered a popular and precious symbol

of extraordinary female bravery—and marital fidelity—in war. As
historian Edward Biddle put it more than fifty years after
Appomattox, in 1916: the Molly Pitcher monument then being
unveiled at Carlisle, Pennsylvania, was "a splendid and lasting
recognition of the lofty virtue which we call courage," and he
added that Molly Pitcher, whose legend by then had absorbed the
identities of Annie Etheridge, Kady Brownell, and hundreds—perhaps thousands—of other Civil War army women as well, had
"come to be accepted as America's most conspicuous exponent of
feminine valor."[18]

From the time of the Revolution and on into the twentieth century, historians and others compressed into the image of one
inimitably noble figure known as "Molly Pitcher" the general evidence about masses of women—and the specific evidence about a
number of individual women—who over the course of American
history had provided paramilitary service to the nation's armies
during war. Moreover, historians and other cultural architects
imbued the legendary figure of Molly Pitcher with didactic purpose, even as they allowed her to obscure the historical reality of
thousands of women who had actually tied their fortunes and
their courage to the military.[19] When J. Clement in 1851 compared
Molly Pitcher to the Greek heroine Artemisia who gave vital assistance to Xerxes at the battle of Salamis, and when he wrote, "If the
queen of Caria is deserving of praise for her martial valor, the name
of the heroic wife of the gunner, should be woven with hers in a
fadeless wreath of song," it seems unlikely that he had in mind
either the working-class roots or the postwar financial struggles of
Corbin or McCauley, or any number of their Civil War counterparts. Moreover, when Edward Biddle in 1916 described Molly
Pitcher as "America's most conspicuous exponent of feminine
valor," his words, laden with romance, did not bring to mind the
actual McCauley, whom others remembered as a woman "at heart
tender and kind" but also "very strict and severe . . . rather rough
in manners, sometimes, when excited, even profane," "a rough,

*"Molly Pitcher at the Battle of Monmouth."* Reprinted from John Landis, *A Short History of Molly Pitcher* (1912).

common woman who swore like a trooper," who "smoked and chewed tobacco"; or the actual Margaret Corbin, whom some described as a woman possessed of a "sharp tongue and quick temper," who though "held in high esteem by all," was nevertheless known for being "commanding and haughty," "not always particular about her dress or person," and who, according to one source, "died a horrible death from the effects of a syphilitic disease."[20] Although individual army women's human complexity should not be permitted to undermine the memory of their indisputably courageous deeds and service during both the American Revolution and the Civil War, it is important to note that a crucial and unfortunate side effect of the enshrinement of Molly Pitcher in legend has been the recession into oblivion of a mass of hard historical detail concerning real women and their real labors in connection with the Continental, Union, and Confederate armies.

In their own way, popular authors who developed romantic fictional representations of army women—specifically daughters of the regiment—during the Civil War similarly set aside the lives and experiences of real women like Etheridge, Brownell, and the others in favor of undoubtedly more marketable images that were, not surprisingly, only partially faithful to the documentary record. A brief look at Joseph Hodgson's 1862 play *The Confederate Vivandière* and Jane Goodwin Austin's 1865 novel *Dora Darling: The Daughter of the Regiment* underscores this point.[21]

*The Confederate Vivandière* begins with the arrival of Clara Brandon, the mute (but not deaf) young daughter of a Confederate general, at the camp of an unidentified Confederate regiment. Presumably to avoid being turned away by those who might recognize and want to protect her from the rigors of army life, Clara has assumed an alias and has disguised herself so successfully that the regiment's commander, Colonel Pembroke, although he is actually betrothed to Clara, fails to recognize her. Within moments of accepting her offer to serve as the regiment's "daughter," Pembroke is glad to have done so: Clara is the first to notice a recently apprehended federal spy reaching for a hidden gun to shoot his captors, and when she does she draws a sword from her belt and, by a quick slash through his arm, disables him. Having displayed from the story's start both martial skill and bravery, daughter of the regiment Clara Brandon goes on to serve as a spy as well, traveling beyond the lines to Union headquarters in Maryland to gather intelligence.

Almost as soon as Clara has infiltrated the enemy's outposts and begun to collect information, Colonel Pembroke and several others from her regiment are brought in as prisoners. This occasion provides Clara with another opportunity to demonstrate her courage, and she unwisely engages in a violent physical struggle with the men's Union captors, only to end up being taken prisoner herself. The Yankee general then calls for her execution, exclaiming that "these rebel women of the South must be taught a lesson."[22] Moments later Pembroke recognizes his betrothed and cries out her name, unintentionally placing himself at the mercy of the Yankee general who now cruelly offers to spare

Pembroke's life if Clara will abandon her commitment to him. In response to this outrage, Clara—like the Yankee spy conveniently but inexplicably still armed—lashes out again, drawing a pistol from the folds of her clothing with which she prepares to kill her adversary. Before she is able to do so, however, soldiers in blue surround her and drag her offstage. Later, just as Pembroke is brought before a firing squad, Clara escapes from the bluecoats' clutches and joins him in what seems likely to be their final embrace. Unexpectedly, however, chaos erupts as rebel troops invade the Yankee camp, sending their enemies fleeing, and the play comes to an end.

*The Confederate Vivandière* is a short play, numbering only a few pages. In contrast, Jane Goodwin Austin's *Dora Darling*—the story of Dora Darley, a twelve-year-old, chestnut-haired girl from an unidentified border state—is well over three hundred pages long. The book opens as Dora is nursing her Unionist mother through her final illness. When her mother dies, Dora's alcoholic, abusive, and staunchly Confederate father sends her to live with an unkind aunt while he himself enlists in the Southern army. Dora's tolerance for life with her aunt is short-lived, however, and before long she runs away, heading, she believes, for the Massachusetts home of her abolitionist aunt, Lucy. Instead, a complicated series of events leads Dora to the encampment of a Union regiment, one of whose soldiers had previously convalesced from a wound at the Darley home. Dora informs the regiment's doctor that she wants to be an army nurse. After warning her that she is setting herself up for some hard work, the doctor refers her to the regiment's colonel, who nicknames her "Dora Darling" and introduces her to the men with enthusiasm. "Boys," he tells them, "here is Dora Darling, who is for the future to act as *vivandière* of this regiment. Remember that every man of you is bound to guard and protect her as if she were his own daughter or sister. She is, in fact, the daughter of the regiment so long as she remains with it. . . . I place her in your care."[23] The colonel's announcement draws cheers from the men in the ranks. Later that day Dora meets up with the young soldier who had stayed at her home. "Captain Karl" is thrilled with her appointment as the daughter of the regiment, and the two become fast friends.

Dora vigorously takes up her duties, her "true, self-denying, patient, and industrious" nature quickly making her popular among the men of her regiment, whom she thinks of as her "six hundred or more fathers." [24] She fashions for herself a proper outfit—a short skirt and some trousers, and a belted coat—which a shoemaker in the regiment augments with a pair of refitted boots. To this a tailor adds a red cap decorated with gold braid and a cloak trimmed in red and boasting military buttons. From other sources Dora receives a wide leather belt and equipment amounting to a small water keg, a flask for liquor, a tin cup, a bottle of smelling salts, and a bottle of hartshorn, a compound—like smelling salts—used for reviving the faint.

Most of Dora's days are occupied by hospital activities, and on Sunday afternoons she spends time reading the Bible to the men and leading them in the singing of hymns. On one occasion, however, Captain Karl invites her to join him on a military expedition, during which Dora has an unexpected opportunity to demonstrate her courage and intrepidity. It is not the first time she has done so in the novel: early on Dora proves her battle-readiness when, while she is hiding in a grove of trees at the edge of an actual battle, a burning shell lands near her and without thinking she seizes the lit fuse in her woolen skirt and smothers the flame. Now, when she and Karl encounter a group of rebels and Karl is wounded, Dora has a chance to prove herself again, positioning herself between Karl and the Confederates on the assumption that they will not shoot at him a second time for fear of wounding her. After she helps Karl drive the rebels back, he remarks, only half in jest: "I never shall dare ride out again without you to protect me, Dora Darling. . . . But I'm in hopes that in time you'll make a man of me, by your own example." [25]

Dora has a number of other adventures as daughter of the regiment, including one in which she wrestles a wolf to the ground and another in which she accompanies the regiment into battle. Through it all, she acts with courage and valor, always placing the men's welfare before her own. As the story winds down, three men in the regiment vie for the opportunity to share (and shape) her future. In the end, Dora goes home as an "adopted" sister to Karl, whom she discovers coincidentally to be a cousin, the son of her Massachusetts aunt.[26]

As in the case of the Molly Pitcher legend, there are certainly ways in which the literary characters of Clara Brandon and Dora Darley accurately reflect the experiences of their historical counterparts among Civil War (and Revolutionary War) army women. Like many historical army women, both Clara and Dora, for example, become attached to their specific regiments by virtue (directly or indirectly) of their connections to one of the regiment's members. For both, a substantial proportion of their service to the army takes the form of nursing. Both also assume other (sometimes paramilitary) responsibilities as well, however, as dictated by their own and the regiment's changing circumstances. And both have occasions to display "manly" courage and soldierlike fortitude and skill when the situation demands it: Dora, for example, is unafraid to march into battle, to wrestle a wild animal to the ground, or to squelch the flame of a burning shell; Clara is daring enough to undertake the dangerous mission of spying on the enemy, and she travels armed, more than once not only pulling a weapon on a challenger but also making it quite clear that she is prepared to follow through on her threat to defend one of "her" men. Dora's resemblance to a historical daughter of the regiment is enhanced by the fact that she wears specific, pseudomilitary clothing and carries certain equipment that betokens her status. With or without a special uniform, however, both characters display the dignity, courage, and devotion to the men under their charge that observers repeatedly noted in historical army women as well. It is clear that authors Austin and Hodgson must have done some research before creating their central characters, and had Dora Darley and Clara Brandon stepped out of the pristine pages of *Dora Darling* and *The Confederate Vivandière* onto the bloodied ground of an actual Civil War battlefield, Kady Brownell, Bridget Divers, and others like them would undoubtedly have recognized in their persons and their wartime contributions elements that were familiar.

On the other hand, however, as in the relationship of the legendary Molly Pitcher to her historical counterparts, neither Dora Darley nor Clara Brandon reflects in any ultimately convincing way the common army woman of the Civil War, or of the Revolution. Rather, one could argue that each woman appears instead as an anomaly, a freak of sorts. Clara, we recall is mute: although this "dumb beauty of Baltimore"[27] writes an occasional note to communicate her thoughts, she remains essentially silent throughout the play. Moreover, in the context of the events of the play, her muteness combines with her virtual invisibility or unrecognizability to become her greatest asset, allowing her access to the regiment of her lover as well as the possibility of providing service as a spy. But muteness and unrecognizability are not qualities associated with real army women, who were instead commonly physically hearty women well known by their regiments; for historical army women such qualities would have represented serious handicaps.

Unlike Clara, Dora has a voice, which she uses freely to speak her mind, sing to the men in the ranks, comfort them with words of good cheer, and instruct them on the Bible. Dora's status as an anomaly instead of as a representative of historical army women is made evident mostly by her extreme youth: she is a mere child—a brave and mature child, but a child nonetheless. Presenting Dora as a child, of course, allows Austin to sidestep important questions regarding her subject's sexuality, an issue that we know was a matter of concern to those who commented on the phenomenon of army women during the Civil War. Instead, Dora appears as a solitary, saintly, virginal child figure, a singular and entertaining example of youthful female innocence, virtue, and patriotic devotion played out in an extraordinary context.

Needless to say, Dora's extreme youth and Clara's muteness are not the only things that set them apart from historical figures such as Brownell, Divers, and the others. As we have already noted, although Civil War army women—like their Revolutionary War predecessors—came from a variety of backgrounds, a sizable proportion were foreign-born, and only a few of the ones we know about abandoned lives of even relative material comfort for the front. A far greater number were women of foreign and/or working-class origins. In contrast, both Dora and Clara are native-born, and both come from what appear to be economically stable backgrounds. Moreover, as was true of Charles Wesley Alexander's fictional Civil War women spies—Pauline D'Estraye, Wenonah, and even Mary Murdock—both Dora and Clara become army women overwhelmingly for the purpose of expressing their ardent patriotism. In Clara's case, of course, her selfless patriotism is augmented by her love for Colonel Pembroke. But what is most important is her determination, despite her handicap, to serve her country however she can. In sum, like the legendary Molly Pitcher, the fictional Dora and Clara offer readers a measure of entertainment on the one hand and, on the other, some prescriptive lessons in female courage, loyalty, purity, and patriotism for which their Civil War service is merely a backdrop. As one should expect of such literary figures, they fall somewhat short of reflecting with precision the lives and experiences—though not the courage and endurance—of historical Civil War (or Revolutionary War) army women, both on the battlefield and off.

Chapter Five

# "The Beardless Boy Was a Universal Favorite"[1]

*Deborah Sampson and a Handful of*
*Civil War Women Soldiers*

I felt called to go and do what I could for the defense of the
right.

*Sarah Emma Edmonds Seelye, alias Private Franklin*
*Thompson, 1886*

Along with the many women who served the Union and
Confederate armies as spies, resistance activists, army
women, and daughters of the regiment, another group of
women has also been hidden in history—probably somewhere
between five hundred and a thousand women who disguised
themselves as men and enlisted as full-fledged soldiers during
the Civil War.[2] Largely lost to memory as well is the fact that, like
the women who participated in the armies' activities in other
ways, Civil War women soldiers took their place in a tradition
that dated back in America at least as far as the American
Revolution.[3]

Undoubtedly the most famous American woman to have
served as a soldier prior to the Civil War, and the one for whom

we have the most documentary evidence, is Deborah Sampson (alternately "Samson"), born in approximately 1760 to a farming family in the small village of Plympton, near Plymouth, in Massachusetts.[4] For Deborah, her brother Ephraim, and her sister Sylvia, early childhood was marked most vividly by poverty and conflict between their parents, followed by the collapse of the household and the children's dispersal among relatives when Deborah was about five years old. Sampson spent the next two or three years with a distant relative, two more in the family of a Mrs. Thacher, and then perhaps eight more in the home of the family of Jeremiah Thomas. In each situation Sampson's adopted family doubled as her employer, expecting her to perform manual and domestic labor in exchange for her upkeep, her moral training, and a measure of education, which she later applied to a short stint as a public school teacher.

Sampson's adolescence coincided with the outbreak of the American Revolution, and living so near Boston, she was surrounded by the political culture of the patriots. The suggestion of her earliest biographer, Herman Mann, that Sampson "not only listened to the least information relative to the rise and progress" of the war but that her thoughts were also, "at times, engrossed with it," is not at all far-fetched.[5] In the spring of 1782, however, Sampson moved beyond mere contemplation of the war to a desire to enlist in the ranks of the Continental army as a soldier, at which point she either made or obtained a suit of men's clothes, donned them, cut her hair, and enlisted for three years or the war's duration.[6] Sampson gave her name as "Robert Shurtliff" (alternately "Shurtleff," "Shurtliffe," and "Shurtlieffe"), and after mustering in to the 4th Massachusetts Regiment under the command first of Colonel William Shepard and later of Colonel Henry Jackson, Sampson marched with her company to West Point, where she drew a uniform, arms, ammunition, and other supplies and equipment and began to learn the business of soldiering.

*The only known image of Deborah Sampson.* Reprinted from Elizabeth Ellet, *Women of the American Revolution* (1900).

Various accounts of Sampson's life and service as a Continental army soldier indicate that she was tall for her sex (perhaps as tall as five feet seven inches), and that she was a sturdy, reasonably attractive, and vigorous individual both serious and deliberate and therefore, presumably, "masculine" and well suited to the rigors of the battlefield.[7] Having enlisted so late in the war, however, Sampson's only combat experience came in some of the patriots' residual skirmishes with the British and their Indian allies which characterized the war's final months. Nevertheless, during one such skirmish near Tarrytown, New York, Sampson was wounded, taking a glancing saber blow to her forehead and a bullet in her leg. Although she was moved to a military hospital for examination, Sampson escaped detection, possibly by removing the bullet from her own leg while the doctor on duty was attending another soldier. In any case, once she was able, Sampson returned to her regiment and her duties as a soldier. In the spring of 1783, however, while Sampson was in Philadelphia, she developed a fever. Laid low, she was put under the care of Dr. Barnabas Binney, who discovered her secret when he examined her. Sources indicate that Dr. Binney saw immediately to Sampson's removal from the hospital, after which he took up care for her in his own home, where he continued to keep her confidence.

Although the doctor did not reveal Sampson's sex to his own family, he did persuade her to deliver a letter of disclosure to General John Paterson, commander of the Continental army's 1st Brigade, at West Point. According to biographer Mann, Sampson presented the letter to Paterson in person, and after he recovered from his shock, and she from her dismay at facing her own certain dismissal, Paterson requested that Sampson resume female dress so that he could introduce her to her surprised commander, Colonel Jackson, and then parade her through the ranks of her fellow soldiers. Though stunned by the news, Sampson's comrades nevertheless had no words of condemnation for the woman who had served faithfully with them for more than a year.

Sampson's discovery led directly to her honorable discharge by General Henry Knox in October 1783. After she left the army, Sampson headed home to Middleborough, making an extended stop with relatives in Stoughton, Massachusetts, where she continued to pose and labor as a man. April 1784 found her living as a woman again, however, and married to a locally respected farmer named Benjamin Gannett (alternately "Gannet"). Together the Gannetts set up house in Sharon, Massachusetts, where they raised four children. Although an 1827 article about Sampson claimed that her postwar life had been one of relative comfort, the evidence suggests that the years after the war were, like her early ones, characterized by hard labor and considerable suffering for herself and her family.[8] In 1792 Sampson composed the first of several petitions to the governments of her state and her nation for assistance. Whatever the initial response of the members of the General Court of Massachusetts was to Sampson's account of her military service, on January 20, 1792, the court declared that it was satisfied that Sampson and "Shurtliff" were one in the flesh, and also that Sampson, although a woman, had properly executed the responsibilities of a soldier and had therefore earned a soldier's wages, which it subsequently paid her.[9] Despite this lump-sum payment of thirty-four pounds and some supplemental government assistance granted in later years, Sampson's family continued to struggle financially, prompting her—like Civil War spies Belle Boyd, Rose Greenhow, and Pauline Cushman—to seek commercial compensation for her military service, which she did through the sale of Mann's biography and through her lectures and performances about her military career and adventures. Deborah Sampson died in 1827, having suffered considerable disability throughout her later life as a consequence of the bullet wound she received during the war: Benjamin Gannett later produced as evidence in his own claim for a pension a stack of his wife's doctor's bills amounting to more than six hundred dollars.[10]

Sampson is by far the best-known woman to have served as a soldier during the Revolutionary War. Among women who followed her example in the Civil War, there are three for whom a sufficient amount of documentary evidence exists with which to reconstruct their stories: Sarah Emma Edmonds, Jennie Hodgers, and Sarah Rosetta Wakeman. As in the case of Annie Etheridge and the other better-documented Civil War army women, Edmonds, Hodgers, and Wakeman all served the Union army.

But their stories provide a solid foundation on which to adjoin the stories of many less fully documented individuals of both the North and the South, for a more thorough understanding of the phenomenon of Civil War women soldiers as a whole.

Born in New Brunswick, Canada, in 1841, Sarah Emma Edmonds grew up on a farm where, as was typical for nineteenth-century farm girls, she and her sisters participated in all the same activities and performed all the same chores as her brother: tending to the animals, chopping wood and milking cows, planting, harvesting, and so forth.[11] Edmonds also learned to ride a horse, to hunt, and to fish. Like Deborah Sampson, she developed through such physical activity the sort of lean, "masculine" physique that was to help her in 1860, when, at the age of nineteen, she decided to head across the border into the United States in the garb and identity of a man. Posing as "Franklin Thompson," Edmonds took a job as a Hartford, Connecticut, publisher's agent, selling Bibles first in Canada, then in Michigan. She was living in Flint, Michigan, when the Civil War broke out, and on May 17, 1861, she enlisted in Company F of the 2nd Michigan Infantry Volunteers, commanded by Colonel Israel B. ("Fighting Dick") Richardson. Mustered in as a three years' recruit at Detroit on May 25, Edmonds was soon on her way to the front.

By mid-June 1861 Edmonds's regiment had encamped on some high ground just outside of Washington, D.C., and Edmonds had taken up the regular life of a common soldier. According to historian Bell Irvin Wiley, the daily routine of "Billy Yank" while in camp began with the sounding of reveille at five or six in the morning, which was typically followed by roll call, a brisk drill, and breakfast, affectionately termed "peas on a trencher." Next came sick call for the ill, who were sent for examination and care to the regimental surgeon; and fatigue call for the well, who spent the next hour or two cleaning and doing chores around camp. Around eight in the morning, the call came for inspection, after which soldiers reported to their respective posts, where they remained until the next period of drill. The noon meal (or, euphemistically, "roast beef") followed, giving way to a period of free time and then more drilling before soldiers returned to their quarters to prepare their uniforms and equipment for the late-afternoon dress parade, "the day's climactic and most impressive ceremony . . . calculated to inspire in the soldiers a pride in the bearing of arms." After dress parade came supper, then another roll call, and finally the return to quarters. While the regiment was in camp, as a private in the 2nd Michigan Infantry Sarah Edmonds participated in all of these daily activities, and at the sound of taps, like the rest of the soldiers in her regiment, she blew out her candles or extinguished her lantern and went to sleep.[12]

Franklin Thompson's military service record indicates that during her first months with the army Edmonds's post was the regimental hospital, where she served as a (male) nurse. Later Edmonds accepted an assignment as the regiment's postmaster (from April 30 to July 12, 1862) and then as its mail carrier (from July 12 to August 31, 1862). Many years later—and armed with the knowledge of Edmonds's true sex—one former superior officer, General O. M. Poe, recalled that "as a soldier 'Frank Thompson' was effeminate looking, and for that reason was detailed as mail carrier, to avoid taking an efficient soldier from the ranks."[13] According to Edmonds herself, as the 2nd Michigan's mail carrier she carried as much as two or three bushels of mail—probably both official and unofficial—back and forth over a distance of fifty to sixty miles at a time. Her "effeminate" look aside, the work that Edmonds was engaged in was not easy, nor was it without its dangers. "Owing to the condition of the roads," she later wrote,

I was often compelled to spend the nights alone by the road-
side. It was reported that the bushwhackers had murdered a

mail carrier on that road and robbed the mail, and there seemed
to be evidence of the fact, for, in the most lonely spot of all the
road the ground was still strewn with fragments of letters and
papers, over which I often passed when it was so dark that I
only knew it by the rustle of the letters under my horse's feet.[14]

While Edmonds faced real hazards in her work as a mail carrier, with her regiment she also faced enemy fire in battle. Like so
many of the other women discussed here, Edmonds's combat ini-
tiation came at First Bull Run in July 1861. Over the course of
1862 she was with her regiment elsewhere in Virginia as well, for
the 2nd Michigan was part of George McClellan's Army of the
Potomac, the principal federal force in the eastern theater,
assigned the threefold task of defending the federal capital, capturing the Confederate capital, and destroying General Robert E.
Lee's Army of Northern Virginia. Edmonds was at Williamsburg
in May; at Fair Oaks in late May and early June; and in the Seven
Days' battle in late June and early July, where despite having far
greater numbers of "effectives" than the enemy under Lee, Union
forces ultimately made a humiliating retreat from their position
just outside Richmond. Edmonds's regiment also endured the
dreadful slaughter at Fredericksburg in December 1862. Through
it all, Edmonds seems to have succeeded in concealing her sex, at
least from most: only one former comrade, himself of the 20th
Michigan, later suggested—again with the benefit of hindsight—
that some of the men with whom Edmonds had served suspected
her secret, but no one else made such a claim. Rather, as a consequence of her tireless performance of the duties of a soldier both
on the field and off, Edmonds earned a reputation among her
comrades for being a "whole-souled, enthusiastic youngster,
frank and fearless."[15] Years later her former comrades offered
unanimous testimony regarding the quality of her military service, which a Congressional report summarized. "Franklin
Thompson," the report indicated, gave his heart and soul to the

regiment, "sharing in all its toils and privations, marching and fighting in the various engagements in which it participated. . . . [He was] never absent from duty, obeying all orders with intelligence and alacrity, his whole aim and desire to render zealous and efficient aid to the Union cause."[16]

As Private Franklin Thompson, Edmonds was admired by the men in her company, regiment, and brigade, but she developed a particularly close friendship with one of them, Jerome John Robbins, a medical steward and assistant surgeon for the 2nd Michigan. From October 1861 through February 1862, Robbins's diary made regular references of one sort or another to "Thompson," who confessed her imposture to Robbins within a month of their meeting. Robbins's October and early November 1861 entries are filled with the delight of finding a true friend. "I had a very pleasant conversation with Frank Thomson [sic] on the subject of religion," wrote Robbins on October 30. "I visited my friend Thompson this eve," he wrote on November 1, "and was highly entertained for the evening in conversing upon the subject of religion and human nature[,] finding him to be a good noble hearted fellow as far as limited acquaintance will allow. . . ." On November 8 Robbins wrote of a conversation the two had had which "to me binds his friendship more firmly. . . ." And on November 13 he wrote, "Had a very pleasant stroll around the guns with Frank. How invaluable is the friendship of one true heart!"[17]

There is no doubt that Robbins and "Thompson" had developed a powerful affinity for one another. Still, Robbins noticed that there was something different about his new friend. On November 11 he wrote, "A mystery appears to me connected with him which is impossible for me to fathom. . . ." Indeed, Robbins worried about the possible consequences of revealing his undefined suspicions: "These may be false surmises," he wrote; "would that I might be free from them for not for worlds would I wrong a friend who so sincerely appreciates confiding friendship." Within a couple of days, however, Robbins found it impossible to avoid dealing with the mystery surrounding Edmonds. On November 16 he penned a rambling entry in his diary in which the central theme was his discovery that "Frank" was "a *female*" who had been masquerading as a man since her initial departure from her home in New Brunswick—a departure Robbins attributed to Edmonds's father's harsh discipline and a love affair that had gone awry. The *"real,"* wrote Robbins, "has been *unmasked*," and not without taxing their friendship, apparently, for Robbins also noted that in response to her confession he had immediately told "Thompson" about his own betrothal to a young woman back home named Anna Corey, and that this revelation had produced in his friend a "dissagreeable [sic] manner." "Earnestly ardently do I try and desire [for] him a prosperous welfare," Robbins noted. But "Thompson," he added, "possesses a nature to[o] willful to be pleasant[,] to[o] jealous to be happy or lend happines[s] to those whom I has [sic] a warm friendship for." Edmonds, it seems, had fallen in love with Robbins, had confessed her true identity to him as a result, and now felt rebuffed by Robbins's profession of love for and commitment to another woman.[18]

Subsequent entries in Robbins's diary indicate that relations between Robbins and Edmonds never quite returned to their previous level of intimacy. Robbins still seems to have valued "Frank's" friendship, but Edmonds had become withdrawn. "Frank is very reserved," Robbins wrote on December 18; "don[']t know what the difficulty is but I am affraid [sic] I have offend[ed] him some way am very sorry if so." On December 23 he wrote: "Frank acts strangely, appears very much out of humor." And on Christmas Day 1861 he remarked with evident sadness: "certain it is there is not so warm [a] friendship existing between us as there formally [sic] has been."[19] It is possible that Edmonds simply could not overcome her affection for Robbins; it is also possible that her newfound reserve reflected her fear that Robbins, in whom she had confided her true identity, might reveal her imposture to the rest of the regiment and her commanding officers.

Robbins did not reveal Edmonds's secret, however, and by the spring of 1862 relations between the two had regained a measure of cordiality which continued through the year. By this time Edmonds had accepted duty as a nurse at the Mansion House Hospital in Alexandria and at the General Hospital in Georgetown, and then as the regimental postmaster and mail carrier. Physical distance from Robbins seems to have diminished Edmonds's frustration. "Frank came in to see me as he was passing with the mail," wrote Robbins on April 4, without any hint of his previous concern about the tone of their friendship. "Yesterday I received a letter from my friend F. Thompson," he reported on October 9. And on Christmas Eve 1862 he noted: "The afternoon I have spent with Frank and a very pleasant agreeable time have I passed." In the back of his journal Robbins kept track of the letters he received and those he sent out. Between May and December 1862, he received eleven letters from Edmonds and wrote her eleven back.[20]

The year 1863 dawned with no further decline in their friendship. Indeed, Edmonds finally seems to have been able to put her fondness for Robbins into some kind of perspective. "Dear Jerome," she wrote in a January letter,

> I am earnest in my *congratulations* & daily realize that had I met you some years ago I might have been much happier now. But Providence has ordered it otherwise & I must be content[.] I would not change it *now* if I could, if my life[']s happiness depended upon it.

"I do not love you less because you have another," Edmonds continued, "but rather more, for your nobleness of character displayed in your love for her." And she concluded, "May God make her worthy of so good a husband. Your loving friend, Emma."[21]

Probably contributing to Edmonds's generosity of spirit was the fact that in her travels she herself had developed a new, deep affection for another man, Assistant Adjutant General James Reid of the 79th New York Volunteers, whom Robbins referred to, on April 20, 1863, as "Frank's particular friend." There is some suggestion that Robbins was in fact at least a bit jealous of the connection between Edmonds and Reid: on April 4 he wrote awkwardly, "It is a sad reality to which we awaken when we learn that others are receiving the *devotion* of one from whom we only claim friendship[']s attention of which too we are deprived."[22]

Any jealousy Robbins felt, however, soon was eclipsed by consternation over his friend's apparent desertion from the army. "I was surprised this evening," Robbins wrote on April 17, 1863, "upon inquiring after Frank to hear he had not been seen since yesterday noon. [T]he present and first thought being he must have gone out of the picket line and found a difficulty in getting back." The following day Robbins noted that "Frank"'s desertion had now been confirmed, though he had not yet uncovered a satisfying explanation for it. On April 20, however, Robbins's tone changed significantly. He now indicated that he had been expecting her desertion but was enraged at her failure to reveal to him in advance either her exact plans or her precise reasons: "Do you know," Robbins wrote with some lack of clarity,

I have learned another lesson in the great book of human nature? . . . [H]e prepared me for his departure in part yet I did not think it would be so premature. [Y]et he did not prepare me for his ingratitude and utter disregard for the finer sensibilities of others. [O]f all others whom I termed friends he was the last I deemed capable of the petty business which was betrayed by his friend at the last moment. A misanthrope would write a chapter in detestation of the human race did he have my experience in this circumstance of life. [A]nd while I own a slight disgust to such a character, I am excited to pity

that poor humanity can be so weak as to repay kindness, interest and the warmest sympathy with deception, almost every
petty attribute of a selfish heart.[23]

Although Robbins continued to be willing to protect Edmonds by
obscuring her true identity in his journal, his anger at her was
unmistakable, fueled no doubt by his unacknowledged jealousy
of James Reid.

Years later Edmonds explained her desertion from the 2nd
Michigan as a choice she made in order to avoid having her sex discovered. While stationed with her regiment in Kentucky in the
spring of 1863, Edmonds claimed, she had fallen ill with a recur-
rence of chills and fever she had initially contracted on the Virginia
peninsula in the campaigns of the spring and early summer of
1862. Fearing that a hospital stay would lead to her exposure, she
had applied for a leave of absence. When her request was denied,
Edmonds deserted because it seemed the only way to protect her
identity. Several of her fellow soldiers from the 2nd Michigan lent
their support to Edmonds's assertion. In his 1882 history of the
regiment, Colonel John Robertson pinned Edmonds's desertion on
her fear of impending discovery: "It is supposed she apprehended
a disclosure of her sex," he wrote, "and deserted at Lebanon,
Kentucky." In 1884, in connection with a government Pension
Bureau inquiry into Edmonds's military service during the Civil
War, a former comrade named William Shakespeare testified that
he had known "Thompson" prior to the spring of 1863 to be a
strong and healthy soldier who never shirked his duty but who
during the Peninsula campaign had indeed contracted bad chills
from which he never quite recovered. Similarly, James Brown, F.
Schneider, and Sylvester Larned all maintained that "Thompson's"
health had been debilitated by hard service, and that she had left
the army after her leave of absence was refused. In an interview
with a journalist from the *Kansas City Times* that same year, Captain
William R. Morse repeated essentially the same story.[24]

It may be that Edmonds's 1884 explanation of her desertion from the army was accurate. Various circumstances, however, cast some doubt on this explanation. For one thing, Jerome Robbins seemed to indicate in his diary that he had been aware in advance of Edmonds's plans to desert. Moreover, Robbins's anger at Edmonds seems most unreasonable if indeed she was ill and trying to hide her sex. He was, after all, the regiment's hospital steward and an assistant surgeon and thus theoretically concerned for the health of the regiment's men; furthermore, he had also clearly demonstrated his own willingness to protect her identity. From a different angle, one could also argue that had Edmonds left the army only because an illness threatened to bring about the discovery of her sex, one might expect that once she had regained her health, her determination to serve would cause her to reenter the ranks, albeit under a new alias and probably in a new area. After all, she had already demonstrated her skills, courage, and determination to provide service to the army as a soldier during her almost two years with the 2nd Michigan. Instead, we know that after leaving her regiment in Kentucky, Edmonds traveled to Ohio and within a month donned women's clothes, resumed her original name and female identity, and set about serving the army in the capacity of a woman nurse. Clearly the reasons for her desertion were not so simple, nor was the explanation she gave years later for her desertion beyond all suspicion. It bears noting that Edmonds's claim that she deserted because of a combination of illness and anxiety about being discovered appeared for the first time—along with her former comrades' corroborating testimony—only in her 1884 application for a federal veteran's pension, when her paramount concern must have been to provide persuasive reasons for her abrupt disappearance from the ranks.

As it turns out, at least one of her contemporaries believed that Edmonds actually deserted because James Reid, whom the source identified as Edmonds's lover, had himself recently left the army.[25] Even if Edmonds and Reid were lovers, however, it is unlikely that Edmonds deserted in order to be *with* Reid: in a letter Edmonds wrote to Robbins in May 1863—only a month after she left the 2nd Michigan—she noted that Reid had invited her to visit him and his wife, who was anxious to meet her. Mrs. Reid's curiosity was probably a function of her having heard about Edmonds's successful imposture as a man and a soldier—which her husband would undoubtedly have mentioned to her—and not a reflection of her desire to trade intimate stories about her husband. In any case, it seems plausible that Edmonds's love for Reid, of which Robbins was perhaps painfully aware, drove her to follow him out of the army, even though she knew she could not be with him. Perhaps the frustration of falling first for Robbins and then for Reid—both of whom were unavailable—became too great, and Edmonds left the army in order to forestall similar disappointments down the line. On top of this, of course, her almost two years of dedicated service with the 2nd Michigan, complicated by the necessary struggle to maintain her imposture, may simply have worn her out. Regardless, Edmonds's desertion from the army drove yet another wedge between her and Robbins. Though they continued to correspond, they did so far less frequently, and Robbins fails to mention Edmonds again in his diary after May 1863.

That June, Edmonds took up the work of a female hospital nurse under the auspices of the United States Christian Commission, one of several civilian organizations established during the Civil War to provide for the physical, emotional, and spiritual needs of the soldiers. Like Belle Boyd and Rose Greenhow, she also turned her hand to writing a memoir recounting her experiences over the past two years. The book, entitled *Unsexed; or, The Female Soldier* when it first appeared in 1864, was reissued in 1865 with the somewhat tamer but also more oblique title *Nurse and Spy in the Union Army*. Curiously, the memoir under either title fails to mention Edmonds's imposture

(a) *Frontispiece of Edmonds's memoir,* Nurse and Spy *(1865), depicting her in conventional woman's dress.* Reprinted from the book.

(b) *Sarah Emma Edmonds, as she appeared in civilian male clothing at the time of the war (inset).* Courtesy of the Clarke Historical Library, Central Michigan University.

as Franklin Thompson, though the publisher's notice that opened the book—and the original title—seemed to wink at those who were already in the know. "In the opinion of many," the notice remarked,

> it is the privilege of woman to minister to the sick and soothe the sorrowing—and in the present crisis of our country's history, to aid our brothers to the extent of her capacity—and whether duty leads her to the couch of luxury, the abode of poverty, the crowded hospital, or the terrible battlefield—it makes little difference what costume she assumes while in the discharge of her duties.—Perhaps she should have the privilege of choosing for herself whatever may be the surest protection from insult and inconvenience in her blessed, self-sacrificing work.[26]

Rather than explicitly discussing Edmonds's career as a soldier, a detail that Edmonds seems not to have been willing to broadcast at that point, the book described her as having "unsexed" herself by means of her work as a female nurse in the male army (one who, in the course of her hospital service, had ironically encountered a woman posing as a male soldier) and, in a new twist on her military career, as a spy, sometimes disguised in male clothes.

Had Edmonds as Franklin Thompson in fact combined espionage work with her regular military service as a private in the 2nd Michigan Infantry? We know that some women served the Union and Confederate armies as both spies and soldiers. On January 7, 1865, the Union's Provost Marshal General of Missouri, J. H. Baker, issued a pass to one Mary M. Pitman, who used the alias "Miss Smith," in connection with her employment by the United States Army as a spy.[27] Pitman had infiltrated a group of rebel sympathizers in the area around St. Louis by posing as one of them and duping them into believing that she, too, was trying to smuggle supplies farther south. In April 1865 Pitman sought instructions from Baker regarding another assignment, for which she would need a disguise. What kind of disguise Pitman utilized on this occasion is not clear, but we do know from other documents that she had masqueraded as a soldier, and earlier in the war as a soldier masquerading as a woman, when she was in fact serving the cause of the Confederacy.

According to one federal government document, dated March 1864, Pitman—a native of Tennessee—had at the beginning of the war dressed as a man, assumed the alias "Rawley," and raised a company of troops whom she then offered for service to Confederate cavalry commander General Nathan Bedford Forrest (who in 1863 sentenced Pauline Cushman to death for espionage). With Forrest and the men she had recruited, "Lieutenant Rawley" proceeded to serve in several battles in Tennessee and Mississippi without anyone discovering her sex. In the winter of 1863, Forrest decided to detail "Rawley" for espionage work, suggesting that the smallish soldier assume the guise of a woman. At this point "Rawley" came clean with Forrest about her true identity, made him promise not to expose her to anyone else, and, taking the alias "Mollie Hayes," began a short career as a Confederate spy and smuggler. At some point during the war, however, Pitman lost faith in the Confederacy and allowed herself to be captured by the Union. Once in Union hands, she provided a substantial amount of information to the federals, including all she possessed with regard to Forrest's future plans. In addition, she provided a thorough exposé of the secret secessionist organization the Knights of the Golden Circle, of which she had once been a member. When the Acting Provost Marshal General of Missouri, Joseph Darr, sent Pitman to Major Frank Bond in October 1864 for assignment, Darr described her most favorably and urged Bond to return her immediately if he could make no use of her espionage skills himself.

There is some evidence to suggest that Edmonds, like Pitman, combined her masquerade as a soldier with espionage work for the Union. Certainly her positions as postmaster and mail carrier would have provided effective covers for some spy activity, and according to regimental historian John Robertson, "Franklin Thompson" was "often employed as a spy, going within the enemy's lines, sometimes absent for weeks."[28] But there is also considerable evidence to suggest that she did not. For one thing, the memoir in which Edmonds claimed to have done so was only loosely based on her actual experiences during the war, being instead primarily a piece of melodramatic pseudofiction written to raise money in part for herself but also for organizations benefiting the soldiers with whom she had served. Publisher A. M. Hurlbert wrote to Edmonds in March 1882 giving an account of the dispersal of the income from the 175,000 copies of her book that had sold. "We, as publishers," he wrote, "gave the Sanitary Commission and other cause[s] hundreds of dollars from the profits of the book; also gave you, I think, two $500 bonds . . . which you used among the sick and wounded soldiers at Harper's Ferry"; and in the same 1884 newspaper interview in which he testified to her valor as a soldier, William Morse also noted that Edmonds had donated $2,000 of the proceeds from the sale of her book to the Christian Commission.[29]

Indeed, more than one source claims that in her later life Edmonds yearned and even attempted to rewrite what she now confessed was her much fictionalized autobiography.[30] Moreover, in a sworn statement written in connection with her pension application, Edmonds herself seemed to deny that she had actually been a spy. "I make no statmement of any secret services," she wrote.

> In my mind there is almost as much odium attached to the word "spy" as there is to the word "deserter." There is so much *mean* deception necessarily practiced by a spy that I much prefer every one should believe that I never was beyond the enemy's lines rather than fasten upon me by oath a thing that I despise so much. It may do in war time, but it is not pleasant to think upon in times of peace.[31]

It is true that this somewhat convoluted denial of having been a spy, like her assertion that she had deserted the army for reasons of health and fear of discovery, was a part of Edmonds's application for a veteran's pension. But it seems unlikely that she would have denied having been a spy in this context simply because she feared that involvement in espionage during the war would have threatened her chances of receiving a pension. Another woman, Emma Porch, had by March 1884 received a federal pension precisely on the grounds of having been a spy during the war.[32] Edmonds probably did not know about Porch. Nevertheless, her denial seems to reflect more her attempt to disclose at last the true (and presumably even more noble and pension-worthy) nature of her military service, which earlier, when she was writing her memoir, she had feared to confess for complicated personal reasons.

In any case, after the war ended, Edmonds returned to New Brunswick, where she married Linus H. Seelye, a carpenter. The couple had three children of their own, all of whom died in childhood. But they adopted two sons, and together the family lived a peripatetic lifestyle. Meanwhile, for over fifteen years the story of Edmonds's imposture was known only to a few people. In 1882, when she began gathering the materials necessary to apply for a veteran's pension, however, she sought all the help she could get from former comrades who could testify that "Franklin Thompson" had been a good soldier and had deserted for one reason alone: the fear of discovery and disgrace. Two years later Edmonds attended a reunion of her regiment where she revealed herself to the men with whom she had served, and they, much to their credit, welcomed her as one of their own and, recognizing her deteriorating health, closed ranks behind her to gain her a pension. The letters that several of them sent testifying to Edmonds's exemplary service as a soldier, her loyalty to the Union, and the reasonableness of her decision to desert helped the Congressional pension committee decide the case in her favor. In July 1884 a special act of Congress acknowledged Edmonds's service with the 2nd Michigan as "Franklin Thompson" and placed her on the pension rolls at a standard rate of twelve dollars per month. At the same time, Congress formally deleted the charge of desertion from her record. Edmonds lived the last years of her life in La Porte, Texas, and at Houston in 1897 she was mustered into the George B. McClellan Post of the Grand Army of the Republic, the premier organization of Civil War veterans. Edmonds died on September 5, 1898, and was buried in Houston's Washington Cemetery with full military honors.[33]

No other woman soldier of the Civil War left the kind of paper trail that Edmonds did. One who left us more than enough to go on, however, is Jennie Hodgers.[34] Born in Ireland in 1844, Hodgers found her way to the United States some years before the outbreak of the war, possibly as a shipboard stowaway, and took up residence in or around Belvidere, Illinois. Not unlike Edmonds, by April 1861 Hodgers had already become accustomed to wearing male attire and using a male pseudonym, in her case, "Albert D. J. Cashier." According to one source, when Hodgers first came to the United States her uncle found her a job in the shoe factory where he worked, and for that job Hodgers was required to wear boy's clothing and adopt a boy's name. It is also possible that Hodgers, who spent her early years helping her father tend sheep, had grown accustomed to wearing boy's clothes in connection with that task. In any case, by the time the war broke out, Hodgers, like Edmonds, had already assumed a male identity and was quite familiar with grinding labor.

Also like Edmonds, the Civil War led Hodgers into military service in the guise of a man. Though diminutive in stature—most descriptions suggest that she was about five feet tall and slight, having noticeably small hands and feet—Hodgers joined the 95th Illinois Infantry Volunteers in August 1862. She was eighteen years old. About a year into her service, in June 1863, Hodgers contracted chronic diarrhea, which threatened her with exposure when it landed her in a military hospital. But like Deborah Sampson, who after her gunshot wound at Tarrytown had somehow managed to avoid a thorough physical examination, within twenty-four hours Hodgers had persuaded the hospital's doctors to treat her for this highly debilitating illness as an outpatient, sparing her the embarrassment of discovery. Her remarkable recovery from one of the "principal killer diseases of the Civil War," which should have left her "incapable of moving from her bed or attending to her own sanitary needs,"[35] permitted her to remain with the regiment until she was honorably discharged in August 1865.

The troops of the 95th Illinois began drilling in August 1862, left for the front in November of that same year to join Ulysses S. Grant's Army of Tennessee, and served in the western theater for the war's duration. The 95th was, as one account puts it, a "fighting regiment," participating in Grant's campaign in northern Mississippi in 1862 and 1863 and—like Belle Reynolds's 17th Illinois—in the siege of Vicksburg, as well as in a number of raids and battles across Mississippi and Tennessee in 1864, on one occasion being "nearly annihilated."[36] The fact that Hodgers's sex was not discovered by those who served with her indicates that she must have done her share of the fighting, and depositions taken long after the war from former comrades who had only recently learned of her sex described her as a thoroughly convincing male soldier. Wrote one comrade, "I never suspected at any time all through the service that Cashier was a woman." Another recalled that she "seemed to be able to do as much work as anyone in the Company," and another called her a "brave little soldier." On the other hand, notably now with the knowledge of her sex, former comrades-in-arms also "remembered" that Hodgers's actions "seemed to be a little funny," that she never seemed to have to shave or go to the toilet, that she did not want to have a bunk mate or to participate in sports or games with the other soldiers, and that she was industrious but reserved. "We sometimes called him half and half," wrote former soldier Robert Horan, using a colloquialism whose specific implications are lost to history. Still, Hodgers's fellow soldiers were not suspicious, and all

# Woman Soldier in 95th Ill.

ALBERT D. J. CASHIER

OF

COMPANY G, 95TH ILLINOIS REGIMENT

Photographed November, 1864

ALBERT D. J. CASHIER

OF

COMPANY G, 95TH ILLINOIS REGIMENT

Photographed July, 1913

*Jennie Hodgers, a.k.a. Albert D. J. Cashier, as she appeared at the time of the war, and in 1913.* Courtesy of the Illinois State Historical Library.

greeted the news of her true sex with the sentiment expressed simply by Charles W. Ives: "I was very much surprised."[37]

After the war, Hodgers returned to Illinois, settling in the small community of Saunemin in 1869, where she resumed her life as a male laborer. Hodgers did not marry but lived out most of the balance of her life peaceably in her own small home, having developed particularly close ties to one local family, the Chesbros, for whom she worked as a handyman for many years and with whom she often ate her meals. At some point after 1890, Hodgers, as

Civil War veteran Albert D. J. Cashier, began collecting a pension and, like Edmonds, became a member of the Grand Army of the Republic. Unlike Edmonds, Hodgers's membership in the GAR was based on the continuing assumption that she was a man.

Ironically, the perilous injury that Hodgers had avoided through three years of army service with the fighting 95th Illinois Infantry caught up with her in Saunemin. In 1911 Hodgers sustained a broken leg in the course of her work and a physical examination by Nettie Chesbro Rose, a daughter of her employer, revealed her sex.[38] Now approximately sixty-seven years of age, Jennie Hodgers, who had lived over fifty years as a man, faced public exposure. Temporarily, however, her secret remained relatively secure, as the Chesbros faithfully determined to bury the knowledge among themselves. But the injury to her leg disabled Hodgers for further labor, and within a few months a consensus emerged among those who were keeping her counsel that she could receive better long-term care in an institution. Thus Hodgers was admitted to the Soldiers and Sailors Home in Quincy, Illinois, where she remained until 1914.

Once she was at the home, knowledge of Hodgers's sex spread, though she continued to receive her pension. Even the conservator appointed to oversee her financial affairs claimed no knowledge of Hodgers's true identity until March 1913, when the state of Illinois declared Jennie Hodgers insane, presumably on the grounds that she had been "posing" as a Civil War veteran named Albert D. J. Cashier (no behavioral explanation was given in the declaration). Within the year the state decided to transfer her to its Hospital for the Insane in Watertown. Over the course of her eighteen months at the state hospital, Hodgers's sex became more widely known—"Let me tell you, it was a shock," said one of Hodgers's former neighbors in Saunemin, Ruth Morehart, when she was interviewed in 1991 about the discovery.[39]

During Hodgers's time in the asylum, the federal government's Pension Bureau solicited depositions of her former comrades—some of whom had visited her at the Soldiers and Sailors Home. The Pension Bureau sought to ascertain whether this Jennie Hodgers was identical to the Albert D. J. Cashier who had been collecting a pension, and also whether Albert D. J. Cashier had in fact served with the 95th Illinois Infantry. The author of one Pension Board of Review report seemed particularly eager to uncover subterfuge: "There is the suggestion," wrote the author of the report, "that Jinnie [*sic*] Hodgers was one of *twins*. . . . If such is the fact it is not improbable that the soldier actually was a man and that the pensioner was not the soldier."[40] In the end, however, the pension board confirmed Jennie Hodgers's identity with "Cashier." During her time at the state hospital, Hodgers was also required to resume the attire of a woman. According to a nurse who worked at the hospital at the time, Hodgers, whom she described as a "dear and loveable patient," never could accustom herself to wearing a dress, having worn pants most if not all of her life. Instead, the nurse reported, with the obvious confusion of pronouns that such a situation produces, Hodgers "would pull his skirt between his legs and pin it together to make pants," a habit to which other women on her ward objected, but which hospital officials decided to permit.[41]

One modern published account of Hodgers's life and career claims that while she lived at the Soldiers and Sailors Home, Hodgers's mental stability did in fact come under question, and that the transfer to the state asylum was justified on the grounds of her shaky mental state. Among the depositions in her pension file, one certainly finds evidence to support this claim. "She had a weak mind when I saw her at Quincy," recalled a former comrade in 1915, and a resident of the Soldiers and Sailors Home noted that Hodgers had been placed "in my care on account of her mental condition. When she was first placed with me her mental condition varied. She had lucid intervals. She was reluctant to divulge any of her previous history," and she provided only disjointed stories about her background.[42]

One could endlessly ponder the roots of Hodgers's alleged mental imbalance: Did it begin with her uncle's (or her father's) early decision to dress her in boy's clothing and call her "Albert"? Was it a consequence of years of gruesome warfare for which her "female nature" did not suit her? Did masquerading as a man for over fifty years cause her to become insane? One could ponder these questions, but it is also crucial not to ignore the evidence in Hodgers's pension file which suggests that she had for years been perceived as "different," evasive, or odd in some way, an impression that, rather than signifying insanity, is what one might expect of a person living under an assumed identity and in the guise of the other sex. Nettie Chesbro Rose, who had known "Cashier" for a long time, noted that "he" had always seemed a bit "queer," and that "some thought he was half witted."[43] Such evidence provokes a different set of questions about Hodgers's purported insanity at the end of her life: if Hodgers was truly mentally incapacitated by 1913, for example, might it not have been a result of the trauma of having her true identity exposed after so many years? Might not the collapse of her lifelong charade, and the requirement that after half a century she must resume a long-since-abandoned female identity complete with women's clothes, bring on a mental breakdown? Or, one could ask, was the state of Illinois's declaration of her mental incapacity even legitimate, given its timing in relation to the revelation that she was a woman? Was the declaration perhaps less a statement of reality than a bureaucratic response to the discovery that this woman had crossed certain boundaries of social and sexual propriety, not only living as a man but also taking up arms as a soldier and thereby apparently staking a claim to a central feature of nineteenth-century American manhood? However one answers these questions, it is important to note that as in the case of Sarah Emma Edmonds, Jennie Hodgers's former comrades-in-arms did not condemn her at the end of her life. Indeed, without exception the deponents in her pension case spoke favorably of her, and members of her GAR local, though aware of her sex, nevertheless insisted on providing Hodgers with a true soldier's burial, sending her to the grave in her soldier's uniform with full military honors when she died in October 1915.

There is one other Civil War woman soldier for whom we have sufficient documentation to flesh out her story in some detail: Sarah Rosetta Wakeman, who served with Company H of the 153rd New York State Volunteers from August 1862 to June 1864 as Private Lyons Wakeman.[44] During her military service Wakeman wrote numerous letters home that her family carefully preserved, along with a photograph of her and a ring she had worn in the army. Wakeman's letters are the only such source for information on Civil War women soldiers that has come to light thus far, and they are profoundly revealing.

Not much is known about Wakeman's early life except that she was born in 1843, the eldest of the nine children Harvey and Emily Wakeman raised on their farm in Afton, New York. By the age of seventeen she had received some formal education and was working as a domestic servant probably not far from her home. By the summer of 1862, however, nineteen-year-old Wakeman seems to have determined that assuming the garb of a man would provide her with a wider range of employment opportunities and perhaps a better means for relieving her family's concerns about her future, as marriage did not seem to be in the offing. "I knew that I Could help you more to leave home than to stay there with you," she later wrote. "So I left." There may also have been some family conflict that drove her to leave home: in the first letter she wrote to her family after she left, she referred to an "old affray" that she hoped they might all be able to put behind them, and a month later she wrote to her mother, "I want you should forgive me of everything that I ever done, and I will forgive you all the same. . . ."[45] In any case, in August 1862 Wakeman donned male clothes and pulled up stakes, soon accepting a job as a boatman on New York's Chenango Canal.

Writing home in November of that year, Wakeman apprised her family of developments since her departure. "When i [*sic*] left you," she wrote,

> i went to Binghamton. . . . I went to work with Stephen Saldon. . . . I work[ed] half a month for 4$ in money. I was only 7 miles from Binghamton up the river. . . . When i got done [with] work I went on the canal to work. I agreed to run 4 trips from Binghamton to Utica for 20$ in money, but this load of coal was going to Canajoharie, Montgomery Co.

When she got to Canajoharie, Wakeman continued, she met up with some soldiers who urged her to enlist, "and so i did." Enlisting for three years or the duration of the war, Wakeman received $152 in bounty money, which she planned to enclose with her letter. "All the money i send you," she wrote, "i want you should spend it for the family in clothing or something to eat. Don't save it for me," she went on, optimistically comparing the wages she had earned as a domestic and as a boatman with the bounty she had gotten for enlisting, "for i can get all the money i want." To Wakeman it was clear that a job in the army, though dangerous, promised a steady income and long-term financial security. "If i ever return," she added, "i shall have enough money for my self and to divide with you." As a parting request, Wakeman asked her family to hold on to a spotted calf to which she was partial and which she perhaps intended to be the centerpiece of a farm of her own after the war.[46]

Wakeman enlisted in Company H of the 153rd New York State Volunteers on August 30 at Root, New York, and mustered in six weeks later at Fonda, also in New York. Wakeman's military service record notes that at her enlistment she misrepresented her age as twenty-one (she was seventeen or eighteen), and that she was small, like Hodgers, five feet tall with a fair complexion, blue eyes, and brown hair. On October 18 Wakeman's regiment headed south to Washington, where it was slated to contribute to the defense of the federal capital. Wakeman wrote home at the end of November from camp in Alexandria, Virginia. By this time she appeared to be well adjusted to the soldier's life, and certainly a month later she was sounding like a cheerful (if not yet battle-tested) veteran. "The weather is cold and the ground is froze hard," she wrote,

> but I sleep as warm in the tents as I would in a good bed. I don't know the difference when I get asleep. We have boards laid down for a floor and our dishes is tin. We all have a tin plate and a tin cup, and a knife and Fork, one spoon. We have to use the floor for a table. I like to be a soldier very well.[47]

In January 1863 measles spread through the camp of the 153rd and men were dying, but Wakeman herself was spared a full-blown battle with the sickness, which might have meant the undoing of her imposture. To her father she wrote: "We have had two men die out of our Company. There has died out of our Regiment about 30 as near as I can learn and there is quite a number sick." In fact, Wakeman may have received a controversial vaccination on January 1, producing a mild case of the disease: her medical record shows that she was hospitalized from January 1 through January 6 in the regimental hospital for "rubeola." Importantly, however, her sex was not discovered. As the epidemic raged, Wakeman placed her faith in God and tobacco to keep her healthy. "Mother," she wrote in a January 15 letter, "I use all of the tobacco I want. I think it will keep off from catch[ing] diseases."[48]

Wakeman continued to write home at least once a month, reassuring her family that she was pleased with her life as a soldier and at the same time excluding any details about the complexities of masquerading as a man. "You mustn't trouble you[r] Self about me," she wrote late in March 1863 from Alexandria, where the regiment was still engaged in the defense of Washington. "I am contented. . . . I don't fear the rebel bullets nor I don't fear the cannon. . . . I like to drill first rate . . . [and] I am getting fat as a hog." Not one to avoid drama entirely, however, in a postscript Wakeman added that "it would make your hair stand out to be where I have been. How would you like to be in the front rank and have the rear rank load and fire their guns over you[r] shoulder? I have been there myself." In mid-April she reemphasized her satisfaction with the army: "I feel perfectly happy," she wrote. In June she claimed to be "enjoying my Self better this summer than I ever did before in this world. I have good Clothing and enough to eat and nothing to do, only to handle my gun and that I can do as well as the rest of them." In July she commented favorably on the regiment's brass band, which played for the soldiers when they were on guard duty, and in September she reported from the regiment's new barracks inside the capital city that she was feeling well and enjoying herself "first rate." (The 153rd's new assignment—to guard the Old Capitol and Carroll prisons—overlapped in time with the second incarceration of Belle Boyd.) Come October 1863 Wakeman insisted that she was still healthy and, indeed, "as tough as a bear." And a few days after Christmas that year, she waxed particularly happy about her life in the military. "I sometimes think that I never will go home in the world," she wrote. "I have enjoyed my self the best since I have been gone away from home than [I] ever did before in my life. I have plenty of money to spend and a good time assoldier[ing]. I find just as good friends among Strangers as I do at home."[49]

In her letters home, Wakeman commented frequently about her plans to send her family money. "We expect to get four months['] pay this week and if I do . . . I will send part of it home to you," she wrote in March 1863. Late in April she reported that she had received her pay, and that she expected to send thirty dollars of it home as soon as she could get to an express office. That November, Wakeman apologized for not being able to send anything: "I got my pay the other day," she wrote,

> but my Clothing bill was so much that I didn't get but 12 dollars and 50 cents, and I Can't let you have any of it, but when we get paid again and if I get money enough so I Can Spare it, I will Send you money. It Cost me a good deal to live for when I have got any money I will have something to eat, as long as I can get it.[50]

In December, Wakeman mentioned that she was considering reenlisting for five years in order to get a promised reenlistment bounty of eight hundred dollars.

Wakeman's letters indicate that her religious faith proved a significant source of comfort to her as she contemplated the dangers that her otherwise enjoyable job entailed. "If I go into battle I shall be alright," she wrote home in April 1863, but she added that "if it is God['s] will for me to be killed here, it is my will to die." In August she reiterated that theme: "I don't know how long before I shall have to go into the field of battle," she wrote, but

> for my part i don't Care. I don't feel afraid to go. I don't believe there are any Rebel's bullet[s] made for me yet. Nor i don't Care if there is. I am as independent as a hog on the ice. If it is God['s] will for me to fall in the field of battle, it is my will to go and never return home.

Wakeman's faith also helped her to resist various temptations associated with army life. In October 1863 she wrote somewhat mysteriously: "I got led away into this world So bad that I sinned a good deal. But I now believe that God['s] Spirit has been working with me." God's spirit did not prevent her from getting into a fight with a fellow soldier, however. In January 1864 Wakeman reported having had a squabble with one of the regiment's troublemakers, Private Stephen Wiley, in which she claimed to have gotten in three or four "pretty good cracks" despite the fact that she was more than half a foot shorter than her opponent.[51]

In one letter Wakeman made reference to an unnamed woman who, like herself, had enlisted as a man in the Union army. Somewhat surprisingly, she did not draw any explicit comparisons with her own situation. Moreover, despite this news that another woman soldier's sex had been detected, Wakeman continued to sign her letters home with her real name, Rosetta. Only in November 1863 did she begin to sign with an alias, "Edwin Wakeman." Why she did not sign using the name under which she had enlisted is unclear, but one source speculates that Wakeman's choice of her pen name may have been an expression of her admiration for her commander, Edwin P. Davis.[52]

Though she repeatedly informed her family that she expected her regiment to go into battle at any moment, by early December 1863, after more than a year in the service, Wakeman had given up on this actually happening. "You needn't be afraid of our regiment ever going to the front," she wrote on December 9, "for it never will. . . ." On February 20, 1864, however, the troops finally left Alexandria heading south, arriving in Algiers, Louisiana, on the last day of the month after nine days on board the transport ship the *Mississippi*. Now Wakeman was sure she and her comrades would be sent to the field, though she did not know where. "Our regiment has gone to raising hell so much that we will get shove[d] to the field of battle," she wrote home on March 2, 1864. And in a tone much more pessimistic than she had ever displayed before, she added: "I don't ever expect to see you again in this world."[53]

About three months later Wakeman's prediction of her own death came true, although she did not fall to rebel fire. On April 14, 1864, she wrote her last surviving letter home, recording the details of the engagement at Pleasant Hill, Louisiana, in which she had faced the enemy with her regiment five days before. "I was under fire about four hours," she wrote, "and laid [sic] on the field of battle all night."[54] Although she was not among those wounded or killed in the battle—a resounding Confederate defeat that nonetheless gave way to a Union retreat from western Louisiana—Wakeman's death was imminent. Shortly after the engagement, she fell sick, and on May 3 she was admitted to the regimental hospital with chronic diarrhea, the same deadly disease that Jennie Hodgers had contracted and survived. A few days later authorities decided to transfer Wakeman to the Marine U.S.A. General Hospital in New Orleans, which admitted her on May 22 after what seems to have been an inordinately long and punishing overland journey. Throughout her hospitalization Wakeman escaped detection: presumably she underwent only the most cursory examinations by staff doctors or nurses because the symptoms of acute chronic diarrhea were self-evident. Wakeman must also have managed, despite obvious weakness, to tend to her own sanitary affairs, or perhaps she presented such a hopeless case that others who might have been assigned to the task decided not to bother. In any case, no one seems to have realized that she was a woman, and she did not recover. On June 19 Rosetta Wakeman died, and her body was buried in a military ceremony at Chalmette National Cemetery in New Orleans. A statement signed by the surgeon in charge at the hospital where she died noted that Wakeman had "served HONESTLY and FAITHFULLY with his Company in the field to the present date," that "he" had last been paid the previous December, and that at his death "he" owed a small amount of money both to the government for clothing and to an army sutler for unnamed supplies.[55] Rosetta Wakeman's military service was at an end.

Chapter Six

# To "Don the Breeches, and Slay Them with a Will!"[1]

✳

*A Host of Women Soldiers*

A sister-soldier's greeting to you, for I too have been, and was, until a few months ago, a soldier.

*Miss Nellie A. K., quoted in* The Life of Pauline Cushman, *1864*

Sarah Emma Edmonds, Jennie Hodgers, and Rosetta Wakeman are three among hundreds of women who dressed as men, adopted male identities, and enlisted in the armies of the Union and the Confederacy during the Civil War. Needless to say, many women who envisioned a military role for themselves in connection with the war, particularly when wanting to defend their homes, did not ultimately enlist as soldiers, although some seemed to come quite close to doing so. A group of women in December 1864 wrote to the Confederate Secretary of War, James Alexander Seddon, requesting—probably not facetiously—that he sanction their organization of a "full regiment of *ladies*, between the ages of 16 and 40," to be armed and "equipped to perform regular service in the Army of the Shenandoah Valley," notably for purposes of local defense. "Our homes have been visited time and again by the vandal foe," wrote Irene Bell, Annie Samuels, and ten other women. "We have been subjected to every conceivable outrage & suffering," for which they blamed "the incompetency of the Confederate Army upon which we depend for defence." In consequence, wrote the women, "we propose to leave our hearthstones, to endure any sacrifice, any privation for the ultimate success of our Holy Cause." Should the Secretary of War approve their plan, Bell and the others concluded, "please favor us by sending immediately properly authenticated orders for the carrying out of our wishes. All arrangements . . . have been effected & we now only wait [for] the approval of the War department."[2]

Many other women, privately and publicly, expressed a similarly strong desire to join the army. In an 1862 letter to the Adjutant General of the Wisconsin National Guard, a Mrs. S. Ann Gordon asked if there was any way she might join the army as a nurse in order to be with her husband, a soldier in the 10th Wisconsin. Although she requested a nurse's position, Gordon clearly believed herself to be soldier material. "As most ladies are considered delicate," she told the Adjutant General, "excuse me for saying that for some weeks past I have accustomed myself to from two to 4 miles walk every day and endure it with very slight fatigue. I have not seen any sickness in twenty years, and I think I should make an enduring soldier." And Louisiana's Sarah Morgan was undoubtedly not the only woman to confide her martial aspirations to her diary: "Oh! if I were only a man," Morgan wrote. "Then I could don the breeches, and slay them with a will! If some few Southern women were in the ranks," she insisted, "they could set the men an example they would not blush to follow."[3]

As we already know, not all women who actually "don[ned] the breeches" during the war served as soldiers. Some, like Mrs. L. A. McCarty, disguised themselves as men for the sole purpose of engaging in espionage and resistance activity. Arrested in

March 1862 while en route to the Confederacy in possession of an item of contraband ordnance, a quantity of contraband medicine, and a weapon tucked into her baggage, McCarty became for a brief time an inmate at "Fort Greenhow," where she caught Rose Greenhow's attention. "Quite an excitement was created throughout the prison. . . ," wrote Greenhow later, "by the arrest of a woman in male attire . . . at the hotel of a man named Donnelly, in Washington. . . . She was very handsome, and was a woman of some cultivation and scientific attainments . . . a keen observer, and both spoke and wrote well."[4]

The vast majority of women who dressed as men during the war, however, did so in order to enlist, and as the stories of Edmonds, Hodgers, and Wakeman (like that of Deborah Sampson) indicate, sustaining an imposture as a male soldier was possible even over an extended period of time. As far as we know, not one of these women was discovered conclusively to be a woman by any observer during the period of her service. Fellow soldiers may have had some suspicions based on the women's relatively small stature, their beardlessness, their more highly pitched voices, and so forth, but in none of these cases is there any indication that such suspicions progressed any further. Rather, we know that Edmonds confessed her sex to her friend Jerome Robbins; that Hodgers lived out the bulk of her life, half a century beyond the end of the war, as a male laborer; and that Wakeman took her identity to the grave. How was it possible for these and so many other women to maintain their impostures, not infrequently for years at a time?

Certain features of mid-nineteenth-century military life and culture helped make cross-gender "passing" possible. For one thing, although in theory women had to overcome the obstacle of a physical examination in order to enlist in the army, in practice the recruitment exam was often quite perfunctory, and thus rarely constituted a serious barrier to a woman's enlistment. This is not to say that there were no army guidelines designed to make the examination process meaningful, for indeed there were. "In passing a recruit," one regulation stipulated,

> the medical officer is to examine him stripped; to see that he has free use of all his limbs; that his chest is ample; that his hearing, vision and speech are perfect; that he has no tumors, or ulcerated or cicatrized legs; no rupture or chronic cutaneous affection; that he has not received any contusion, or wound of the head, that may impair his faculties; that he is not subject to convulsions; and has no infectious disorder that may unfit him for military service.[5]

Moreover, after being examined as a raw recruit, the soldier who was accepted into the service was supposed to undergo a second examination upon joining his regiment.

But thanks to the combination of an equally inexperienced medical staff and the rush of so many soldiers to enlist, in the first part of the war in particular an army recruit rarely faced a physical examination "more rigorous than holding out his hands to demonstrate that he had a working trigger finger, or perhaps opening his mouth to show that his teeth were strong enough to rip open a minié ball cartridge." According to one soldier, the recruitment examination he received from the "fat, jolly old doctor" assigned to perform it was both typical and absurd. "He requested me to stand up straight," the soldier recalled,

> then gave me two or three little sort of "love taps" on the chest, turned me round, ran his hands over my shoulders, back, and limbs, laughing and talking all the time, then whirled me to the front, and rendered judgment on me as follows: "Ah, Capt. Reddish! I only wish you had a hundred such fine boys as this one! He's all right, and good for the service."

According to historian Bell Wiley's research, of two hundred federal regiments who were the subject of an investigation by the watchdog United States Sanitary Commission towards the end of 1861, 58 percent were cited as failing to have made even a pretense of examining the health of their recruits at the time of their enlistment. At least one examiner had a reputation for being able to evaluate ninety recruits per hour. From this perspective alone, it is no wonder that women were often able to slip into the ranks undetected.[6]

Women soldiers who evaded or made it through the physical examination process soon discovered that many of the features of regular Civil War army life also provided effective shields against the discovery of their sex. Army life in the 1860s was significantly different from army life in the late twentieth century. For one thing, recruitment was rarely if ever followed by anything resembling modern-day boot camp with its intensive physical training. Rather, the focus was generally on learning how to drill. Wrote one Pennsylvania soldier after six months in the army: "The first thing in the morning is drill, then drill, then drill again. Then drill, drill, a little more drill. Then drill, and lastly drill. Between drills, we drill and sometimes stop to eat a little and have a roll-call." In new units at least, "drilling" meant learning how to handle, load, and fire guns and how to parry and thrust with a bayonet, practicing simple maneuvers, and marching. In the early weeks of their military service, women soldiers' efforts, like those of their male comrades, centered on such gender-neutral exercises. Of course, women soldiers also had to learn to carry their own gear, which typically included a gun, a bayonet and scabbard, ammunition, blankets, a canteen, clothing, stationery, photographs, toiletries, and a mending kit, plus equipment for cooking and eating rations. But once they grew accustomed to the forty to fifty pounds of matériel they had to carry, as many men also needed to accustom themselves, women soldiers rarely had to fear that additional biologically based differences in physical strength would lead to their disclosure.[7]

Moreover, camp life, although intimate in some ways, allowed for sufficient freedom of movement to enable women soldiers to avoid notice when bathing and dealing with other personal matters. Civil War soldiers lived and slept in close proximity to one another, but they rarely changed their clothes. Furthermore, they passed the bulk of their time, day and night, out of doors, where they also attended to their bodily needs. Thus, a female soldier could often maintain a certain amount of physical distance from her comrades, which was particularly important in connection with her toilet. Prevailing standards regarding modesty in such matters worked in a woman soldier's favor, writes the editor of Sarah Rosetta Wakeman's papers, Lauren Burgess, "ensur[ing] that no one would question a shy soldier's reluctance to bathe in a river with his messmates or to relieve himself in the open company sinks [long trenches soldiers dug for sanitation purposes wherever they camped]."[8]

Of course, attending to one's personal needs on the march or in battle was a rather different matter. Though generally loose-fitting for the sake of easy sizing (and thus beneficial to the woman soldier trying to disguise her physical form), Civil War soldiers' uniforms consisted of many pieces, overlaid with a great deal of equipment—or "impedimenta," as Wiley calls it. Much of this clothing and equipment had to be removed if a woman did not want to soil herself, and at least one modern student of the phenomenon of women soldiers during the Civil War has argued persuasively that in order to avoid detection while on the march or on the field, women soldiers simply drank as little as possible given the weather conditions to which they were exposed, and if they could not get away to some private place to relieve themselves, just went ahead and did so in their clothing, as discreetly as possible, while on the move. Regarding the question of menstruation, one suspects that many women soldiers, who often became lean and athletic in the service, simply stopped menstruating. Those who continued to do so simply had to find ways to dispose of the evidence of their menstrual periods: bloody rags that they probably managed either to burn or bury themselves, or to combine surreptitiously with similar-looking "laundry" from soldiers wounded in battle.[9]

That there were so many young men and even boys in the ranks during the Civil War also helped women soldiers avoid exposure. Whereas armies composed only of fully mature men might have been less tolerant of the odd enlisted man whose build was slighter or whose cheeks were strangely smooth, Civil War armies drew their soldiers from a wide range of age groups. Despite various regulations to the contrary, untold numbers of boys seventeen and younger lied about their ages and joined the Union and Confederate armies as regular soldiers. The presence of so many youngsters who looked and sounded similar to women provided women soldiers with an added measure of security.[10]

Rigid codes of dress typical of the mid-nineteenth century also reinforced an assumption among Civil War soldiers that "if it wore pants, it was male."[11] Wrote one soldier after he discovered that a former comrade was a woman, "A single glance at her in her proper character leads me to wonder how I ever could have mistaken her for a man, and I readily recall many things which ought to have betrayed her, except that no one thought of finding a woman in a soldier's dress." In 1902 Captain Ira B. Gardner, formerly of the 14th Maine, recalled enrolling a woman soldier in his company who went on to serve for two years before he realized his mistake. "If I had been anything but a boy, I should have probably seen from her form that she was a female," Gardner wrote, but clearly the woman's clothes had been enough to deceive him.[12] Dominant mid-century notions about differences in men's and women's capabilities had a similar result: women were considered unfit for military service in consequence of their presumed physical, emotional, and intellectual weaknesses (though such presumed weaknesses clearly did not apply to working-class and slave women). Thus, few expected to find them in the ranks or thought to look for them there. Interestingly, there is considerable evidence to suggest that women soldiers, who knew what signs to watch for, recognized each other with relative ease.[13]

Almost certainly the bulk of women who served as soldiers during the Civil War were never discovered. Some, like Jennie Hodgers, were discovered only years after their military service had come to an end. According to a Chicago *Times-Herald* story published shortly after "his" death, a coroner's examination revealed that Civil War veteran "Otto Schaffer" was a woman. "Schaffer" had spent many years after the war in Butler County, Kansas, living as a hermit. One day a major thunderstorm caused "Schaffer" to take shelter in his cabin moments before a bolt of lightning demolished it. Neighbors found the body on the floor and called the coroner, who became aware of "Schaffer's" secret while he was preparing the body for burial. Perhaps because "Schaffer" was known to have participated in so many battles during the war, local veterans rose to the occasion and gave "him" a soldier's burial, during which they honored the veteran's remains with a final gun salute.[14]

A somewhat different case is that of Emma A. B. Kinsey. Whether or not she ever actually served in the Civil War military, her husband later in life claimed that she had. An undated memo at the National Archives notes his request for information regarding her service. According to the memo, Kinsey's widower claimed that his late wife had reached the rank of lieutenant colonel with the 40th New Jersey Infantry before she received an honorable discharge from the regiment's commander, Augustus Fay, Jr., in July 1865. The author of the memo in turn insisted that Kinsey's name was not to be found on the rolls of the 40th New Jersey. Needless to say, however, the fact that her name did not appear on the rolls hardly precludes the possibility of her having served: like other women soldiers,

Emma Kinsey would have enlisted under an alias that her husband may not have known.[15]

Other women soldiers' identities came to light shortly after they received their discharges as men. In 1863 a Detroit newspaper described the arrest of a discharged soldier on suspicion of being a woman. Following her arrest, Ida Remington of Rochester, New York—who was still wearing her uniform—informed police that she had served with the 11th New York for two years through several battles, including the September 14, 1862, battle of South Mountain in Maryland, where the 11th New York helped to foil General Lee's plans for a successful invasion of the North; and the bloodbath at nearby Antietam that came a few days later. Because she had already left the army, authorities had no cause to hold her, and upon her release, the article noted, Remington left town. "Her whole story . . ." the article concluded, "shows that 'when a woman will, she will,' regardless of consequences."[16]

Women soldiers sustained their impostures through all sorts of complicated situations and sometimes for the duration of their postwar lives. Still, there were circumstances during the war under which exposure became virtually unavoidable. Certainly any situation that caused her to come under close scrutiny put a woman soldier's imposture in jeopardy. One woman soldier is mentioned in the letter an Indiana cavalryman wrote to his wife in February 1863: "We discovered last week a soldier who turned out to be a girl," he wrote, and who had already been in service for almost two years, during which time she was wounded twice. "Maybe she would have remained undiscovered for a long time if she hadn't fainted. She was given a warm bath which gave the secret away."[17]

In some cases, an unexpected encounter with a particularly observant family member or friend was enough to put an end to a woman soldier's career. In October 1862 the Owensburg, Kentucky, *Monitor* remarked on the commotion that the discovery of a woman soldier had provoked among the men of the 66th

Kentucky. During her four weeks with the regiment, the woman had apparently conducted herself in such a way as to allay suspicions among her comrades about her sex. But an unexpected visit by her uncle to the regiment's camp—he had probably come to see others in the regiment whom he might have known from his community—led to her undoing. When he recognized her, her uncle saw immediately to her discharge.[18]

In February 1863 the Detroit *Advertiser and Tribune* reported that authorities had arrested one Mary Burns after she was recognized by an acquaintance, and had dismissed her from the service. Burns, it seems, had—with his knowledge—followed her lover into the 7th Michigan Cavalry under the alias "John Burns" and had succeeded in maintaining her disguise for two weeks. Similarly, a woman who enlisted with her brother in a Confederate regiment by using the pseudonym "Joshua Clarke" was quickly recognized by someone who knew her and discharged. Upon her departure, "Private Clarke" expressed her determination to reenlist as soon as possible in a different regiment, and one suspects that the lessons she learned as a result of having been discovered once only helped her to disguise herself more effectively in the future. In contrast, Marian Green of Michigan was forced to return home after several weeks, not because someone unexpectedly recognized her, but because her fiancé, whom she had followed into the army against his will, chose to inform her unhappy parents that she was with him.[19]

Some women soldiers inadvertently gave themselves away by displaying behavior that aroused observers' suspicions about their sex. When Sarah Collins of Wisconsin cut her hair, donned men's clothes, and enlisted with her brother after the war broke out, she hoped to have an opportunity to engage the enemy in battle. Instead, she failed to make it out of town with her regiment. Described as a "robust girl" for whom the soldier's life should have presented few challenges she could not meet, Collins nevertheless aroused suspicion—and brought on her dismissal—by her "unmasculine manner of putting on her shoes and stockings." Similarly, shortly after the war, in his history of wartime Secret Service activities, Albert Richardson wrote of a twenty-year-old woman who served with the 1st Kentucky Infantry for three months before the regimental surgeon guessed that she was a woman. "She performed camp duties with great fortitude," wrote Richardson, "and never fell out of the ranks during the severest marches." Nevertheless, her "feminine method of putting on her stockings" gave her away. A particularly careless female recruit in Rochester, New York, unwittingly exposed herself as a woman when in a brief moment of awkwardness she was seen trying to pull her pants on over her head. Sources indicate that when Lizzie Cook of Iowa tried to enlist with her brother at St. Louis, she gave herself away by displaying surprisingly refined table manners. And despite being "inspected, accepted, and sworn in" with her regiment and participating fully in the regiment's establishment of its initial camp site near Cincinnati—"handling lumber, doing sentry duty, &c."—one young woman who followed her brother into the 3rd Ohio Infantry lasted only two weeks before she provoked suspicion by displaying an unusual degree of familiarity with him.[20]

Sometimes a woman soldier aroused observers' suspicions for reasons that they later failed to record. When Civil War nurse and soldier relief activist Mary Livermore wrote her memoirs, she recalled her encounter with an unidentified woman enlisted in the 19th Illinois, the initial regimental home of John and Nadine Turchin. On a visit to the regiment, Livermore wrote, she had been observing a drill when an officer approached her and asked her if she noticed anything peculiar about the appearance of one of the soldiers drilling. Immediately, Livermore claimed, she realized that the soldier was a woman. After sharing her thoughts with the officer, who had suspected the masquerade himself, Livermore then watched as the woman soldier was called out of the ranks and charged with being an impostor. "There was a scene in an instant," Livermore recalled.

> Clutching the officer by the arm, and speaking in tones of passionate entreaty, she begged him not to expose her, but to allow her to retain her disguise. Her husband had enlisted in his company, she said, and it would kill her if he marched without her. "Let me go with you!" I heard her plead. "Oh, sir, let me go with you!"

The woman's pleas were in vain, however, and shortly thereafter she attempted suicide by jumping into the Chicago River, only to be rescued by a police officer and placed in a charity home where Livermore found her depressed and incapable of being comforted. "It was impossible to turn her from her purpose to follow her husband," wrote Livermore. Some days later the woman disappeared from the home, presumably with the intention of finding her way back into the ranks.[21]

Though it did not ultimately prove so in the cases of Jennie Hodgers or Rosetta Wakeman, landing in a hospital as a result of illness or a battle wound was, not surprisingly, the most common precursor of discovery. In July 1862 seventeen-year-old Mary Scaberry of Columbus, Ohio, enlisted as "Charles Freeman" in Company F of the 52nd Ohio. Sixteen weeks later, when she was admitted to the general hospital at Louisville, Kentucky, the doctors diagnosed "Freeman" not only with "remittent fever" but also with "sexual incompatibility," and on December 13 Scaberry received her discharge. In July 1863 the feminist reform journal *The Sibyl*, which had published an article on Kady Brownell at New Bern, published one in which it described the discovery of a woman in the ranks of the 1st Kansas Infantry. The unnamed woman, who had been with the regiment for almost two years and who had reportedly participated in a dozen battles and skir-mishes, had just died in the hospital, her sex having been revealed upon examination. The article described her as "rather more than average size for a woman, with rather strongly marked features" such that "with the aid of man's attire she had quite a masculine look." According to the article, the unnamed woman had a good reputation as a soldier, and was remembered by the men of her regiment with respect and affection for being "as brave as a lion in battle" and for never having failed to perform her duty under any conditions. "She must have been very shrewd," the article continued, "to have lived in the regiment so long and preserved her secret so well." In January 1864 *The Sibyl* noted the arrival in Louisville, Kentucky, of a sixteen-year-old Canadian woman who had already been in the army for a year and a half. The article associated this young woman with a num-ber of regiments, claiming that she had fought in several battles and had been wounded more than once. Each time the authori-ties discovered her sex, they mustered her out of the service. Each time she convalesced, she mustered back in from some other location. Despite her foreign heritage and her repeated dis-covery and dismissal, the article made clear, this young woman was "bound to fight for the American Union."[22]

One young woman who enlisted in the 2nd East Tennessee Cavalry regiment in mid-1862 survived for five months without being discovered. Despite having experienced the grisly December contest at Stones River, Tennessee, for control of Nashville's sup-ply lines which saw almost thirteen thousand Union casualties (Confederate losses were equally severe), the woman masquerad-ing as "Frank Martin" was wounded in the shoulder, and a med-ical examination revealed her secret and resulted in her discharge. "Martin," however, showed no signs of giving up on her determi-nation to be a soldier, and as soon as she was able she reenlisted, this time in the 8th Michigan, with which she served as an orderly sergeant and a scout for several more months, during which time some evidence suggests that her sex again became known but was ignored. A journal of the time described "Martin" as about eighteen years of age in 1863, amiable, loquacious, and "quite small" with auburn hair, blue eyes, and a fair complexion that had become tanned from months of living outdoors.[23]

Other cases of female soldiers being discovered as a consequence of hospitalization are abundant. In October 1863 an article in *Frank Leslie's Illustrated Newspaper* commented that authorities had recently detected the presence of a twelve-year-old girl posing as a drummer in the ranks of a Pennsylvania regiment, with which she had already seen five battles. Now ill with typhoid fever and a patient at the Pennsylvania Hospital in Philadelphia, the girl—whom a later source identified with the alias "Charles Martin"—was scheduled to go home. In August 1864 the *New York Herald* republished an article that had originally appeared in the Memphis *Argus* and which described a nineteen-year-old woman from Long Island, New York, named Fanny Wilson. Wilson, whose identity had been discovered in Memphis, claimed to have served for two years in the 24th New Jersey Infantry regiment before she fell sick, her sex was revealed, and she was discharged. A brief interlude as a ballet dancer at a theater in Cairo, Illinois, preceded Wilson's return to the ranks, this time as a member of the 3rd Illinois Cavalry, with whom she served until her sex was detected again and she was sent north. Two days later the *Herald* published a story about Mary Wise, a "female private" of the 34th Indiana Volunteers. Wise, the article claimed, had participated in several battles in the western theater and been wounded three times, most recently by a bullet in her shoulder at Lookout Mountain in Tennessee. Upon being taken to a hospital, Wise's sex was discovered and she, like so many others, was mustered out of the service.[24]

During October 1863 both the Wellsburg, West Virginia, *Weekly Herald* and *Frank Leslie's Illustrated Newspaper* published articles about a native of Minnesota named Frances Clayton (alternately "Clalin") who enlisted with her husband in a Minnesota regiment in 1861 and served with him for about a year until she was wounded, and her husband was killed, while engaging in a bayonet charge at the late December 1862 battle of Stones River. Clayton was hospitalized with a bullet in her hip, and an examination led to the discovery of her sex and her eventual discharge. Prior to that, however, Clayton had concealed her sex successfully, in part because she displayed personal habits that marked her as a soldier—drinking, smoking, chewing tobacco, and swearing—and partly because she unfailingly performed her duty in all sorts of weather both on the field and when on guard or picket duty. Her fellow soldiers considered Clayton "a good fighting man"; the author of one of the articles described her as a "very tall, masculine looking woman, bronzed from exposure to the weather" with a "masculine stride" and a "soldierly carriage." The article also noted that once she had recovered from her wound, the widowed Clayton had made her way back to her former regiment, ostensibly to recover some papers belonging to her husband, but probably in the hope of reenlisting. Instead, she was sent home.[25]

Many women soldiers' identities came to light after they were captured by the enemy. Such was the case with a woman who appears in the sources alternately as "Amy Clarke" and "Anna Clark." According to a December 1862 article in the Jackson *Mississippian*, Amy Clarke of Iuka, Mississippi, was thirty years old when she enlisted with her husband in a Confederate cavalry regiment, fighting with him until his death at the battle of Shiloh, whereupon she left the regiment and reenlisted in the 11th Tennessee. It was during her second period of enlistment, the article claimed, that Clarke was wounded in battle and captured by the federals, who discovered her sex and tried to put an end to her army career (in the same inconclusive manner that federal officials had attempted to put a stop to Confederate women's espionage activities) by sending her beyond the Confederate lines.[26]

*Frances Clalin (alternately "Clayton"), in uniform and in female dress.*
Courtesy of The Trustees of Boston Public Library.

In fact, the *Mississippian* was not the first paper to report the Clarke story. A few days earlier the Cairo, Illinois, *City Gazette* had noted the discovery in the ranks of the 11th Tennessee of a "Mrs. Anna Clark," the widow of one Walter Clark and a native of Luka [*sic*], Tennessee. "Not above medium height, rather slight in build, features effeminate but eye full of resolution," the article commented, Clark had been taken prisoner as a private in the Confederate army only to have her masquerade—perpetrated under the alias "Richard Anderson"—discovered. To her federal captors Clark purportedly explained that when her husband had enlisted early in the war, she had tried to manage their home without him but had not been particularly successful. In addition, in his absence (he subsequently died in the service, though the article did not say under what circumstances), Clark had fallen in love with a trooper in a Louisiana cavalry regiment. Procuring a horse for herself, Clark had enlisted in her lover's company and for four months had remained at his side until the demands of a life on horseback made her yearn for the infantry, for which she considered herself better suited. Joining the 11th Tennessee as "Richard Anderson," Clark served the Confederate army for another half year, by her own account performing such "prodigies of valor" as "having to stand upon the dead body of a comrade to obtain a sight of the enemy, upon whom she continually emptied the contents of her musket," until Yankee soldiers took her and some of her fellow Confederates prisoner. Now, her imposture having been exposed, she asked to be returned south, where she promised to resume her female identity and stay out of the ranks. The *City Gazette* article concluded with the news that Clark was expected to be sent on to Vicksburg shortly. According to one source, a short time after her arrival in Vicksburg, this determined Confederate woman was seen making plans to reenlist. Another source indicates that Clarke/Clark succeeded in doing so—undoubtedly under a different name—only to be discovered again in Tennessee in August 1863, by which time she had achieved the rank of lieutenant.[27]

Union nurse Anna Morris Holstein wrote of a Confederate woman artillery sergeant captured in the summer of 1864 near Port Royal, Virginia, not far from Belle Boyd's hometown of Martinsburg. This woman, Holstein pointed out, "was the *last* to leave the gun" when the troops were captured by the federals. When Annie Wittenmyer wrote her 1892 memoir of her work as a nurse and a leader in wartime soldier relief, she recalled coming across a wounded woman soldier in the hospital where she was working. According to Wittenmyer, this unnamed Union woman had been with her regiment for over a year before being captured by the Confederates after the September 1863 battle of Chickamauga and sent beyond federal lines with the note "As Confederates do not use women in war [sic], this woman, wounded in battle, is returned to you." Wittenmyer, who recommended that the woman return home once she was healed and forget about any future military service, noted that the woman instead swore her determination to reenlist as soon as possible. In 1934 the New York Times published a story about a woman known as Florena (alternately "Florina") Budwin who had enlisted in an unidentified Union regiment with her husband. Having served with him in battle for some time, Budwin was subsequently captured by the Confederates with her husband, and together they were transferred to the crowded, inadequately supplied, and critically unsanitary Confederate prison at Andersonville, Georgia, where Budwin's husband—like almost thirteen thousand other Union soldiers—died. Late in 1864, following a transfer to another prison in Florence, South Carolina, Budwin herself became ill. Discovered in the hospital to be a woman, she was released from the prison only upon her death in January 1865. After the war, Budwin was buried at the National Cemetery in Florence along with other federal soldiers who had died in prison there, her simple tombstone listing only her name. Budwin was not as lucky as one "Madame Collier," who had enlisted with a federal regiment from eastern Tennessee and whose exposure as a woman while imprisoned at Belle Isle, Virginia—the second-largest Confederate prison after Andersonville—led to her safe removal to the north under a flag of truce.[28]

Frances Hook also devoted herself to the Union cause, serving under the name of "Frank Miller." Described by one contemporary source as "of about medium height, with dark hazel eyes, dark brown hair, rounded features, and a feminine voice and appearance," Hook enlisted with her brother in the 65th Illinois Home Guards shortly after the outbreak of the war, and served three months without discovery before being mustered out.

Brother and sister then reenlisted in the 90th Illinois Infantry and fought together until Hook's brother was killed at the battle of Shiloh in April 1862. Hook remained with the regiment after her brother's death, however, until she was taken prisoner by the Confederates at Florence, Alabama, probably in late 1863. In an escape attempt some weeks later, Frances Hook took a bullet in her left leg, and when Confederate authorities examined her, they discovered her sex and promptly sent her to Nashville in a February 1864 prisoner exchange. There, Union officials hospitalized Hook until she was well enough to travel, then sent her north. According to an April 1864 article, during her captivity Hook received a letter from Confederate President Jefferson Davis offering her a lieutenant's commission if she would join the Confederate army. Hook, claimed the article, responded in the negative, informing Davis that she "preferred to fight as a private soldier for the stars and stripes, rather than be honored with a commission from the Rebs."[29] Whether or not Hook resumed her military service under a different name once her wound healed is unknown.

Of course, some women soldiers simply chose for personal reasons to reveal their identity after a period of service. Such was the case with Sarah Malinda Pritchard Blalock (alternately "Blaylock").[30] Born in Alexander County, North Carolina, in 1839 and married in 1856 to William ("Keith") McKesson Blalock, Malinda Blalock followed her husband in March 1862 into Company F of the 26th North Carolina, posing as Keith's younger brother and using the alias "Sam Blalock." Enlisting for three years or the duration of the war, Malinda Blalock received a bounty of fifty dollars.

Whether or not she saw fighting during her brief tenure with the 26th North Carolina is unclear: at least one source indicates that Blalock fought in three major battles and may even have been wounded before she left the service. Malinda Blalock was only with her regiment for about a month, however, and the more persuasive evidence suggests that her service as a soldier did not take her beyond the boundaries of the 26th's camp. Nevertheless, during her weeks with the regiment, Malinda Blalock learned the drill and did exemplary duty as a new soldier, earning an early spot on the regiment's honor roll. Her service might have been more protracted had her husband not received a discharge, as a consequence of a probably feigned disability: Keith Blalock claimed to have a hernia and severe sumac poisoning. In fact, Malinda Blalock's husband was a Unionist at heart who seems to have enlisted in order to avoid conscription and who had planned to desert until he found that it was more difficult to do so than he had expected. In any case, once her husband received his medical discharge, Malinda Blalock immediately confessed her imposture to the company's commander—and the future governor of North Carolina—Zebulon Vance. Vance dismissed her right away, demanding that she return the bounty money she had accepted under false pretenses. Malinda and Keith Blalock subsequently returned home to take up the work of Unionist resistance in North Carolina and eastern Tennessee, leading raids and escorting prison escapees to safety. Malinda Blalock died in 1903.

A woman soldier's sex necessarily came to light, of course, if—as happened on very rare occasions—she became visibly pregnant while in the service, though some continued to hide their true identity until the delivery of the child. In December 1864 the Sandusky, Ohio, *Commercial Register* reported a "strange birth" in the Confederate army. "We are credibly informed," wrote the article's Yankee author with obvious glee,

> that one day last week, one of the rebel officers in the "bull pen," as our soldiers call it: otherwise, in one of the barracks in the enclosure on Johnson's Island [prison on Lake Erie in Ohio], in which the rebel prisoners are kept, gave birth to a "bouncing

*Malinda Blalock, holding up a photograph of herself in uniform.* Courtesy of the North Carolina Collection, University of North Carolina Library at Chapel Hill.

boy." This is the first instance of a father giving birth to a child we have heard of; nor have we read of it "in the books."[31]

Pregnancy in the ranks was not confined to the Confederate army: according to one source, Union General William S. Rosecrans became outraged when an unnamed sergeant under his command *"was delivered of a baby*, which," he irately noted, "is in violation of all military law and of the army regulations." On August 21, 1862, Civil War nurse Harriet Whetten reported in her diary the discovery of a woman among the hospitalized Union soldiers in her care, and to whom she had just brought some jelly. "She is obliged to go home for a womanly reason," Whetten noted.[32] According to Lauren Burgess, at least six pregnant women soldiers went undiscovered until their babies were born, including one who went into labor while on picket duty and another who fought at the bloody battle of Fredericksburg in December 1862—and was promoted for her valor there from corporal to sergeant—not long before she gave birth. Wrote a soldier in this woman's regiment to his family at home: "What use have we for women, if soldiers in the army can give birth to children?"[33]

Death, of course, offered a belated opportunity for the detection of a woman soldier's true identity, but it did not guarantee it, as the story of Rosetta Wakeman attests. Most female soldiers' corpses underwent the same cursory burial on the field or on the grounds of the hospital as did those of their male counterparts. On July 17, 1863, however, when Brigadier General William Hays reported on the burial of the dead at Gettysburg, he noted that among those he counted was a "female (private) in rebel uniform." At least one woman's body went undiscovered at the Shiloh battleground in Tennessee until 1934, when Mancil Milligan unearthed the remains of several Civil War soldiers while planting in the flower bed of his home on the outskirts of the Shiloh National Military Park. Summoning the authorities, Milligan observed the excavation of the bones of nine soldiers, one of whom was determined to have been a woman, along with bits of the soldiers' uniforms and gear, and the ammunition that killed them. The bones, including those of the woman, were subsequently reinterred at the National Cemetery.[34]

The final revelation of at least one woman soldier's true identity—Frances Day, who served with the 126th Pennsylvania under the alias "Frank Mayne"—seems to have come at the very moment of her demise. Day enlisted as a nine months' recruit at Mifflin, Pennsylvania, on August 5, 1862, and mustered in at Harrisburg on August 9. Eighteen years old at the time of her enlistment, with "complexion light, eyes light, hair light," Day deserted the regiment about three weeks later, despite having received a rapid promotion to sergeant. Apparently Day had followed her lover, William Fitzpatrick, into Company F of the 126th, but when Fitzpatrick died of an illness while in camp, Day went absent without leave. According to the author of the

126th Pennsylvania's regimental history, Day resurfaced much later in the war as a soldier in the Far West. When she was mortally wounded and unable to conceal her sex any longer, she told her story to a comrade, explaining that the "abandon and despair" she had experienced when Fitzpatrick died had driven her to reenlist.[35]

Because the information surrounding so many women soldiers' stories is so limited, it is often impossible to know precisely how an individual woman's imposture was revealed. An unidentified nineteen-year-old woman enlisted as "John Williams" in Company H of the 17th Missouri Infantry in October 1861, only to be discharged a few days later. Her service record reads simply, "Discharged (Proved to be a Woman)." In April 1862 at Natchez, Mississippi, a woman using the alias "William Bradley" mustered in to Company G of an organization of Louisiana volunteers known as "Miles's Legion." Though she signed on for the duration of the war, "Bradley" was discharged at the end of June. The remarks on her service record for June 30 indicate only that she was "mustered in through mistake, was of female sex." In July 1862 *Frank Leslie's Illustrated Newspaper* reported the frustration of a woman from Chenango County, New York—the same region where Rosetta Wakeman had worked as a boatman—who had repeatedly attempted to join the army, first following her husband into the 61st New York as a nurse but then, having become separated from the regiment and being without resources, posing as a man and joining a Pennsylvania regiment. By some unknown means her imposture was detected, however, and she was discharged, after which she wandered about in desperation until a group of sympathetic soldiers underwrote her trip home. "The woman's sex could easily have been discovered," the article boasted with all the confidence of hindsight. "Voice, looks, actions and shape were all tell-tales, yet she had successfully passed guards and broke through orders."[36] And a March 1864 article in the Platteville, Wisconsin, *Witness* reported the return from the army of Georgianna Peterman, a native of Ellenboro, Wisconsin, who had served for two years as a drummer in the 7th Wisconsin Infantry. "She lives in Ellenboro," the article noted, "is about twenty years old, wears soldier clothes, and is quiet and reserved."[37]

We know little, too, about the means by which the true identity of "John Hoffman" of Battery C, 1st Tennessee Artillery (Union), became known. In September 1864 the *Richmond Daily Examiner* reported without explanation the discovery in Nashville, Tennessee, that "John Hoffman" was in fact Louisa Hoffman, a native of New York City and a "very good looking and respectable soldier girl." Hoffman disclosed that she had initially served with the 1st Virginia Cavalry up through the second battle of Bull Run in August 1862, and had then, switching her allegiance to the Union, taken a position as a cook with the 1st Ohio Infantry before deciding to join the artillery corps. Possibly the revelation of her sex while in Nashville ended Hoffman's career as a soldier; given her history, it is more likely that she went on to find a new regimental home somewhere else.[38]

In February 1865 the *Richmond Whig* reported, also without bothering to explain, the discovery of a woman named Mollie Bean in the ranks of the 47th North Carolina. Bean, who used the alias "Melvin Bean," had been picked up a few days earlier for questioning and had told investigators that she had been with the regiment for over two years and had been wounded twice in the service. Although the *Whig* presumed that others in her company knew that Bean was a woman, there is no reason to believe that they did.[39]

Clearly a key reason why we know of the wartime service of so many women soldiers is that they received so much attention in the newspapers when their impostures were exposed. Indeed, newspaper notices relating to women's military service during the Civil War continued to appear years after Appomattox. In 1896 an article appeared in the St. Louis *Star* which considered the case of Mary Stevens Jenkins (alternately "Mary Owens Jenkins"). Jenkins, the article claimed, had been a Pennsylvania schoolgirl when the war broke out. Although a schoolgirl, Jenkins was also in love with a young man identified as William Evans, whom she followed into the army. For approximately two years Jenkins served with William Evans in Company K of the 9th Pennsylvania Infantry under the alias "John Evans." After William died in battle, Jenkins remained with the regiment and continued in the service, possibly being wounded on several occasions. It is not clear whether her sex was ever discovered while she was in the service: the sources disagree. In any case, after the war Jenkins married a coal miner named Abraham Jenkins. When she died, in about 1881, Jenkins was buried in a village graveyard in Ohio. Shortly thereafter, the St. Louis *Star* noted, when the story of her military service became widely known, Jenkins's grave was quickly decorated by local veterans "with honors equal to those bestowed upon any other of the grass-grown mounds."[40]

In 1898 the Charlestown, West Virginia, *Farmer's Advocate* printed a poignant article about Mary Walters, who had followed her husband, William—without his knowledge—into the 10th Michigan Infantry. Wounded at Antietam in the fall of 1862, Mary Walters had refused the advice she received from the doctor who examined her and discovered her sex, namely, that she return home. Instead, as soon as she was well enough, Walters returned to her regiment. Only when her husband disappeared while on a scouting expedition did Walters apply for a discharge and go home to Michigan. Meanwhile, William was wounded in the head and lost his memory, making a reunion of the two unlikely. Thirty-four years later, however, a bizarre set of circumstances conspired to bring them together again. "The happy couple," the article concluded, "have returned to Michigan where they will spend the remaining years of their lives." In 1915 the *New York Times* published a piece that mentioned Mary Siezgle, the wife of a soldier in the 44th New York Infantry who had first entered the military ranks as a nurse but had soon exchanged her skirts for the uniform of a soldier in order to fight the enemy directly. According to the article, Siezgle's battlefield experience included Gettysburg. In 1920 a Raritan, New Jersey, newspaper noted the death of Elizabeth Niles, who, it claimed, "with close-cropped hair and a uniform, concealed her sex and is said to have fought beside her husband through the civil war." A newlywed at the time of the war's outbreak, the article continued, Niles had followed her husband Martin into the 4th New Jersey and had acted the soldier's part through a number of engagements, her sex remaining undiscovered to the end of her service.[41]

Snippets of material about various other women soldiers appear in a variety of sources, modern and otherwise. We learn, for example, about Lizzie Compton, whose sex was detected after she was wounded and who claimed, upon discovery, to have enlisted at the age of fourteen and to have served for eighteen months in seven different regiments, pursuant to the repeated discovery of her sex. We learn, too, of Margaret Henry and Mary Wright, Southern women discovered in uniform shortly before the end of the war, when they were captured by federal authorities while in the act of burning the bridges around Nashville; Catherine E. Davidson of Sheffield, Ohio, who after her discharge told interviewers that she had seen her lover killed at Antietam, where she herself sustained a wound; Satronia Smith Hunt, who enlisted with her husband in an Iowa regiment and who, after he died in battle, remained in the regiment until the end of the war, unwounded and her sex undetected; and Annie Lillybridge of Detroit, who enlisted in the 21st Michigan in order to be near her fiancé, but who managed to hide her identity even from him until she was disabled by a wound in her arm and was discharged following the discovery of her sex.[42] Especially if we assume that the majority remained undetected, it is clear that an impressive array of women joined the armies of the Union and the

Confederacy in the guise of men, and that as long as they were able to sustain their impostures, they commonly fulfilled with fierce determination the responsibilities they had assumed as soldiers. As in the cases of women spies, resistance activists, army women, and daughters of the regiment, the individual women soldiers for whom we have the most substantial documentation are only a small proportion of those who felt compelled to "don the breeches" and serve as men.

Chapter Seven

# "A Devoted Worker for Her Cause"[1]

*The Question of Motivation*

All appear to have belonged to the higher social levels. . . .
Their work as spies appears to have stemmed from motives
of loyalty to the cause they served.

> *Oscar Kinchen,* Women Who Spied
> for the Blue and Gray, *1972*

Some went to avoid separation from those who were dearer
to them than ease, or life itself; others, from a pure love of
romance and adventure; and others, from a mental hallucination that victory and deliverance would come to the war-
burdened land only by the sacrifice of their lives.

> *Frank Moore, speaking of women soldiers,*
> in Women of the War, *1866*

So why did they do it? Why did women serve the armies of the
Union and the Confederacy as spies, resistance activists, army
women, daughters of the regiment, and full-fledged soldiers?
Certainly for women in espionage and resistance, the traditional
explanation has centered on pure, unadulterated patriotism.
Charles Wesley Alexander's Civil War-era spy stories are only
some of the many sources to identify women's unbridled devotion
to their respective national causes as their fundamental motivation for such work. In Alexander's fiction, Pauline, though a
native of France, is profoundly dedicated to the Union, a fierce
defender of the paired principles of liberty and law. To her father's
remark that she must learn to love her new homeland, the United

States, Pauline responds, "Oh my dear Papa, I shall love them, I know I shall!" And when her dying father drapes over her shoulders a flag presented to him after the American Revolution by the French hero the Marquis de Lafayette, Pauline proudly receives his instruction to wed herself to the cause of her adopted country. "This starry flag," D'Estraye tells her, "is the veil that you now take. . . . America, I give you my child, the offering of my heart." Pauline's service as a spy for Generals McClellan and Grant represents her fulfillment of her father's charge.[2]

Alexander's Wenonah similarly dedicates herself to the defeat of the enemies of the United States: Wenonah seeks to "help the good pale faces" because she loves them and because "pale face blood and Indian blood, Tecumseh's blood, runs in my heart together, like brother and sister."[3] As for Mary Murdock, in Northerner Alexander's eyes, her passion for the Confederacy arises from nothing less than a pact with the devil, and even Mary herself sees her own enthusiasm for the Confederate cause as a satanic perversion of her better nature. To Jefferson Davis she explains that her "mission" is "to render your cause assistance, not because it is holy . . . but because it is the most diabolical that could be conceived of."[4] For better or worse, each of Alexander's beautiful, bewitching heroines is motivated by pure devotion—holy or unholy—to the cause of the nation she serves.

Alexander's fictional representations of Civil War women spies' underlying motivations reinforce the standard representations (and in some cases self-representations) of their historical counterparts. In most accounts, both contemporary and more recent, Belle Boyd, Rose Greenhow, and other espionage and resistance activists have been characterized (and have characterized themselves) as women who acted only on the basis of pure, ardent patriotism, devoid of any expectation that their wartime service should elicit more than a simple expression of their nation's gratitude. Wrote Greenhow in her memoir: "I only performed my duty"; and speaking of why she did not give in to advice that she should go into hiding once the federals had begun closing in on her operations, she added: "I could have escaped the snare set for me, but I should thereby have done great injury to our cause. . . . I felt it to be my post of duty whatever danger threatened . . . [so] that every woman's heart, throughout the South, would make my cause their own; and that, so far from intimidating, the knowledge that one of their own was suffering for the same faith, in the prisons of the tyrant, would nerve the most timid to deeds of daring."[5]

In the course of her analysis of the broad phenomenon of Civil War women's engagement in espionage and resistance, historian Mary Elizabeth Massey characterized the primary motivation of each of her subjects as a simple desire to respond to her nation's call to service, although Massey noted secondarily that women's patriotism had to be augmented by their spirited and imaginative natures if they were to succeed in the work. In his *Women Who Spied for the Blue and Gray*, Oscar Kinchen, too, insisted on patriotism as the fundamental motivating force behind women's espionage and resistance activities during the Civil War. Few if any, he claimed, were paid for their work, though some Unionists—such as Elizabeth Van Lew—received government clerkships after the war.[6]

But was it really unalloyed patriotism that motivated *all* women to engage in espionage and resistance work during the war? In fact, some evidence suggests that Boyd's well-documented "insane devotion" to the Confederacy and "Crazy Bet" Van Lew's "lively sense of . . . fidelity" to the Union fail to fully explain at least some women's involvement in such admittedly dangerous enterprises, and that there were women whose actions grew out of an ardor for the cause enhanced not only by their basic adventurousness but also by their hope of fiscal reward.[7] Indeed, Alexander's fictional characters may protest a bit too much on the question of payment for services rendered: when Generals McClellan and Grant each offer Pauline D'Estraye money—to cover disguises and other expenses—she responds with indignation and insists on paying her own way: "The best and only reward I should ever desire for my poor services," Pauline tells McClellan, "would be that, when I die, your people coming to my grave should say: 'She loved our nation; she was our sister.'"[8] Like Pauline, Wenonah refuses to accept any money from General Sherman. "Wenonah," the young woman informs the general in no uncertain terms, "will give her heart and life to the cause of the good pale faces, but she will never sell them!"[9] We have little choice but to accept uncritically the claims made by or about these fictional characters, and may even choose to do the same with regard to the claims made about (and by) the more familiar women spies and resistance activists whose stories have come down to us—namely, that they served either the Union or the Confederacy simply because they loved the cause. At the same time, however, we must acknowledge that some of these women's service to their military organizations, however patriotic in its essential motivation, however exciting in comparison with what most mid-century American women could expect from their normal daily lives, was compensated by wages.

Indeed, the *Official Records of the Union and Confederate Armies* describe a number of women as being formally employed as spies or scouts, most commonly for the Union. In a September 1863 letter, the Union's Brigadier General George Washington Getty noted the arrival of a Mrs. Charles Swartz, a "spy in the Government employ" who often used the alias "Mrs. C. Wilson" in her work. In February 1864 Captain W. T. Leeper wrote to Brigadier General Clinton B. Fisk, commander of the Union's District of Northern Missouri, from the town of Patterson, informing him that "our good, loyal friend Mrs. Byrne, has been a regular spy since the commencement of the war. I have no doubt of this, and we have many of them." (Were Mrs. Byrne a man, Leeper added pointedly, "and guilty of the crimes that she is, she would not live here twenty-four hours.") From Nashville on

October 3, 1864, B. H. Polk relayed to General George H. Thomas the report of Mary McNell, employed as a Union scout, to the effect that the Tennessee River had risen sufficiently for the Union troops to ford it. On April 1, 1865, Major A. M. Jackson of the 10th U. S. Colored Heavy Artillery at New Orleans wrote to Lieutenant Colonel C. T. Christensen about the activities of a Mrs. Whitely, "a spy in the employ of this office."[10]

If there is any doubt that the references to "employment" in these women's cases indicated payment for labor, such doubt fades considerably in the light of documentation—in the *Official Records* and elsewhere—involving other women, such as a Mrs. Susan Bond, who appeared in Special Orders No. 260 issued at Springfield, Missouri, in September 1864: "Capt. R. B. Owen Chief Quarter Master," the order read, "is hereby authorized and directed to take up and bear upon his Rolls, as scout in Government Employ, the following persons to date from the 17th day of September 1864, viz., Mrs. Susan Bond. . . ." This same Mrs. Bond reappeared in Special Orders No. 306, dated November 16, as due to be paid for services rendered. "Capt. R. B. Owen," the order read, "is hereby directed to settle with and pay Mrs. Susan Bond for her services as scout from the 17th day of September to the 25th day of October both inclusive." Similarly, Charlotte Rhoden received pay for her espionage work: in March 1865, acting upon an order from the provost marshal's office in Huntsville, Alabama, Lieutenant Colonel John W. Horner, commanding post, ordered Captain George W. Bullock to "pay to Charlotte Rhoden the sum of $50 fifty Dollars for services as a Detective."[11]

The federal government hired and paid for spying, scouting, and related work many other women as well, including Frankie Abells—described by one source as a "spy belonging to [General Nathaniel] Banks's command," later a detective employed by the Union's "Middle Department at Baltimore," and still later as a detective for Lafayette Baker and the United States Secret Service.

Abells—who used a number of disguises and aliases and was probably the agent who visited Antonia Ford's house and solicited the bold confession that resulted in Ford's arrest and imprisonment—received over $450 for her services and expenses beginning in January 1863. The records mention many others who were similarly paid for their labor on behalf of the Union, including a Mrs. M. J. Childers, paid $150 for Secret Service work for the Union army in May 1862; a Miss Mary Jane Hensley, hired as a spy on August 17, 1864, in Springfield, Missouri, at a wage of $5 per day, and given a horse for her use; a Mrs. Nutter, paid $100 on February 24, 1864, for her services as a scout; Lucinda Phillips, paid in conjunction with her husband, William, $100 on May 23, 1864, for their joint service to the Union as detectives; Mrs. Matilda Rogers, paid $322.60 in U.S. Treasury notes and $400 in Confederate bills on March 27, 1864, in acknowledgment of her Secret Service activities; a Miss Eleanora Shell, paid $400 on February 11, 1864, for special services ordered by General Sherman; and a Mrs. Hester A. Myers, paid on several occasions between April 5 and June 19, 1863, a total of $165 for detective work.[12]

We know of some women spies' wage arrangements with the United States Army because various documents testify to the women's demands for overdue pay. On February 12, 1865, for example, Nora Winder wrote to General Sherman regarding the service she had thus far provided to the Union, urging him to see to it that she receive her long-expected wages. "Honorable Sir," Winder wrote from Hilton Head, South Carolina, "I will write you the most important news I know." Winder began with a report of the activities of the Confederate forces, and particularly of General John B. Hood's Army of Tennessee, as she had observed them during December and January. (Deeply frustrated by his inability, following Sherman's capture of Atlanta, to win victories against the Union army in Tennessee, Hood resigned from field command at the end of January 1865.) Winder continued with a summary explanation of the resourceful way in which she had managed to finance her espionage work when the funds promised by the federal government had not materialized in a timely manner. "General," Winder wrote,

> The young man who was to hand me the money the day I left Milledgeville [Georgia] forgot to do so, and consequently I had to work my way a part of the time. Weaving pays well in the Confederacy, and I am a splendid weaver; so I stopped in Warren County and Jefferson County and wove for families, and by that means I paid my son's and my own way to Savannah, though we had to walk; though if we had been riding we would have been suspected to be going farther than five or seven miles. I came to you as soon as I could under those circumstances, having to work my way back. I would like to go to New Orleans as soon as possible. I cannot go until the commander of the post at this place hears from you. I have no means to go on. I have my only child with me. He is in his twelfth year. I want him to go to New Orleans with me.[13]

Mrs. Mary E. Clements similarly addressed a letter to General George Thomas in March 1865, pleading that she at least be granted rations for herself and her three children as partial payment for her work as a Secret Service agent in Atlanta. ("Give this woman rations until May," Thomas responded, "after which time she will have to seek some employment which will subsist her & her children.") Emma C. Rowell, of Burlington, Iowa, in June 1865 requested information on the proper procedures for resigning her commission in the United States Secret Service and receiving payment for her past work. "I have since the 16th of July last been a member of the U. S. D[etective] Corpse [sic]—in the Citty [sic] of Memphis Tenn.," wrote Rowell with an unintended hint of the macabre. "What I wish to know is this in what manner shall I proceed to secure the remuneration due me &

resign my orders." In November 1863 a Mrs. Carter issued a claim for $500 in back wages. Noted General William S. Rosecrans in his communication to General Thomas on the matter: "If she has received nothing on this ap[plication] it ought to be paid. If I am not mistaken however there was a dispute as to whether she ought to receive so large a sum for what she did and suffered, and I was under the impression that $200 or $300 had been paid on it." Concluding that the provost marshal general could undoubtedly sort out the details in the case, Rosecrans nevertheless urged that Thomas see to it that the "poor woman's" claim was settled.[14]

Although its resources were more limited, it is clear that the Confederacy also hired women to serve as spies. Such was the case with the French-born Augusta Morris (alias "Mrs. Mason"), who was arrested in Washington in February 1862 for providing the Confederacy with information on the strength and position of federal troops and fortifications in and around the capital.[15] Morris was imprisoned at the Old Capitol during the same period that Rose Greenhow was an inmate there, and indeed the two seem to have developed a strong mutual dislike. According to Morris, Greenhow saw her as a rival in the business of doing good for the Confederacy. Greenhow, Morris complained, was a woman "drowned by mean ambition for being known [as the only one] in the good work and jealous of everything that surpasses her in loyalty and courage."[16] In any case, by the coincidence of their imprisonment, the two women were linked together in the popular and official mind: Allan Pinkerton himself referred to Morris as a "second Mrs. Greenhow" on account of her skillful collection and communication of information to the South.

But whereas there is no evidence to suggest that Greenhow was paid for her work for the Confederacy, there is strong evidence to suggest that Morris was. That evidence comes in the form of an October 1861 letter to Confederate President Jefferson Davis from Major Edward Porter Alexander, in which he mentions Morris as a "lady . . . whom I design employing in Washington City" and whom he deems "most admirably adapted mentally, socially, and physically to her task," and having also the sort of motives that would "carry her to any necessary lengths" in her service to the Confederacy. Notably, Alexander does not count raw patriotism among Morris's impulses. Instead, he mentions Morris's claim that she was married to a wealthy and influential Confederate officer—with whom she had two children—who had now decided to deny his paternity and his marriage to Morris in order to marry someone else. Morris, Alexander explained to Davis, was looking to serve the Confederacy in order to gain influence of the sort that might help her to press her claims for support for her children. But she also needed money in the interim. President Davis responded to Alexander's letter with a curt message approving Morris's employment as a spy in exchange for wages. Morris, Davis wrote back, "may be sustained with money."[17] Perhaps Davis should have used more caution in his choice of hired operatives: once imprisoned, Morris seems to have been more than willing to compromise her Confederate loyalties for a price. Hoping to effect a quick release from the Old Capitol, she claimed intimate knowledge of the signal code of the rebel army, which she offered to reveal to whoever could pay her the exorbitant price of $100,000. Unfortunately for Morris, she made her offer in vain.

One former employee of the United States Secret Service left an unusually extensive record of her determination not only to be paid for her work at the time she performed it but also to win a pension years later for her wartime service. Emma Smith Porch, known as Miss Katie Smith during the war, had been a schoolteacher when she took a job as a scout for the Union's Department of Missouri in late 1864. According to documents in her pension file, Porch served as a dispatch bearer and spy between October and December of that year, and in the course of her service, which included more than one imprisonment, she claimed to have contracted a number of ailments that ultimately produced a state of "general debility." In January 1865 Porch haggled at length with Brigadier General Egbert B. Brown, commander of the District of Southwest Missouri, at Rollo, regarding her pay. "General," she wrote,

> I have received those vouchers from Captain Case, but there is nothing said about the voucher for the twenty five ($25) dollars promised on the night I went out for you with Captain Ames, when I spoke to you about it you told me you would have it attended to and that is the last I ever heard of it. General, was it the understanding that I was to pay my own expenses while employed by you! the six dollars paid to me by your order was taken out of my wages when the vouchers was [sic] made out. that of course was all right, and you gave me ten dollars at Brownsville, which I expected to pay back to you, but from that time until I returned my travelling expenses were $102.55 cts. my transportation was twenty eight ($28.80 cts) and eighty cents and board at the different places I was at was Seventy three dollars and seventy five cents. ($73.75) making the sum total $102.55 cts. now General what I want to know is this, must I lose all that I receive and more besides? . . . I supposed that I was to receive a scout[']s pay, but I see I do not receive half as much as other scouts.

"General [John B.] Sanborn paid me five dollars a day for the time I was on his roll," Porch scolded Brown, and "General [James G.] Blunt offered me ten dollars per day as long as I would belong to his department [the districts of Upper Arkansas and South Kansas]. . . . If you think you can do anything for my case," she concluded in a more conciliatory tone, "please write and let me know."[18]

We do not know the results of Porch's January 1865 request for a righting of the accounts, but we do know that she filed an application for a pension in June 1874, on the basis of the accumulated disabilities she associated with her government service. Initially, the federal government rejected Porch's claim on the mistaken grounds that she had not been in the military service at the time she became disabled. Ten years later, however, Congress passed a special act acknowledging that despite the fact that she had not worn a soldier's uniform, Porch had "served with such heroic spirit and fortitude" at the time of her nation's great need that she should be granted $20 per month "for her services as Scouts and Spies U. S. Vols." "Her sex," the report concluded, "prevented [her] enlistment, but it enabled her to gain access to the enemy, to pass safely by and through their lines, and thereby to render to the Government a service as valuable as the soldier who bore a musket." As historian Jane E. Schultz has put it, in the eyes of her government, "Porch was no less a man for being a woman."[19]

Subsequently Porch applied to the Pension Bureau for the pension funds that would have accumulated to date had the 1884 act on her behalf been retroactive. She was denied. When she applied in 1896 for a second pension on the basis of her status as the widow of a former soldier, she was refused again, this time on the grounds that she could not receive a pension in her own name as well as another one in the name of her late husband. Even Porch's persuasive letter on her own behalf—after the war she had gone on to become a pension attorney—did not prove successful in overturning the government's decision. Porch would have to be satisfied with her original pension.[20]

There were women who sought reimbursements other than money for their work in Civil War espionage and resistance: the Confederacy's Mrs. Catherine V. Baxley was concerned not so much with the rewards she herself might earn as a spy but with the rewards she might commandeer for a friend.[21] Arrested in December 1861 by Union officials for being a spy and for carrying forbidden correspondence between Washington, D.C., and Richmond, Baxley was imprisoned first at "Fort Greenhow" and then at the Old Capitol. A resident of Baltimore, Baxley had confessed to fellow passengers aboard a boat on which she was traveling that she was smuggling secret papers and letters on her person. When the boat docked in Baltimore, Baxley was taken into custody and a search produced a hundred items of correspondence, some fifty of which were stashed in her bonnet. It also produced a Confederate army commission appointing one Dr. Septimus Brown an army surgeon, a privilege that Union officials claimed Baxley had admitted having "procured by personal application . . . as a consideration or reward for the safe conveyance of letters, &c, to the chief of the rebel Government."[22]

A far greater number of women, however, sought rewards for their loyal service which they could literally bank on. It is undoubtedly true that many women who served the Union and Confederate armies as espionage and resistance operatives did so, like Belle Boyd, Rose Greenhow, Elizabeth Van Lew, and others, out of a desire to serve their nations, with little concern for any reward or remuneration whatsoever down the line. But one cannot escape the conclusion that there were also some women whose patriotism—and whose eagerness for adventure—were mixed with a measure of financial aspiration, if not outright financial need.

What of women soldiers? Why did women leave their regular lives and their identities behind, transform themselves into men, and undertake the tedious, often brutal, and potentially fatal work of soldiering, work made considerably more difficult by the challenge of sustaining a complicated imposture, and personally more risky given the price in embarrassment, even public humiliation, that a woman soldier might have to pay for her discovery? A year after Appomattox, Frank Moore laid the foundation for an enduring triad of explanations: some women soldiers, he wrote, "went to avoid separation from those who were dearer to them than ease, or life itself; others, from a pure love of romance and adventure; and others, from a mental hallucination that victory and deliverance would come to the war-burdened land only by the sacrifice of their lives."[23] As an example of the latter, Moore offered the story of "Emily," a native of Brooklyn, New York, who had enlisted early in 1863 and had died from a battle wound later that year. Aged nineteen and just out of school when she enrolled in the Union army, wrote Moore, Emily "conceived the idea that Providence had destined her, as an American Joan of Arc, to marshal our discouraged forces, rally them to new efforts, and inspire them with a fresh and glowing enthusiasm." Despite the efforts of her parents, friends, relatives, doctor, and pastor to dissuade her, young Emily disguised herself as a boy while visiting an aunt in Michigan and joined the drum corps of a Michigan regiment. With the regiment she traveled to Tennessee, where she was mortally wounded at Chickamauga. When she was examined by the surgeon, Emily's sex became apparent, and with her dying breath she dictated a telegraph message to her parents asking them to forgive her for her deception. "I expected to deliver my country," Moore quoted Emily as saying, "but the Fates would not have it so." Emily died a few weeks after the battle in which she fell.[24]

Moore suggested that women who enlisted as soldiers in the Civil War did so for love of a man, for love of adventure, or because, like Emily, their patriotic fervor deluded them into believing that they had significant contributions to make to their nation's cause. Postwar historians Linus Brockett and Mary Vaughan reinforced Moore's thesis in 1867 when they identified "romance, love or patriotism" as the most likely explanations for women's enlistment in Civil War armies.[25] More recently other students of the phenomenon have reiterated the same basic assumptions that love of a good man, love of adventure, and/or love of country lay at the heart of individual women's decisions to take up the life of a Civil War soldier.[26]

Certainly the stories recounted in previous chapters provide solid support for the theory that women's enlistment in the Union and Confederate armies as soldiers was often closely tied to their devotion to their husbands, lovers, or brothers,[27] although many women stayed in or returned to the ranks—often for an extended period of time—after they were separated from their loved ones, sometimes by death.[28] Undoubtedly the explanation emphasizing individual women's connections to particular male soldiers as a motivating force behind their own enlistment is at least partially accurate: among other things, having the confidence of at least one man in the ranks would have made it easier for a woman to maintain her imposture. At least partially accurate, too, is the explanation that fervent patriotism drove women, just as it drove men, into the military service, although it is also important to recognize the various other means by which a woman during the Civil War could express her dedication to the Union or Confederate cause besides donning a uniform and assuming a man's identity. Besides serving as spies and resistance activists and as army women and daughters of the regiment, Civil War women frequently became nurses or hospital personnel; they created or staffed local and national soldiers' aid societies; they became activists in their communities promoting men's enlistment, and so forth. Still, a woman's patriotic desire to do something substantial on behalf of either the Union or the Confederacy must have figured somehow in her decision to put herself in the line of enemy fire. If a loved one had put himself there first, it could only have made her decision easier. Patriotism, too, may help to explain why so many women remained in the army even after they could no longer serve side by side with those they had initially followed into the service.

Regarding the raw spirit of adventure that Moore and others have cited as being at the root of some women's enlistment as soldiers during the Civil War, [29] we can only assume, again, that the women who chose this particular avenue of wartime service shared some if not all of the impulses that characterized women spies as well as their male comrades-in-arms. Given the numerous opportunities for contributions to the military which existed for women on the home front, one must believe that many of the women who became soldiers—like other women of the Civil War armies—sought a life different than that which conventional standards offered them. Surely women who decided to enlist were not ignorant about the distinctions between home life and life on the battlefront (a distinction that admittedly became blurred for many women in the South as the war dragged on). Many women who enlisted as men in the Union and Confederate armies must have yearned for a wider sphere of activity than was available to them in their normal lives. Especially if they were impelled by patriotism and by a strong connection to a man who had already decided to enlist, women endowed with an adventuresome nature must have seen that imposture and military service could fulfill a range of personal yearnings. In short, Moore's triad of explanations for women's enlistment in the armies of the Civil War—like traditional explanations for women's engagement in espionage and resistance—holds a good amount of water. But there is also, predictably, more to the story than Moore and others have typically revealed.

Perhaps not surprisingly, some have suggested that "baser motives" underlay at least some women's decision to enlist. According to historian Wiley, a number of the women who joined the ranks of the Union and Confederate armies were "persons of easy virtue who enrolled as soldiers to further their lewd enterprises."[30] Indeed, among the women who served as soldiers during the Civil War, there were some who were accused of taking on the soldier's life for reasons that were either partially or entirely immoral. When he published his memoirs in 1891, the Union cavalry's General Philip Sheridan recalled his January 1863 discovery of two women under his command: one from eastern Tennessee who had been detailed as a teamster with the wagon train, and the other a cavalry private who had temporarily been assigned to escort duty at his headquarters. While on a foraging mission, the two women, in a manner surely not unlike that of many of their fellow soldiers, had gotten drunk on hard cider and had nearly drowned in a river. While other soldiers were attempting to resuscitate them, the women's sex became apparent. Subsequently Sheridan called the two in for questioning and dismissed them from the service, having seen to it that they were first provided with appropriate women's clothing. Of the two, Sheridan remembered the woman from Tennessee as the more convincing soldier: "Her features were very large," he wrote, "and so coarse and masculine was her general appearance that she would readily have passed as a man." In contrast, the other woman was more "feminine"-looking, a "rather prepossessing young woman" who, "though necessarily bronzed and hardened by exposure" must have had a more difficult time concealing her sex. In any case, when Sheridan made his discovery known, Colonel Joseph Conrad of the 15th Missouri Infantry claimed that these same women had for some time been busy "demoralizing" his men—presumably having sexual relations with them. Regardless of whether Conrad was speaking truthfully or was simply covering his embarrassment at not having discovered the imposture himself, Sheridan was more concerned with the women's display of drunkenness than with the charge of harlotry. Like any male soldier, a woman soldier who could not hold her liquor posed a threat to the security and the discipline of the troops around her.[31]

The motives underlying other women's decisions to serve as Civil War soldiers came under similarly harsh judgment. Under the alias "Henry Fitzallen," eighteen-year-old Marian McKenzie joined the Union army's 23rd Kentucky Infantry, signing up for three years or the duration of the war. The company descriptive book attached to "Fitzallen's" military service record notes McKenzie's Scottish origins as well as her dark complexion, light blue eyes, black hair, and height of just under five feet three inches. Though she enlisted as a three years' recruit, in a statement she signed in December 1862, McKenzie explained that her sex had been discovered after she had been in the service for only four months, at which time authorities agreed to assign her to nursing duty in the regimental hospital, where she worked for two months more. For reasons she did not explain, McKenzie then left the 23rd Kentucky, subsequently signing on with the 92nd Ohio and then the 8th Ohio before settling in with the 1st Illinois. Most likely McKenzie's sex was discovered repeatedly, causing her to switch regiments several times. At least one federal official, however, suspected that McKenzie was simply in the habit of "frequenting our camps in male attire" for purposes of prostitution. "Fitzallen" was finally mustered out for good in January 1865, "on acc't of proving to be a female."[32]

Seventeen-year-old Molly and twenty-four-year-old Mary Bell faced similar accusations concerning their purposes in joining the army. Cousins from Pulaski County, Virginia, both Molly and Mary Bell grew up on farms, and their early knowledge of hard work and horseback riding came in handy when they enlisted under the command of Confederate General Jubal A. Early in 1862. Molly and Mary Bell served respectively as "Tom Parker" and "Bob Martin" (alternately "Morgan") until they were reported by a comrade to whom they had confessed their imposture in the fall of 1864. Following the revelation of the women's true identities, Confederate authorities briefly imprisoned them at Castle Thunder in Richmond, then sent them home to their families. At least one journalist at the time reported that advocates of the Bells insisted that they had dutifully performed the work of soldiers without arousing any suspicions about their sex among the men with whom they served. But more decisively the same journalist argued that in fact Molly and Mary were nothing more than "common camp followers" who had been busy "demoralizing several hundred men" in Early's command. "They adopted the disguise of soldiers the better to follow the army and hide their iniquity," he concluded.[33]

It is possible, of course, that the author of the article was correct and that the Bell cousins were prostitutes who camouflaged their activities by pretending to be soldiers. As with Marian McKenzie and the women discovered in Sheridan's command, however, it seems unlikely that Molly and Mary Bell would have gone to the trouble of enlisting under assumed male names in order to ply a trade for which actual enlistment and military service were hardly necessary. It seems unlikely as well that the Bells could have remained in the service for over two years without doing the work of soldiers. Indeed, according to a modern source, the Bells' fellow soldiers considered them "gallant, first-class fighting men," and one had earned a promotion to sergeant, the other a promotion to corporal.[34] As it turns out, the author of the article condemning Molly and Mary Bell as "common camp followers" actually betrayed the philosophical underpinnings of his own accusation when he tried to explain the Confederacy's inability to win the war on the presence of rampant immorality in the ranks. "The country," he wrote,

> has here an insight into one of the probable causes of the utter worthlessness and inefficiency of some of the commands in the [Shenandoah] Valley. Hidden in Early's camp like the stolen Babylonian garment and silver in the camp of the Hebrews, defeat and disaster ever follows, and ever will continue to cling to it, like the shirt of Nemisis [sic], until purged of the unclean presence.[35]

Defying all evidence to the contrary, this writer automatically associated the presence of women in the ranks with prostitution and thus with a decline in the moral force necessary to permit the Southern armies to win the war. Rather than being responsible for the regiment's (and the Confederacy's) failures, however, Molly and Mary Bell were described by those who fought with them as contributors to the army's and the nation's successes. Even the archconservative Southern activist Edmund

Ruffin declared at the time of their dismissal that the Bells had "proved themselves fine soldiers . . . and should be allowed to stay in the service."[36]

For the vast majority of the women who enlisted as soldiers in the ranks of the Union and Confederate armies, the accusation of immorality was unfounded. Too many women proved that they had come to do the work of soldiers and nothing else as long as they could maintain their disguises. Admittedly, a few women were discovered in uniform for whom there was just cause for suspicion regarding their intentions. Probably the most famous women to fall into this category were the two who accompanied Union Generals H. Judson Kilpatrick and L. G. Estes when they set up their headquarters near Durham Station, North Carolina, in April 1865. Kilpatrick and Estes brought with them to Durham Station two individuals whom they introduced as "Charley" and "Frank" but whom locals, including the owner of the house that became the generals' headquarters, insisted were "vulgar, rude and indecent" women "of dissolute character." These women dressed at least partially in soldier's clothing and rode astride their horses, but they were also known to have raided the wardrobes of their host's daughters on occasion. Moreover, one former servant in the home recalled seeing "Charley" naked and commented that "no man was ever made like her," noting as well that a third woman who traveled with the group as a servant had been spied washing the women's undergarments. Another former servant recalled that he knew "Charley" and "Frank" were women because he had seen them "making water and they always let down their pantaloons and squatted down and I also saw the shape of their breasts." Obviously "Charley" and "Frank" were traveling under false pretenses. "I have often seen General Kilpatrick in bed with Charley hugged up close together," noted one observer; and another recalled that he had seen Kilpatrick kissing "Charley" with great affection.[37]

It seems clear that "Charley" and "Frank" posed as men for

less than honorable reasons. It is important to remember, however, that these women never intended to serve as actual soldiers: there is no evidence, for example, that either woman formally enlisted in the ranks using an alias, or ever carried weapons or equipment. The masquerade seems to have been a complicated and morally questionable game for which responsibility lay not only with themselves but also with the officers with whom they associated. A somewhat less scandalous but also complicated situation arose in connection with nineteen-year-old Harriet Merrill of Watertown, New York, who in the fall of 1861 enlisted in Company G of the 59th New York Infantry Volunteers. When the 59th's Captain Jerome B. Taft came before a general court-martial in the spring of 1862, he faced the charge of conduct unbecoming an officer and a gentleman for, among other things, allegedly persuading Merrill to join the army as a common soldier in order that she might become his mistress. Taft's lengthy statement, written in response to the charges against him, contended that Merrill was known to be the "most lieing [sic] creature living," and that one of Taft's fellow officers had for political reasons prompted her to disseminate false rumors that she and Taft were lovers. In fact, Taft insisted, Merrill was the mistress of another officer, James Miller, who had brought her with him to the camp of the 59th. "Is it reasonable," the married Taft demanded to know, "to suppose that I would thus risk my then at least *fair* public and private reputation, as well as my name as an officer upon the association and person of a common prostitute?"[38]

Taft might have done well to be less hostile to Merrill and to have directed his ire instead at those who seem to have been trying, for whatever reason, to sabotage his military career. As it turned out, in her own testimony Merrill gave no indication whatsoever that her enlistment was connected to an agreement to become Taft's mistress. Rather, Merrill—who refused to answer any questions about her previous occupation—asserted that she had first met Taft at a "dining saloon" in Watertown, and had at that time voiced an interest in enlisting in the military, for undisclosed reasons. Some days later, now clad in civilian men's clothing and having mysteriously received a train ticket that could carry her as far as New York City and the headquarters of the 59th, Merrill encountered Taft again at the Watertown and Rome train station, where he asked her if she had received her transportation. Acknowledging that she had, Merrill continued on her way to visit a friend in Utica, then proceeded to New York, where she took the oath of allegiance and enlisted as "Frederick Woods." Asked if she had undergone the usual physical examination by a medical officer, Merrill responded that she had not and that she did not know why she had not. Asked what duties she had performed while in camp at New York, Merrill replied, "I performed all the duties that the rest of the soldiers did," and she elsewhere noted that she had consistently "performed the duties of a soldier, and shared a soldier's part." Asked how many among the other soldiers in camp knew that she was a woman, Merrill answered: "I don't know how many there were knew me, in soldier's clothes. Almost all our company knew or had heard the report. I could not say who they were." Merrill laid no claim to having been intimately involved with Taft, and the court ultimately found Taft not guilty.[39]

Harriet Merrill's precise reasons for enlisting in the Union army are unclear, but as in the case of other women soldiers who were the subject of similar accusations, it seems highly unlikely that she joined the army for the sole purpose of engaging in illicit sex with her fellow soldiers and officers. Enlistment brought with it far too many other responsibilities and hazards to make it an attractive avenue to such activity, especially when other avenues were available. Such accusations of calculated sexual impropriety were generally groundless. What they tend to reflect is the often negative opinion of Civil War women soldiers held by wartime, postwar, and even more recent observers.[40] Observers in their own time and interpreters since then have frequently made the point that a woman who enlisted as a man in the Union or Confederate army performed an unnatural act, and explanations that revolve around the issue of a woman's moral debasement—like the state of Illinois's claim about Jennie Hodgers's "insanity"—can be understood as deriving primarily from the distaste shared by many observers from the time of the war down to the present for the phenomenon of women posing as men and serving as soldiers. Given this attitude, it makes sense that observers would seek to emphasize reasons for women soldiers' transgressive behavior that provided some comfort: moral debasement on the one hand, or love of a man, pure adventuresomeness, and ardent patriotism on the other. As Lauren Burgess notes, "Women who followed a husband, sweetheart, or brother into the army . . . received more favorable press when their stories became public."[41]

As in the case of women who engaged in espionage and resistance activities and those who served as army women and daughters of the regiment during the Civil War, women soldiers of the Union and Confederate armies were not without their counterparts in American fiction, and the majority of these fictional heroines are driven to disguise themselves as male soldiers because of their love for a good man.[42] Perhaps the most famous pre-Civil War work of this sort—and a somewhat surprising one, given its apparently feminist overtones—is *Fanny Campbell, the Female Pirate Captain*, published by Maturin Murray Ballou in 1844.[43] In Fanny Campbell readers encounter what one scholar has described as the "model of bravery, beauty, and pluck . . . deserving in romance, able in war, and rewarded in love,"[44] and it is no wonder that at least one source has claimed that the Civil War's Sarah Emma Edmonds found in Fanny Campbell the inspiration for her own miltiary service.[45]

Fanny Campbell's story begins in 1773 in a small Massachusetts fishing community where rugged living conditions and an era characterized by open, often violent political conflict, writes Ballou, produced a generation of strong, bold, and adventurous men and women, of whom Fanny was one. As the story begins, seventeen-year-old Fanny is bidding farewell to her beloved, William Lovell, who is about to go off to sea. Fanny confesses to William that she envies him the opportunity to experience the world in this way, and insists that if she were a man, she would do the same herself. Needless to say, the chance soon presents itself to her: when William's ship is wrecked off the coast of Cuba and he and his mates are imprisoned by Cubans who suspect them of piracy, the faithful Fanny determines to go to his rescue. For this purpose she assumes the identity of a sailor named "Channing" and accepts work on board the brig the *Constance*, bound for the West Indies.

Conveniently, the British captain of the *Constance* early on proves to be an evil man, and in short order Fanny, as "Channing," engineers a mutiny, puts herself in charge, and turns the ship towards Cuba. En route the *Constance*, under Fanny's command, successfully engages a British ship in battle and Fanny thwarts a second mutiny by the men she previously removed from duty, killing one in cold blood to demonstrate the seriousness of her commitment to control. Fanny completes the rescue mission without further incident, bringing William and his mates on board.

It is not long before William becomes curious about his new, mysterious, and vaguely familiar captain, and when the two meet privately, Fanny reveals herself to him. William greets Fanny's disclosure with respect and admiration, and for a time, by mutual agreement, Fanny—still as "Channing"—remains in charge of the *Constance*, bringing the ship and its crew successfully through a number of other adventures. Finally, after repeatedly proving herself to be a wise and compassionate commander of men, Fanny leaves the ship and secretly abandons her masquerade, making way for William to become the new captain of the refitted *Constance*. William and Fanny marry and return to sea with Fanny on board as William's primary military adviser as well as his wife. The story ends with an account of the later lives of the char-

acters and a review of the importance of each to the telling of the
tale. Of the character of Fanny Campbell, Ballou writes—in
words reminiscent of Moore's introductory comments about
daughter of the regiment Bridget Divers—"We have designed to
show that among the lower classes of society, there is more than
the germ of true intellect and courage, nobleness of purpose,
and strength of will than may be found among the pampered and
wealthy children of fortune."[46]

In the gallery of American female warrior heroines, Fanny
Campbell stands tall, a powerfully independent, forceful, unin-
hibited, capable figure—notably of the "hearty lower class"—
whose exploits, wisdom, and courage certify that she is a match
for any man. Fanny's story suggests that, pushed to the extreme
for whatever reason, a woman may prove herself able and worthy
and thus may claim, as Ballou does for her, to be a "man at
heart."[47] Fanny Campbell displays only confidence and pride
when acting as a ship's captain; she is no lovesick puppy requiring the steady hand of a man to save her from herself. She is
instead a master of men and a master of her own emotions, a
woman whose reason and judgment repeatedly prove reliable.
Fanny is indeed a worthy hero on all fronts.

Nevertheless, Fanny is a woman who has donned a military
uniform because of her love for a man. The same is true of the
heroine of The Lady Lieutenant, allegedly the autobiography of
Kentucky native Madeline Moore, published in 1862 and set in
the Civil War.[48] Having benefited early on from wealth and a
good education, Madeline Moore at eighteen crowns her promising youth by falling in love with one Frank Ashton, the son of a
good family in her community and himself a law student.
However, Madeline's sanctimonious and ill-tempered aunt, with
whom she has been living, disapproves of Frank and seeks to
throw whatever obstacles she can in the path of their union.
Thus, when Sumter falls and Frank decides to enlist in the Union
army, Madeline determines to leave her unkind aunt's home and

follow Frank to war. Securing the necessary disguise, complete with whiskers and a mustache, Madeline signs on as "Albert Harville" with a company in Frank's regiment. Typical of such literature, when Madeline introduces herself in her new identity to Frank, he fails to recognize her.

On board ship heading for the battlefront, "Albert Harville" and Frank Ashton become inseparable, and they are side by side when they confront the enemy for the first time in a skirmish. Both are wounded, however, which leads to their separation. Not long thereafter, "Albert"—who has healed quickly—fights without Frank at her side in the first battle of Bull Run, during which action she proves herself to be a skilled equestrienne and a good soldier. Once the battle ends, however, she decides that she must go in search of Frank, whom she finds barely alive in a makeshift hospital. Over the course of the next several weeks Madeline remains by Frank's side, nursing him back to health while sustaining her imposture as "Albert." Finally, when Frank seems to be fully on the mend, Madeline decides to make her true identity known, a feat she achieves simply by telling Frank to look at her more closely. Frank recognizes Madeline at last, and with a burst of delight throws his arms around her and collapses into tears of joy. The two subsequently return home, marry, and live out their lives in a state of conjugal contentment.

Like Fanny Campbell, although she proves herself to be a credible soldier, Madeline is initially motivated to serve in the military because of her great love for and devotion to a man. Like Fanny, Madeline goes to war in the first place only because she wants to be at her lover's side, not because she yearns to assume the role of a soldier for its own sake, or even for her nation's sake. Although once she is engaged in battle Madeline—like Fanny—performs her duties with honor, when the time comes she quickly and happily shifts into the role of nurse and thereby fulfills her "true" calling. Though she has proven herself to be a good soldier under fire, it is much more important to the story that she prove herself to be a good woman; and although the behavior she manifests while in the role of a male soldier is exemplary, the author of *The Lady Lieutenant* clearly suggests that the role itself is fundamentally an improper one for women. From the author's perspective, women did not belong in the armies of the Civil War as soldiers. At most, women should at most be tending to the sick and wounded in the war's hospitals. Even better, they should be at home tending the hearth.

By the time of the Civil War, fictional women in uniform from the pages of American literature commonly shared as the fundamental motivation for their imposture and their military service the desire to be with a much loved man, in some cases amplified by a desire for adventure.[49] A work that appeared just over a decade after Appomattox, however, offers a somewhat more complicated interpretation, one that may in fact be more consistent with the complexity of the actual motivations of women for entering the military service as soldiers or as spies and army women, for that matter. Loreta Janeta Velazquez's *The Woman in Battle* is ostensibly a narrative account of the author's four years of service to the Confederate army as both a spy and a soldier.[50] It is a fantastic tale in many ways, but there is evidence as well that the narrative's contents—like the protagonist's reasons for joining the military—are rooted in real experience.

The book begins with Velazquez's explanation of the conditions that led to her decision to join the Confederate army. In April 1856, Velazquez—the daughter of Cuban immigrants—explains, she fell in love and eloped with an American army officer whom she identifies only as William. Together they had three children, all of whom had died by the fall of 1860. When the Civil War broke out in 1861, the now childless Velazquez was ready for action, in part, at least, as a means to divert her attention from the loss of her children. "As for me," she writes, "I was perfectly wild on the subject of war."[51] In line with this, Velazquez lay before her husband a plan for disguising herself as a man and entering the

Confederate service, a plan to which she became more committed when William refused to accept it. When her husband departed for the front in June 1861, Velazquez headed for New Orleans, where she cut her hair, purchased a uniform and a false mustache, and stained her face to make it look tanned. "Everything," she writes, "was now in proper trim for me to commence operations in earnest. . . . I was ready to start on my campaign with as stout a heart as ever beat in the breast of a soldier."[52]

Velazquez's initial plan is to raise a battalion at her own expense and then present the men to her husband and offer him their command. Gather troops she does: 236 men in four days—not enough for a battalion but certainly enough for the core of a regiment. With her "Arkansas Grays," Velazquez then heads for William's encampment in Pensacola, Florida. When she presents the men to him, William is displeased to discover that his wife has disobeyed his orders; his displeasure, however, shortly becomes moot, for soon after Velazquez's arrival in Pensacola, William is killed in an accident. Rising above her grief and leaving the Arkansas Grays in someone else's command, Velazquez heads out to search for her next role with the army.

Subsequent chapters detail Velazquez's struggles under the pseudonym of "Harry T. Buford" to gain a lieutenant's commission and a formal attachment to a specific Confederate regiment (at one point she does join the 21st Louisiana Infantry). Over the course of the war Velazquez participates in a number of battles, including the first battle of Bull Run, during which she is assigned temporary command of a company whose senior officer has been killed. October 1861 finds Velazquez also participating in the battle of Ball's Bluff, in which a small number of Confederate troops surprised a Union force attempting to cross the Potomac and scale a seventy-foot bluff into Virginia. After this, frustrated—like army woman Nadine Turchin—with the periods of prolonged inaction that seem to follow every major engagement, and also with her failure to achieve a regular commission, Velazquez somewhat reluctantly decides to turn her hand instead to the work of spying on behalf of the Confederacy.

The bulk of the rest of the book weaves together Velazquez's experiences as a spy and as a soldier for the Southern army. She continues to take part in various battles, including Shiloh, where she temporarily assumes command of her old Arkansas Grays when their lieutenant falls to enemy fire. She also provides service as a smuggler of drugs, matériel, and correspondence, sometimes in the guise of "Lieutenant Harry Buford" and sometimes not. Velazquez also serves briefly as a double agent for the Confederacy under the alias "Mrs. Williams." On occasion Velazquez comes under arrest; on occasion she is suspected or even discovered to be a woman. Always she manages to find her way back under cover and into the Confederate army's service. Reflecting on her years of devotion to the military at the end of the book, Velazquez celebrates her own achievements. At the same time, she demands recognition from her readers of the appropriateness and the moral rectitude of her choice of wartime work, despite its unconventionality on the basis of her sex. "All I claim," she writes,

> is, that my conduct, under the many trying and peculiar circumstances in which I have been placed, shall be judged with the impartiality and candor and that due credit shall be given me for integrity of purpose, and a desire to do my whole duty as I understand it. For the part I took in the great contest between the South and the North I have no apologies to offer. I did what I thought to be right; and, while anxious for the good opinion of all honorable and right-thinking people, a consciousness of the purity of my motives will be an ample protection against the censure of those who may be disposed to be censorious.[53]

Velazquez was right to expect censure. Almost as soon as *The Woman in Battle* appeared, it met with serious challenge, specifi-

*Two etchings depicting Loreta Velazquez in female attire, and as she would have appeared as Lieutenant Harry T. Buford during the war.* Reprinted from her memoir, *The Woman in Battle* (1876).

cally with regard to its authenticity. In 1878 former Confederate General Jubal Early (under whose command Mary and Molly Bell had served in cognito for two years) penned an outraged letter to Southern Congressman W. F. Slemons in which he took Velazquez's assertions to task one after the other. "When I was in New Orleans last winter," Early wrote with considerable heat, "I came across Madame Velazquez's book . . . and gave it a cursory examination, from which I was satisfied that the writer of that book . . . had never had the adventures therein narrated." Moreover, Early continued, the book's "several inconsistencies, absurdities, and impossibilities" made it clear that Velazquez "could not be what she pretended to be." Early claimed to have had a personal interview with Velazquez as well, with the result that he was "satisfied that she had not written the book of which she professed to be the author, or that it had been very much changed and influenced in style by the editor."[54]

In fact, Velazquez acknowledges in her preface to *The Woman in Battle* that like all good editors, hers was instrumental in preparing her manuscript for publication. Editor and publisher C. J. Worthington—himself a Union naval officer during the war— also admitted having put his hand to refining Velazquez's prose for a popular audience and having corrected certain errors of detail. Both Velazquez and Worthington, therefore, confessed up front that *The Woman in Battle* was not a pure memoir per se—if such a thing exists—but rather a product of their combined efforts, a product of memory as well as research which also benefited from the stylistic skill and judgment of an editor sensitive to the demands of a popular readership.

Jubal Early's intention, however, was not to criticize the book on this level. Rather, to him the entire work was nothing more than an insult to its readers' intelligence, to the Confederacy, and to Southern womanhood. It was, as one scholar has put it, an "atrocity" that Velazquez had "perpetrated . . . on the American literary audience."[55] Indeed, in his letter to Congressman Slemons, Early argued that even if *The Woman in Battle* were presented as a work of pure fiction, it would be one which Southerners should consider libelous, and he went on to detail the many aspects of the book that defied both history and good common sense, at the same time raising serious questions about Velazquez's moral integrity. Velazquez, he concluded, was "no true type of Southern woman."[56]

Others down to the present have relentlessly questioned the overall authenticity of Velazquez's purported memoir. As one modern scholar points out, "Almost nothing that Velazquez included in her book can be authenticated." On the other hand, this same scholar rightly notes that the records of the Confederate Secretary of War contain a reference to a request for an officer's commission, received on July 27, 1863, from a soldier named "H. T. Buford."[57] Although it is not possible to confirm a direct link between an historical Loreta Janeta Velazquez and the commission-seeking soldier identified as H. T. Buford in 1863, there is additional evidence in other sources to support the theory that at least the broad outlines and even more precise details of the Velazquez story, as presented in *The Woman in Battle*, have their basis in fact. As early as October 1861, for example, the Louisville, Kentucky, *Daily Journal* reported the arrest of a woman soldier in Richmond. "A lady, who gave her name as Mrs. Mary Ann Keith, of Memphis, Tenn.," the article noted,

was arrested in Lynchburg, Va., recently. When arrested she was rigged out in a full suit of soldiers' clothes, and had registered her name at the Piedmont House as Lieut. Buford. She said she had been married twice—her first husband having been a member of Sherman's famous battery; her second husband was in the Southern army; but she stated that she separated from him for some reason she did not make known. She

declared she was all right on the Southern question, and scout-
ed the idea of being a spy. She said her reason for dressing in
soldier clothes was that she had determined to fight the battles
of her country, and thought such disguise more likely to enable
her to accomplish her object. She was sent to Richmond for a
further hearing.[58]

Almost two years later the Richmond, Virginia, *Whig* republished a detailed article from the Jackson *Mississippian* describing
the "adventures of a young lady in the army," adventures that put
her, notably, "in the ranks of the Molly Pitchers of the present
revolution." According to this article, at the outbreak of the war,
a Mrs. Laura J. Williams (a name hardly inconsistent with a pseudonym like Loreta J. Velazquez) of Arkansas, who demonstrated
"little of the characteristic weakness of her sex, either in body or
mind," and who was motivated by a desire to "offer her life upon
the altar of her country," disguised herself as a Confederate soldier, took the alias "Henry Benford" (also not inconsistent with
"Harry Buford") and

proceeded to Texas, where she raised and equipped an independent company, and went to Virginia with it as first lieutenant. She was in the battle of Leesburg [another name for
the battle of Ball's Bluff] and several skirmishes; but, finally,
her sex having been discovered by the surgeon of the regiment
. . . she returned to her home in Arkansas. After remaining
there a short time she proceeded to Corinth, and was in the
battle of Shiloh, where she displayed great coolness and
courage. . . . She then visited New Orleans . . . where she
employed herself in carrying communications, assisting parties
to run the blockade with drugs and cloths for uniforms. She
was informed on by a negro and arrested and brought before
[Union] General [Benjamin] Butler. . . . Butler denounced her
as the most incorrigible she rebel he had ever met with. By

order of the Beast she was placed in confinement, where she remained three months. . . .[59]

Two weeks later, in July 1863, the Richmond *Daily Examiner* noted the arrival in that city of a "female lieutenant." "Yesterday," the article explained,

the hero or heroine, whichever you please, was received in the city from the Provost Marshal of Mobile, and lodged in Castle Thunder. She bears her assumed name, Lieutenant Benford, and persists in wearing the uniform of an officer of that rank. We did not undersand that any charge, except that of unsexing herself, is alleged against her.[60]

And in January 1867 the New Orleans *Daily Picayune* published a story about a woman using the name Mary DeCaulp who had served as a Texas cavalry lieutenant and whom the reporter had spotted in New Orleans during the war "dressed in a rough gray jacket and pants, the suit rather the worse for wear, with her hair cut short, and supporting a bandaged foot with a crutch of the most primitive pattern.[61] According to *The Woman in Battle*, DeCaulp was the last name of Velazquez's second husband.

Not only newspaper accounts from the period of the war but also the *Official Records of the Union and Confederate Armies* lend credence to at least the basic outlines of author Velazquez's claims in *The Woman in Battle*. In the *Official Records* we find an October 1865 letter from Sanford Conover to Brigadier General Joseph Holt in which he notes that a Miss Alice Williams received a commission in the Confederate army as Lieutenant Buford. The name Alice Williams appears as well in the Union Provost Marshal General's List of Scouts, Guides, Spies and Detectives, in a November 1863 memo signed by William S. Fish of the 8th Army Corps. This document certifies the appointment of one Alice Williams as a "special agent" and sets her fee at two dollars per day. Another document in the same file indicates that Williams surrendered her commission as a detective in July 1864.[62]

In short, various sources combine to create the impression that there was at least one Confederate woman—originally Mary Ann Keith? Mary DeCaulp? Laura J. or Alice Williams?—whose wartime movements, activities, and use of aliases were consistent with those recorded by Velazquez in *The Woman in Battle*. At least one woman masqueraded as a soldier named Harry Buford (and/or Henry Benford), served in a number of battles, and became a spy (perhaps playing on both sides of the fence) and a smuggler.[63] In any case, the individual who claimed to be the book's author and subject responded with passion to Jubal Early's challenges to the book's fundamental authenticity. In a letter to Early, the woman who signed her name "Madame L. J. Velasquez or H. T. Buford (C. S. A.)" insisted that the tales contained in the book, though they were for a variety of reasons somewhat inaccurate in detail, were nonetheless true at their core.[64]

*The Woman in Battle* lies at the nexus of many of the issues regarding women's service to the armies of the North and the South (and the Continental army as well) as soldiers and spies in particular, and also as army women: What was the scope of their service? How were such women perceived by observers in their own time and later? What is the relationship between the representations of such women's activities in popular literature and their actual experience? *The Woman in Battle* also brings us back to the question of women's motivation in taking up the work of aiding their respective military organizations during the war, for what is truly startling about Velazquez's narrative is her forthright statement of the impulses that lay behind the choices she made.

Among these impulses Velazquez identifies her lifelong desire to be a man. "It was frequently my habit," she writes of her childhood, "after all the house had retired to bed at night, to dress myself in my [male] cousin's clothes, and to promenade by the hour before the mirror, practising the gait of a man, and admiring the figure I made in masculine raiment."[65] She points as well to her personal ambition to attain glory on the battlefield regardless of her sex: along with countless other "great souled women" of history "who have stood in the front rank where the battle was hottest and the fray most deadly," Joan of Arc was her inspiration, she writes, "an example of what a woman may do if only she dares, and dares to do greatly."[66]

Perhaps even more important than her confessed desire to experience life as a man, however, is Velazquez's ready admission that she enjoyed the financial benefits her chosen work offered her. Notably, she admits to sharing a desire to "earn a dollar or so when I could, and, if possible, without stealing," and she delights particularly in the lucrative nature of her work as a smuggler. "Drugs of all kinds," she writes,

> were very scarce within the Confederate lines, and consequently brought enormous prices; so that any one who could manage to smuggle them past the Federal outposts was certain of reaping a handsome profit. I succeeded in obtaining a good quantity of this kind of merchandise from the different hospitals, and, as I could carry many dollars' worth about my person without attracting particular attention, I much more than made my expenses on the several trips I undertook.[67]

Indeed, war's end did not bring an end to Velazquez's determination to find a way to make some money: in her preface to *The Woman in Battle*, Velazquez admits that she was more interested in the income from her book's sales than in the praise of her readers; and in her rebuttal to Jubal Early she reserved her deepest resentment for what she perceived to be his undermining of her own and her son's economic future. "Now General," she wrote,

> my Book and Correspondence with the Press is my entire support of myself and little son. . . . I have had trials Enough to

have driven almost any proud spirited woman to madness, or to commit suicide, but I have struggled and born[e] my lot with the hope of prosperity before me, casting the buffeting of my inferiors beneath my feet and with god[']s Protection I have lived above it all, and all I now ask from you is justice to my *child*.[68]

Whether as Harry T. Buford during the war or as the author and defender of a wartime memoir of uncertain authenticity, the individual known as Loreta Velazquez unhesitatingly laid claim to the fiscal rewards she believed were her due.

Given the ways in which contemporary observers typically explained Civil War military women's motivations, one suspects that a good part of Jubal Early's discomfort with Velazquez's story—his insistence that she was no example of a true Southern woman—had less to do with his questioning of the details than with his disgust at Velazquez's blatant confession of her financial motives. Indeed, a century after Early's response to *The Woman in Battle*, at least one critic revisited the theme of Velazquez's presumably unseemly self-interest.

One cannot read [this book] without concluding that [Velazquez] was at the very least an opportunist. She admitted that her reasons for writing the book were pecuniary rather than patriotic, educational, or literary. Certainly the character she revealed in her book was capable of taking advantage of a reading public inclined to buy romantic literature . . . she was quite capable of using her wits and the gullibility of her readers in order to support herself and her child.[69]

Ten years, even a hundred and ten years after Appomattox, commenters expressed disgust at the idea that a woman would do what Velazquez claimed to have done, serving not only for the glorious cause but also for money as a Civil War soldier and spy, and then writing a memoir about her military adventures for profit.[70] Such disgust aside, however, Velazquez's story encourages us to revisit the question of motivation in the cases of the most fully documented women soldiers of the Civil War, Sarah Emma Edmonds, Jennie Hodgers, and Rosetta Wakeman, and of their Revolutionary War predecessor, Deborah Sampson.

Perhaps not surprisingly, in her 1792 petition for aid to the General Court of Massachusetts, Sampson indicated that it was her "zeal for the good of her Country" that had provoked her to enlist in the Continental army.[71] A decade after her 1792 petition, while lecturing on her Continental army service, Sampson reinforced the notion that it was indeed patriotism first and foremost that had led her into the military. Passionately Sampson recalled the swell of nationalistic fervor that had preceded her decision to enlist. "Confirmed by this time," she told her audiences,

in the justness of a defensive war . . . my mind ripened with my strength; and while our beds and our roses were sprinkled with the blood of indiscriminate youth, beauty, innocence and decrepit old age, I only seemed to want the *license* to become one of the severest *avengers* of the wrong.[72]

Although Sampson boldly declared the patriotic impulse behind her enlistment, one must acknowledge that her claims of ardent patriotism as her sole motive for joining the army came in the context of a request for back pay from a government body that most likely would have been highly skeptical about her claims of service, and in the context of her performance before curious, perhaps even incredulous audiences who were likely to be uncomfortable with the idea of her "unsexing" herself, and who wanted an explanation that could comfortably justify such behavior.[73] Under these circumstances, it must be presumed that Sampson would have suggested only a motive for enlistment which her various audiences would have found unobjectionable.

Claims about the purity of her patriotic impulses must be considered with care.

Indeed, there is strong evidence to suggest that Sampson had at least two other possible motives for enlisting as Robert Shurtliff in the Continental army: a desire on the one hand to escape a fiancé whom her mother had foisted upon her and who purportedly manifested the "silliness of a baboon," and, on the other hand, a desire to avoid the punishment that her community had in store for her for a previous indiscretion, provocatively termed by one historian the "Timothy Thayer fiasco."[74] Of these two possible explanations, the latter holds the greater interest: it refers to an earlier short-lived enlistment by Sampson as "Timothy Thayer" sometime early in the spring of 1782, before she assumed the identity of Robert Shurtliff. On this occasion Sampson does not seem to have had any real intention to go into battle. Rather, with the bounty money she received from her enlistment as Thayer, she apparently proceeded straight from the recruiting office to a tavern where she reportedly became visibly drunk. She then returned home and resumed her own attire, and "Timothy Thayer" promptly disappeared. Sampson's indiscretion might have gone undiscovered had not a local woman subsequently reported to authorities that the missing Thayer had manifested the same familiar but unconventional style of holding a pen as Sampson.

In her preliminary imposture as Timothy Thayer, of course, Sampson may simply have been trying to determine whether a longer-term imposture could possibly succeed. More likely, as some have suggested, the Thayer incident reflected what biographer Mann described as Sampson's frustration with the limitations of the "woman's sphere" in her time.[75] Indeed, it was Mann who in 1797 first suggested that Sampson's desire to travel more freely than convention allowed preceded her decision to assume a male identity and join the army. Mann proposed that Sampson was profoundly patriotic, but also that she was deeply dissatisfied with her lot as a late eighteenth-century woman, and indeed one could interpret the Thayer incident as an expression of this sort of dissatisfaction. Certainly her community had for some time recognized (and condemned) Sampson's tendency to rebel against the restrictions imposed on her sex: a September 1782 document from the records of the First Baptist Church in Middleborough, where Sampson was a member, notes that Sampson's imposture as Thayer, far from being an isolated instance, actually fit an established pattern of misguided conduct. Sampson, the document noted, had behaved in a manner "very loose and unchristian like" prior to the Thayer incident. Moreover, once her charade as Timothy Thayer was discovered, Sampson had responded not with contrition but rather with what appeared to be disdain, or perhaps embarrassment: she "left our parts in a suden maner [sic], and it is not known among us where she is gone." As a consequence, the church decided to terminate Sampson's membership until she returned and made "Christian satisfaction."[76] Evidently Sampson had for some time been at odds with her church for engaging in conduct that exceeded the bounds of propriety. Indeed, if she was already frustrated with social constraints and sought a larger world to explore, her experience of stern community disapproval for the Timothy Thayer incident probably only added to her desire to find an avenue to greater freedom, which real enlistment in the army seemed to offer.

The Timothy Thayer incident helps to explain Sampson's decision to enlist as Robert Shurtliff because it shows that she was already a rebel of sorts who was willing to defy convention by posing as a man eager to serve the army, and who subsequently was also willing to ignore community censure of her initial defiance and commit another offense of the same sort that was potentially even more serious. The Thayer incident also raises another issue, however: the issue of Sampson's financial situation at the time she joined the army. For it seems more than reasonable to assume that, having experienced poverty and hard labor throughout her youth, a perhaps patriotic, undoubtedly rebellious and hard-nosed

Sampson saw the army as a setting in which she could apply her skills as a laborer to the alleviation of some of her financial distress.[77] We have already noted that after she enlisted as Timothy Thayer, Sampson spent a portion of her bounty money on an evening's revelry in a tavern, undoubtedly a liberating experience for one who had lived such a long time so close to the bone. Another chunk of "Thayer's" bounty money seems to have gone to clothes for herself as well as to a pair of long gloves that she presented to a woman friend to whom she felt indebted.[78] From what we know about her preenlistment life, there is little cause to doubt that Sampson would have rejoiced in having some cash to spend—in the form of bounty money or in the form of the regular wages promised to the soldiers of the Continental army.

Sources that consider the phenomenon of the enlisted woman soldier in early modern Europe provide strong evidence to support the notion that Sampson's decision to join the Continental army was rooted in her economic situation, in her desire to earn a steady wage in a line of work not generally open to women of that era. According to historians Rudolf M. Dekker and Lotte C. van de Pol, almost all early modern European women who disguised themselves as men and took up the work of soldiers or sailors for any length of time came from the working class, and most of the women had already engaged in forms of paid labor considered appropriate for women (preeminently domestic service) before trying their hand at military service. Many of these lower-class women, like Sampson, also came from particularly unstable families, and most were young—between sixteen and twenty-five years of age at the time they decided to "unsex" themselves—unmarried, and childless.[79]

Certainly Deborah Sampson, who was young, single, and childless, who came from a broken family in the lower ranks of early American society, and who had a history of hard labor behind her when she enlisted, fits this model quite closely. What of Civil War women soldiers? That economics may have been a factor in women's decision to enlist in the armies of the Union and the Confederacy is not an entirely new idea: a few writers have suggested, with varying degrees of emphasis, that women became soldiers during the Civil War because they needed or wanted the financial security that a steady, if dangerous, job supposedly could provide. Historian and military archivist DeAnne Blanton in particular has argued the probability that "working class and poor women were probably enticed by the bounties and the promise of a regular pay-check," and Lauren Burgess points out that "among the documented cases of women combatants for whom background information is known, the majority were from poor and agrarian classes. . . ."[80]

If we turn to the story of Sarah Emma Edmonds, we can hardly fail to recognize the strong evidence supporting an economic motive as part of the explanation for her enlistment. Like Sampson, Edmonds was young, single, and childless at the time she joined the army; she was the daughter of a troubled farming family and had behind her a history of hard physical labor. Perhaps not surprisingly, some in her own time and since—including she herself—have sought to justify Edmonds's enlistment in ways that do not even hint at the question of financial distress. In his diary, Jerome Robbins recalled that Edmonds had explained her decision to leave home in the first place as one based on her dislike of her tyrannical father and a desire to escape a love affair gone awry. The congressional committee that ultimately granted her request for a pension spoke of the "strange impulse" (apparently her overweening patriotism for her adopted country) that had led Edmonds to feel "constrained to enter the service."[81] A rather bizarre and melodramatic article that appeared in an 1884 issue of the *Weekly Monitor* of Fort Scott, Kansas (where Edmonds and her family were living at the time), and which claimed to report the results of an interview with her, reinforced the idea that Edmonds's father's tyranny and her own desire to resist it had driven Edmonds from her family home, and that her devotion to the Union cause had subsequently propelled her into the army. "I was in the vicinity of

Flint, Michigan, and was present when the first troops bade
farewell to home and friends and marched to their place of ren-
dezvous at Detroit . . ." Edmonds purportedly told her interviewer.
"It was while witnessing the anguish of that first parting that I
became convinced that I, too, had a duty to perform in the sacred
cause of Truth and Freedom."[82]

Hatred of her father, a desire to escape her family home, a
thirst for adventure, and a passion for the Union cause—these are
the factors that figure in most explanations of Edmonds's decision
to enlist in the army.[83] Although there is evidence in the sources
to support each and also some combination of these theories, one
cannot ignore the additional evidence supporting economic motivation as well. Indeed, it seems that financial considerations
(quite reasonably) were a factor in all of Edmonds's adult decisions, including the decision to enlist in the 2nd Michigan as
Franklin Thompson. Even the Fort Scott *Weekly Monitor* article
lends some weight to the notion that Edmonds as a young, single
woman had determined to find ways to earn her own keep. "I
greatly preferred the privilege of earning my own bread and but-
ter," the article quoted Edmonds as saying. Indeed, in its discussion of her prewar career as a bookseller, the article left the
impression that finding a way to earn a lot of money was a matter
of paramount concern to Edmonds, who knew that as a woman
her options were limited. "The publishing company," Edmonds
was reported as saying,

> told me that they had employed agents for thirty years, and
> they never had employed one that could outsell me. I made
> money, dressed well, owned and drove a fine horse and
> buggy—silver-mounted harness and all the paraphernalia of a
> nice turnout. . . .[84]

For Edmonds, earning her own money made her feel, in her own
words, "manly," though her lavish lifestyle had harsh conse-

quences: by 1861, according to the same article, she had used up most of her earnings and her job with the publishing company seems to have fallen through.[85] That the war offered a new opportunity for "manly" independence and a paycheck cannot be denied. In 1861 Edmonds was a woman on her own who had come from a poor farming family and who needed a steady income. The employment opportunities available to her as a woman were exceedingly limited, and the lure to don men's clothing and enhance those opportunities was irresistible. When the Civil War came, it brought steady jobs for many of the sons of poor farming families across America. If the pay turned out not always to be as steady as the work, there was still the work itself, along with some food, and some shelter, and, of course, adventure and patriotic purpose. The independent daughter of a poor farming family, Edmonds went to war for perhaps many of these reasons, but not least of all because soldiering offered her a paying job. [86]

Edmonds's story suggests that for the most famous woman soldier of the Civil War, economics was a factor in her decision to enlist. As for Rosetta Wakeman, there is no question whatsoever that she left home in disguise as a man to take a job as a boatman and then as a Union soldier because she and her family needed the money; and as the editor of her letters notes, "after joining the army, Rosetta sent home substantial sums of money, in amounts that she could not have earned as quickly in any position open to her as a woman, with the possible exception of prostitution."[87] What of Jennie Hodgers? We know from Hodgers's military service record and from other sources as well that she came from the ranks of the laboring classes and from a life in which she, like Edmonds and Wakeman, was already masquerading as a man. The occupation Hodgers claimed when she enlisted was "farmer," and in her case as well, there is little doubt that the decision to join the army reflected at least in part the very practical demands that resulted from being poor and female and needing to engage in a form of waged labor that was accessible only to men in the middle of the nineteenth century. In Hodgers's case, the financial benefits of enlisting must have had great appeal: several documents note that by August 1862, when Hodgers signed up with the 95th Illinois Infantry, the town of Belvidere had raised its initial $40 enlistment bonus to $302.[88] We also know that Hodgers remained a laborer throughout her life and, like Edmonds, was ready and willing to claim a veteran's pension as soon as Congress made it available. Hodgers, like Edmonds and Wakeman, was not a rich woman but rather a poor one who was used to hard work. When war came to the land with the promise of steady employment, Hodgers took the opportunity despite its numerous and obvious hazards.

In discussing Rosetta Wakeman, Lauren Burgess points out that in terms of her background and her experience of the war, Wakeman was representative not only of the sorts of women—but also the sorts of men—who typically enlisted in the ranks of the Civil War military. "Like many of her male counterparts," Burgess writes, "Rosetta Wakeman came from a modest and unsophisticated rural background."[89] Although Civil War women soldiers came from a variety of backgrounds, they overwhelmingly had their roots in the rural heartland, North and South, and they tended to be individuals whose prewar lives had conditioned them for hard work and harsh living conditions. Not surprisingly, those who were most successful were those who readily took to the outdoor life, the gun, and the drill.

The same is also true of Civil War army women and daughters of the regiment. When postwar and more modern writers discussed Annie Etheridge, Kady Brownell, and other Civil War army women and daughters of the regiment, they typically emphasized the women's ardent patriotism as their primary motivation for going to war. And although Frank Moore and others occasionally conceded that an army woman's patriotism represented only one among several motives driving her into the military's service, they bypassed the economic question entirely.

On the question of why Kady Brownell joined the Union army, Moore gave a three-point explanation that others would commonly apply in connection not only with Brownell but also with others like her: Moore attributed Brownell's decision to join the army to her military heritage, her love for her husband, and her love for the Union. "Accustomed to arms and soldiers from infancy," he wrote,

> she learned to love the camp; and it was not strange years later, when she had come to America and married a young mechanic in Providence, that the recollections of the camp fire in front of her father's tent, as well as the devotion of a newly-married wife, and loyalty to the Union, prompted her to follow her husband, stand beside him in battle, and share all his hardships.[90]

Moore might well have been describing Nadine Turchin. Similarly, the creators of fictional daughters of the regiment such as Dora Darley and Clara Brandon highlighted their characters' passionate devotion to their respective causes. And as in the cases of women spies and soldiers, we have no reason to doubt that Annie Etheridge, Kady Brownell, and the other army women whose stories have been told here were lacking in patriotic sentiment; nor have we reason to doubt that in many—though not all—cases an army woman's service to the military was predicated upon her connection to a man who had gone into the military before her, or who let her follow him (sometimes less than willingly).[91]

Nevertheless, we must also recall that, unlike fictional Dora Darley and Clara Brandon, a significant proportion of Civil War army women came to military life during the Civil War from the immigrant or native working class, and as such can be assumed to have chosen army life not only because it offered an opportunity to follow loved ones or to express political commitment to the cause of the North or the South, but also because it provided a superior alternative to the limited forms of waged work available to such women in civilian life. Along with the possibility of following loved ones, serving their country, and enjoying admittedly dangerous adventures, if military service did not always provide army women and daughters of the regiment with a living wage, it typically provided them with its rough equivalent in rations and shelter.

In short, stereotyping the Civil War woman spy, resistance activist, soldier, army woman, or daughter of the regiment as a selfless defender of her flag, or a reckless adventurer, or a hopelessly smitten lover, limits us to an understanding of only a portion of the larger picture of women's service to the Civil War armies. It simultaneously distracts us from more pedantic, less romantic, but nonetheless historically certifiable considerations bearing on women's wartime activities: namely, that some women who took up the work of serving the armies chose to do so in part because it offered an opportunity to make ends meet. Reporting the birth of a baby to a rebel soldier discovered while in prison to be a woman, the Sandusky, Ohio, *Commercial Register* in December 1864 commented, with intended derision, that "it was in all probability profit, not patriotism, or love . . . which led this accidental mother into the rebel ranks." Ironically, the stories of many women soldiers, spies and resistance activists, and army women during the Civil War lend credibility to such apparently facile conclusions.

# Afterword

---  ✳  ---

On December 28, 1862, Sarah Emma Edmonds dropped by for
a visit with her friend Jerome John Robbins. Wrote Robbins
in his diary that day: "Had quite a lengthy call from Frank
but all his social qualities were given to a new work entitled
'Pauline of the Potomac or Gen[']l McClellan[']s Spy'[;] he pro-
nounces it a low quality of fiction and from a very brief examination I agree with my *literary friend*."[1] Perhaps in her criticism of
*Pauline of the Potomac*, Edmonds merely meant to reprimand
Charles Wesley Alexander for his exceedingly melodramatic
prose. One suspects, however, that having already served for over
a year as a soldier in the Union army's 2nd Michigan Infantry,
Edmonds knew that on numerous counts Alexander's heroine,

Pauline D'Estraye, failed to embody some of the key experiences and motivations of the women like herself who actually served the Civil War armies in a range of capacities. As a real woman soldier and already a veteran of many of the battles in which General George McClellan's Army of the Potomac had been engaged in Confederate Virginia, Sarah Edmonds knew what it meant, and what it required, to be a woman in Civil War military service. Not least of all, she knew the range of impulses that might drive a woman into such work, impulses that Alexander's beautiful but uncomplicated heroine did not manifest.

Sarah Edmonds was merely one of the hundreds of brave women who disguised themselves as men and fought as soldiers in the Union and Confederate armies during the American Civil War. Moreover, when she enlisted in the 2nd Michigan Infantry in May 1861, Edmonds perpetuated a tradition of American women serving as undercover soldiers in the nation's armies, a tradition some might associate more readily with the Revolutionary War's Deborah Sampson. At the same time, Edmonds took her place among the host of women who, by April 1865, would perpetuate the long-standing tradition of women serving America's armies not only as soldiers but also—like Mary McCauley and Annie Etheridge—as army women and daughters of the regiment, and—like Lydia Darragh and Belle Boyd—as activists engaged in espionage and resistance.

Unfortunately, far too few of the women who lived and served the military during the first century of United States history have left us the quantity of documentary evidence about their army experiences with which Edmonds inadvertently graced posterity. It is also the case, however, that considerably more evidence is available regarding such women's activities and experiences than historians have previously acknowledged or appreciated. In *All the Daring of the Soldier*, I have attempted to bring more of these daring brave and high-spirited women's stories forward, in order to shed light on their sheer numbers and on the range of contributions they made to the military organizations and the political causes they served. Furthermore, I have tried to demonstrate clearly that at a time in American history when most women were generally perceived to be far too frail—either mentally or physically—to withstand the hurly-burly of public civilian life let alone the chaos and brutality of war, many more women than we have previously realized proved themselves—in the language of their culture—"manly" by virtue of their courage, intelligence, and physical endurance in the thick of war. Finally, I have attempted to offer some clarification about the possible motives women such as these may have had for undertaking military service, with all its deadly perils both on the battlefield and off. If I have done any of these things in a manner that Sarah Emma Edmonds would find more persuasive than Alexander's *Pauline of the Potomac*, I will be satisfied.

# Notes

———— ✳ ————

*Introduction*

1. The Aletta Jacobs story appears in Rudolf M. Dekker and Lotte C. van de Pol, *The Tradition of Female Transvestism in Early Modern Europe* (New York: St. Martin's Press, 1989), p. 99.

2. On the matter of Revolutionary War soldiers' failure to receive in a timely manner the wages that they expected for their military service, see, for example, Charles Royster, *A Revolutionary People at War: The Continental Army and the American Character, 1776–1783* (New York: W. W. Norton, 1979); and James Kirby Martin, ed., *Ordinary Courage: The Revolutionary War Adventures of Joseph Plumb Martin* (St. James, N.Y.: Brandywine Press, 1993).

3. *The Joan Baez Songbook* (New York: Ryerson Music Publishers, 1964), pp. 80–81. See also Dianne Dugaw, *Warrior Women and Popular Balladry, 1650–1850* (New York: Cambridge University Press, 1989).

4. Rita Mae Brown, *High Hearts* (New York: Bantam Books, 1988).

5. See my notes to chapter five for a full discussion of the various cal-
culations that have been made over time of the number of women who
served as soldiers during the Civil War.

*Chapter One*

1. Harnett T. Kane, *Spies for the Blue and Gray* (Garden City, N.Y.:
Hanover House, 1954), p. 12.

2. Sources for the material on Darragh include, among others, a sec-
tion of an article entitled "American Biography," which appears in the
*American Quarterly Review* 1 (March 1827): 1–37; George Barton, *The
World's Greatest Military Spies and Secret Service Agents* (Boston: Page,
1918); Henry Darrach, *Lydia Darragh: One of the Heroines of the Revolution*
(Philadelphia: City History Society of Philadelphia, 1916); Elisabeth
Anthony Dexter, *Colonial Women of Affairs: Women in Business and the
Professions in America Before 1776* (Boston: Houghton Mifflin, 1924;
reprint, Clifton, N.J.: Augustus M. Kelley, 1972); Sophie H. Drinker,
"Lydia Barrington Darragh," in Edward T. James and Janet W. James,
eds., *Notable American Women, 1607–1950: A Biographical Dictionary*
(Cambridge: Belknap Press, 1971), vol. 1, p. 434; and Elizabeth F. Ellet,
*Women of the American Revolution*, 2 vols. (Philadelphia: George W.
Jacobs, 1900).

3. There have been several attempts to challenge the credibility of the
Darragh story. However, as Henry Darrach notes, there are too many reliable, independent sources to judge it merely apocryphal (see Darrach,
*Lydia Darragh*, p. 400). For one thing, oral traditions about Darragh's
espionage activities on behalf of the Continental army developed early on
within her family: Lydia's daughter Ann, who was twenty-one years old
and living at home in the winter of 1777–78, herself later frequently
described the events in question to her great-niece, Margaret Porter
Darragh, who wrote them down, providing the foundation for the 1827
article in the *American Quarterly Review*.

4. *Pennsylvania Mercury and Universal Advertiser*, January 2, 1790.

5. Barton, *The World's Greatest Military Spies and Secret Service Agents*, p.
112. The Darraghs were Quakers, but during the war Lydia and her son
Charles allied themselves with the "Fighting Quakers," a breakaway

group that rejected the Society of Friends' pacifism for the duration of the conflict. Mother and son both met with rebuke from their Monthly Meeting, but in Lydia's case, at least, the breach was not permanent: when she died in 1789, she was buried in the Quaker burial ground in Philadelphia.

6. Sources for the material on Boyd include several full-length biographies as well as shorter sketches of her in works dealing with Civil War intelligence operations, and her own memoir (edited by Curtis Carroll Davis), entitled *Belle Boyd in Camp and Prison, Written by Herself* (New York: Thomas Yoseloff, 1968). See, among others, John Edwin Bakeless, *Spies of the Confederacy* (Philadelphia: J. B. Lippincott, 1970); Barton, *The World's Greatest Military Spies and Secret Service Agents*; William Gilmore Beymer, *On Hazardous Service: Scouts and Spies of the North and South* (New York: Harper Brothers, 1912); Joseph Hergesheimer, *Swords and Roses* (New York: Alfred A. Knopf, 1929); Kane, *Spies for the Blue and Gray*; Oscar A. Kinchen, *Women Who Spied for the Blue and Gray* (Philadelphia: Dorrance, 1972); Ruth Scarborough, *Belle Boyd: Siren of the South* (Macon, Ga.: Mercer University Press, 1983); Louis Sigaud, *Belle Boyd: Confederate Spy* (Richmond, Va.: Dietz Press, 1944); Leonora Wood, *Belle Boyd: Famous Spy of the Confederate States of America* (Keyser, W. Va.: Mountain Echo, 1940); and Richardson Wright, *Forgotten Ladies: Nine Portraits from the American Family Album* (Philadelphia: J. B. Lippincott, 1928). See also various articles by Curtis Carroll Davis cited in the Bibliography, and his lengthy introduction to Boyd's memoir.

Boyd herself claims to have been born in 1844 (Davis, *Belle Boyd in Camp and Prison*, p. 117), but others have convincingly argued that the correct birth year is 1843.

7. *New York Herald*, August 3, 1862. An 1864 article in *Frank Leslie's Illustrated Newspaper* called her an "eccentric and over-loyal female" (*Frank Leslie's Illustrated Newspaper*, June 18, 1864).

8. Allan Pinkerton, *The Spy of the Rebellion: Being a True History of the Spy System of the United States Army During the Late Rebellion* (New York: G. W. Carleton, 1883), p. 251.

The *Official Records of the Union and Confederate Armies* contain a number of documents outlining the general policies that the Union instituted with regard to spies. We can assume that the Confederacy's policies were similar. General Orders No. 100 ("Instructions for the Government of

Armies of the United States in the Field"), issued on April 24, 1863, by United States Secretary of War Edwin Stanton, delineated the sorts of activities that characterized an individual as a "war-rebel," "spy," "traitor," "war-traitor," "messenger," or enemy "agent," and warned that in each case, the appropriate punishment might well be imprisonment or death. "The law of war," the order concluded, "like the criminal law regarding other offenses, makes no difference on account of the differences of the sexes, concerning the spy, the war-traitor, or the war-rebels" (*The War of the Rebellion: The Official Records of the Union and Confederate Armies* [Washington, D.C.: Government Printing Office, 1881–1902], ser. 3, vol. 2, pp. 157–59 [hereafter cited as *Official Records*]. As Oscar Kinchen and others have pointed out, however, although both male and female spies during the Civil War were "regarded as outlaws and due to be hanged if apprehended," there is in fact "no record of any woman being put to death as a spy during the war between the blue and the gray" (Kinchen, *Spies for the Blue and Gray*, p. 1).

9. Boyd herself claimed to have killed the soldier (see Davis, *Belle Boyd in Camp and Prison*, p. 134), but the best evidence suggests that she probably only wounded him (see Davis, "'The Pet of the Confederacy' Still? Fresh Findings About Belle Boyd," *Maryland Historical Magazine* 78 [Spring 1983], p. 36).

10. Davis, *Belle Boyd in Camp and Prison*, p. 135.

11. Henry Kyd Douglas, *I Rode with Stonewall* (Chapel Hill: University of North Carolina Press, 1940), pp. 50–52. See also Richard Taylor, *Destruction and Reconstruction: Personal Experiences of the Late War* (New York: Longman's, Green, 1955), pp. 53–54.

12. Davis, *Belle Boyd in Camp and Prison*, p. 167. Jackson's note to Boyd has not survived. In 1863 D. A. Mahony noted that Jackson's victory in the Shenandoah was widely attributed to Boyd. See D. A. Mahony, *The Prisoner of State* (New York: G. W. Carleton, 1863), p. 268. See also James M. McPherson, *Ordeal by Fire: The Civil War and Reconstruction* (New York: Alfred A. Knopf, 1982), p. 188.

13. Davis, "'The Pet of the Confederacy' Still?," pp. 40, 41.

14. *Official Records*, ser. 2, vol. 4, pp. 309–10.

15 William Doster, *Lincoln and Episodes of the Civil War* (New York: G. P. Putnam & Sons, 1915), p. 76.

16. William F. Broaddus Diary, Library of Virginia, Richmond, Va.

17. Mahony, *The Prisoner of State*, pp. 268–79; Doster, *Lincoln and Episodes of the Civil War*, p. 102.

18. *Official Records*, ser. 2, vol. 4, p. 461. See also ser. 2, vol. 4, p. 349.

19. Davis, "'The Pet of the Confederacy' Still?," p. 43.

20. Curtis Carroll Davis, "The Civil War's Most Over-Rated Spy," *West Virginia History* 27 (October 1965): p. 5. Harding's dismissal followed his arrest and trial in connection with the escape of the Confederate captain of the *Greyhound*.

21. *New York Times*, June 13, 1900.

22. An undated *New York Times* article inaccurately described Boyd as a "much-married woman" who had "six husbands in all" (undated clipping, "Belle Boyd, the Spy" [originally published in the *New York Tribune*], in RG 94, Records of the Adjutant General's Office, Administrative Precedent File ["Frech File"] #3H36, National Archives, Washington, D.C.).

23. *New York Times*, November 12, 1874. As far as I know, neither the *Times* nor the *Atlanta News* ever acknowledged the error.

24. *New York Times*, June 13, 1900; *New York Times*, June 16, 1929.

25. Sources for the material on Greenhow include her own memoir, *My Imprisonment, and the First Year of Abolition Rule at Washington* (London: Richard Bentley, 1863); and Bakeless, *Spies of the Confederacy*; Beymer, *On Hazardous Service*; Nash K. Burger, *Confederate Spy: Rose O'Neale Greenhow* (New York: Franklin Watts, 1967); Edwin C. Fishel, *The Secret War for the Union: The Untold Story of Military Intelligence in the Civil War* (Boston: Houghton Mifflin, 1996); Kane, *Spies for the Blue and Gray*; Kinchen, *Women Who Spied for the Blue and Gray*; Margaret Leech, *Reveille in Washington, 1860–1865* (New York: Harper & Brothers, 1941); Mary Elizabeth Massey, *Bonnet Brigades* (New York: Alfred A. Knopf, 1966); Pinkerton, *The Spy of the Rebellion*; and Ishbel Ross, *Rebel Rose: Life of Rose O'Neal Greenhow, Confederate Spy* (New York: Harper & Brothers, 1954).

26. Doster, *Lincoln and Episodes of the Civil War*, pp. 79–80.

27. Pinkerton, *The Spy of the Rebellion*, p. 252.

28. See *Official Records*, ser. 2, vol. 2, pp. 564–65.

29. Ibid., ser. 2, vol. 51, pt. 2, p. 688; Greenhow, *My Imprisonment*, p. 18.

30. Greenhow, *My Imprisonment*, pp. 23–24;

31. Letter dated "21st," in RG 107, Seized Correspondence of Mrs. Rose Greenhow, Records of the Office of the Secretary of War, Records Concerning the Conduct and Loyalty of Certain Union Army Officers,

Civilian Employees of the War Department and U.S. Citizens During the Civil War, National Archives, Washington, D.C.

32. Greenhow, *My Imprisonment*, pp. 86–87.

33. Kane, *Spies for the Blue and Gray*, p. 54. Regarding other inmates at Fort Greenhow, see reports in the *New York Times* dated September 25 and November 2, 1861. Regarding Betty Hassler's arrest and imprisonment, see *Official Records*, ser. 2, vol. 2, p. 295. See also *Official Records*, ser. 2, vol. 2, p. 237.

34. A brief summary of Greenhow's case up until the middle of February 1862 appears in the *Official Records*, ser. 2, vol. 2, p. 561.

Greenhow's letter to Seward, which was published in the local papers, was later referred to by Confederate enthusiast Mary Chesnut in her diary. See C. Vann Woodward and Elisabeth Muhlenfeld, *The Private Mary Chesnut: The Unpublished Civil War Diaries* (New York: Oxford University Press, 1984), p. 212.

In contrast with Greenhow's harsh characterization of prison conditions, John C. Babcock, a Union officer stationed as a guard at Fort Greenhow, wrote to his aunt that "the fair captives are allowed the freedom of the house and premises, and are permitted to receive from their friends such necessaries, and luxuries, as they may wish, beyond what the government furnish[es] them" (John C. Babcock to Mrs. Horace Clark, December 26, 1861, in the John C. Babcock Papers, Library of Congress, Washington, D.C.).

35. *Official Records*, ser. 2, vol. 2, pp. 575–76.

36. Ibid., pp. 279, 577; *New York Times*, June 2, 1862.

37. Greenhow, *My Imprisonment*, p. 322.

38. See *Official Records*, ser. 2, vol. 5, pp. 699–700.

39. Sources for material on Ford include Lafayette Charles Baker, *History of the United States Secret Service* (Philadelphia: L. C. Baker, 1867); Garnett Laidlaw Eskew, *Willard's of Washington: The Epic of a Capital Caravansary* (New York: Coward-McCann, 1954); Kane, *Spies for the Blue and Gray*; and Kinchen, *Women Who Spied for the Blue and Gray*. Ford did not compose a memoir, but she did leave behind assorted personal papers. See the Antonia Ford Willard Papers, Willard Family Papers, Library of Congress, Washington, D.C.

40. Eskew, *Willard's of Washington*, p. 73. See also unidentified, untitled typescript in the Antonia Ford Willard Papers which refers to

Stuart's commission; and John Esten Cooke, article on Antonia Ford in the *Southern Illustrated News* (August 15, 1863), in the Antonia Ford Willard Papers.

Many Northerners who later learned of the commission treated it as worthy of nothing more than a good sneer: an April 1863 article in *Harper's Weekly* magazine cheerfully exaggerated the status of "General Stuart's New Aid [sic]" when it reported that "the rebel cavalry leader . . . has appointed to a position on his staff, with the rank of Major, a young lady residing at Fairfax Court House, who has been of great service" (*Harper's Weekly*, April 4, 1863, p. 211).

41. Eskew, *Willard's of Washington*, p. 76.

42. According to both Jeffry Wert and Howard Coffin, Mosby's initial target in this raid was not Stoughton but rather the commander of a federal cavalry brigade named Percy Wyndham who had once insulted Mosby publicly. When they went to find Wyndham on the night of March 8, however, Mosby's troops discovered that Wyndham was in Washington. Upon receiving this news, they turned their attention to Stoughton instead. (See Jeffry Wert, *Mosby's Rangers* [New York: Simon & Schuster, 1990], pp. 18–19; Howard Coffin, *Nine Months to Gettysburg: Stannard's Vermonters and the Repulse of Pickett's Charge* [Woodstock, Vt.: Countryman Press, 1997], 117–19.) I thank William T. Racine of Bath, Maine, for bringing this to my attention.

43. Baker, *History of the United States Secret Service*, pp. 107, 171–73. See also a document with the heading "Answering an inquiry" in the Antonia Ford Willard Papers.

44. *New York Times*, March 18, 1863.

45. Antonia Ford to Joseph Willard, January 31, 1864, in the Antonia Ford Willard Papers. The letter is actually dated "1863," but the internal evidence clearly indicates that the correct year is 1864.

46. See *Official Records*, ser. 1, vol. 25, pt. 2, p. 858. See also J. D. Ferguson to John Mosby, March 24, 1863, in the Antonia Ford Willard Papers. There is no record of Mosby's response.

47. Unidentified, undated letter that begins, "I would gladly write a long letter," in the Antonia Ford Willard Papers. In connection with Willard's resignation from the army, see Special Military Orders, War Department, February 12, 1864, in the Antonia Ford Willard Papers. These orders recognized Willard's resignation as of March 1.

48. David D. Ryan, *A Yankee Spy in Richmond: The Civil War Diary of "Crazy Bet" Van Lew* (Mechanicsburg, Pa.: Stackpole Books, 1996), p. 115.

49. Sources for material on Van Lew include James H. Bailey, "Crazy Bet, Union Spy," *Virginia Cavalcade* (Spring 1952): pp. 14–17; Beymer, *On Hazardous Service*; Kane, *Spies for the Blue and Gray*; Ryan, *A Yankee Spy in Richmond*; and Richard P. Weinert, "Federal Spies in Richmond," *Civil War Times Illustrated* 4 (February 1965): pp. 28–34.

Van Lew's diary and papers, most of which appear in Ryan's *A Yankee Spy in Richmond*, are housed at the New York Public Library. Writes Ryan:

Elizabeth Van Lew's "Occasional Journal" originally consisted of over 700 handwritten pages. . . . It was buried for a time, however, and many pages are lost or damaged. In some places as many as 50 pages are missing. What survives of the journal is about 400 pages. On her deathbed in 1900, reported John Albee, Elizabeth asked for the journal to be brought to her. When she saw it, she was disappointed. "Oh, that is not half," she exclaimed. (Ryan, *A Yankee Spy in Richmond*, p. 22)

50. Benjamin Butler to John A. Rawlins, April 19, 1864, quoted in John Y. Simon, ed., *The Papers of Ulysses S. Grant*, vol. 10, January 1–May 31, 1864 (Carbondale, Ill.: Southern Illinois University Press, 1967), p. 560. See also *Official Records*, ser. 1, vol. 33, pp. 519–21. Ryan, who reprints much of Van Lew's correspondence with various federal officials, claims that Van Lew had been communicating with the Union's military leadership since early 1862 (see Ryan, *A Yankee Spy in Richmond*, pp. 12, 83–85).

51. Ryan, *A Yankee Spy in Richmond*, p. 37.

52. Ibid., pp. 109–10.

53. Ibid., pp. 11–12. Bowser was inducted into the U.S. Army's Intelligence Hall of Fame, located at Fort Huachuca, Arizona, in June 1995 (ibid., p. 136).

54. Ibid., p. 10.

55. *New York Times*, April 4, 1915.

56. See St. Clair A. Mulholland, *The Story of the 116th Regiment, Pennsylvania Infantry* (Philadelphia: F. McManus, Jr., 1899), p. 328. Almost fifty of the officers were later recaptured.

57. Why Van Lew would involve herself in such a plan is a curious

question. There is some suggestion that she felt personally responsible for Dahlgren's death. Of the many dispatches she sent through the Confederate lines, the only one that still exists, dated January 30, 1864, and addressed to Benjamin Butler, urged Butler to attack the town with "not less than 30,000 cavalry supported by 10,000 to 15,000 infantry" (*Official Records*, ser. 1, vol. 33, p. 520). Some analysts believe that this order may have been instrumental in Dahlgren's decision to make a raid, and therefore instrumental in his death. Van Lew's journal itself contains an extended discussion of the Dahlgren affair (see Ryan, *A Yankee Spy in Richmond*, pp. 67–82). See also Duane Schultz, *The Dahlgren Affair: Terror and Conspiracy in the Civil War* (New York: W. W. Norton, 1998).

58. On Van Lew's later years and her death, see, among other things, the articles about her that appeared in the *New York Times* on September 26 and 30, 1900.

59. Sources for material on Cushman include Linus P. Brockett, *The Camp, the Battlefield, and the Hospital; or, Light and Shadows of the Great Rebellion* (Philadelphia: National Publishing, 1866); Kane, *Spies for the Blue and Gray*; Frank Moore, *Women of the War: Their Heroism and Self-Sacrifice* (Hartford, Conn.: S. S. Scranton, 1866); Irwin Richman, "Pauline Cushman: She Was a Heroine but Not a Lady," *Civil War Times Illustrated* 7 (February 1969): pp. 38–44; F. L. Sarmiento, *Life of Pauline Cushman: The Celebrated Union Spy and Scout* (Philadelphia: John E. Potter, 1865); *The Sibyl* 8 (January 1864): p. 1207; and Agatha Young, *The Women and the Crisis: Women of the North in the Civil War* (New York: McDowell, Obolensky, 1959).

60. *The Sibyl* 8 (January 1864): p. 1207; Sarmiento, *Life of Pauline Cushman*, pp. 20, 36.

61. *New York Times*, May 28, 1864.

62. One government document relating to Cushman's service to the Union as a spy connects her with both Truesdail and Morgan. In May 1863 Truesdail wrote to Morgan apparently trying to convince him that Cushman was in fact a Confederate agent. "Sir," he wrote, "I have not arrested Miss Cushman, and would not arrest a lady without reasonable cause—and in such case, I should send the papers to you, for your order" (William Truesdail to John Morgan, May 23, 1863, in RG 110, Provost Marshal General's Bureau, List of Scouts, Guides, Spies and Detectives, National Archives, Washington, D.C.).

63. *Frank Leslie's Illustrated Newspaper*, June 25, 1864. See also Kane, *Spies for the Blue and Gray*, p. 191; Moore, *Women of the War*, p. 175; Sarmiento, *Life of Pauline Cushman*, p. 346.

64. Richman, "Pauline Cushman," p. 43.

65. *New York Herald*, August 3, 1862; *Frank Leslie's Illustrated Newspaper*, June 25, 1864; *New York Times*, June 13, 1900.

Twentieth-century students of the Boyd story have been less consistent on the point of the effectiveness of her espionage activity. Some have given her mediocre marks at best (see, for example, Bakeless, *Spies of the Confederacy*; Davis, "The Civil War's Most Over-Rated Spy"; and Fishel, *The Secret War for the Union*). Others have been more generous, in some cases arguing that her effectiveness has in fact been consistently underrated (see, for example, Hergesheimer, *Swords and Roses*; Scarborough, *Belle Boyd*; Sigaud, *Belle Boyd*; and Wood, *Belle Boyd*). Debates over the authenticity of specific details in Boyd's memoir have also persisted (see, for example, Wright, *Forgotten Ladies*). What is most important here is that during the war her contemporaries on both sides of the struggle believed her various actions to be of great value to the Confederate military, and they praised her or punished her accordingly.

66. *Official Records*, ser. 2, vol. 2, p. 271.

Debates about her effectiveness as a spy have also dogged Rose Greenhow into the twentieth century (see, in particular, Fishel, *The Secret War for the Union*). As with Boyd, however, Greenhow's effectiveness was not a matter of any significant debate among her contemporaries. Fishel's interesting but ultimately unpersuasive contention is that federal officials such as the U.S. Secret Service's Allan Pinkerton themselves exaggerated the extent and the importance of Greenhow's activities because they had an investment in conveying to the public how much the federal government had managed to bring the situation in Washington under control now that the secret service was in place (ibid., pp. 64–66).

67. Ryan, *A Yankee Spy in Richmond*, pp. 113, 119–20. Among the few who have more recently considered the question of Van Lew's importance to the Union cause, there is evidence of some difference of opinion (see, for example, Weinert, "Federal Spies in Richmond"). But even the ever dubious Fishel insists that she was coleader of the "most productive

espionage operation of the Civil War, on either side, that has ever been documented . . ." (Fishel, *The Secret War for the Union*, p. 551).

68. *New York Times*, December 3, 1893.

## Chapter Two

1. *The War of the Rebellion: The Official Records of the Union and Confederate Armies* (Washington, D.C.: Government Printing Office, 1881–1902), ser. 1, vol. 35, pt. 2, p. 315 (hereafter cited as *Official Records*).

2. Sources for material on the Moon sisters include Anne Funderberg, "Women of the Confederacy," *Southern Partisan* 14 (second quarter 1994): pp. 18–22; Harnett T. Kane, *Spies for the Blue and Gray* (Garden City, N.Y.: Hanover House, 1954); and Oscar A. Kinchen, *Women Who Spied for the Blue and Gray* (Philadelphia: Dorrance, 1972).

3. Sources for material on the Sanchez sisters include Funderberg, "Women of the Confederacy"; and J. L. Underwood, *The Women of the Confederacy* (New York: Neale Publishing, 1906).

4. Sources for material on Floyd include Kinchen, *Women Who Spied for the Blue and Gray*; *Official Records*, ser. 2, vol. 4; and the *New York Times*, December 12, 1905.

5. Kinchen, *Women Who Spied for the Blue and Gray*, p. 27; *New York Times*, December 12, 1905.

6. Sources for material on Polk include Mary Elizabeth Massey, *Bonnet Brigades* (New York: Alfred A. Knopf, 1966); and Francis Butler Simkins and James Welch Patton, *The Women of the Confederacy* (New York: Garrett & Massie, 1936; reprinted, St. Clair Shores, Mich.: Scholarly Press, 1976).

7. See Simkins and Patton, *The Women of the Confederacy*, p. 76.

8. Sources for material on Pollock include Matthew Page Andrews, *The Women of the South in War Times* (Baltimore: Norman, Remington, 1920); Kinchen, *Women Who Spied for the Blue and Gray*; and Underwood, *The Women of the Confederacy*.

9. Sources on Williams and Wright include Kinchen, *Women Who Spied for the Blue and Gray*; and Massey, *Bonnet Brigades*.

10. Sources for material on Tubman include Sarah Bradford, *Harriet Tubman: The Moses of Her People* (New York: Carol Publishing, 1991); Earl Conrad, *Harriet Tubman* (Washington, D.C.: Associated Publishers,

1943); Jane Ellen Schultz, "Women at the Front: Gender and Genre in Literature of the American Civil War" (Ph.D. diss., University of Michigan, Ann Arbor, 1988); and the *New York Times*, March 11, 1913, and March 14, 1913.

11. On Beattie, see Massey, *Bonnet Brigades*, p. 105. On Bruckner, see Massey, *Bonnet Brigades*, pp. 105–6. On Faulkner, see Massey, *Bonnet Brigades*; and *Frank Leslie's Illustrated Newspaper*, August 9, 1862. On Goldsborough, see Curtis Carroll Davis, "Effie Goldsborough: Confederate Courier," *Civil War Times Illustrated* 7 (April 1968): pp. 29–30; and Eileen F. Conklin, *Women at Gettysburg, 1863* (Gettysburg, Pa.: Thomas Publications, 1993), pp. 347–67. On Harland, see Simkins and Patton, *The Women of the Confederacy*, p. 78. On Hutchings, see Massey, *Bonnet Brigades*; p. 100; and *New York Herald*, November 26, November 30, 1864, and January 8, 1865. On Jamieson, see Massey, *Bonnet Brigades*, p. 98; and *Frank Leslie's Illustrated Newspaper*, August 9, 1862. On Kirby, see Andrews, *Women of the South in War Times*, pp. 116–19. On Larue, see Schultz, "Women at the Front," pp. 297–98; and *New York Herald*, July 14, 1862. On Tynes, see Funderberg, "Women of the Confederacy," p. 18.

See also Massey, *Bonnet Brigades*, p. 104 (Anna Campbell, Ella Herbert); Massey, *Bonnet Brigades*, p. 105, and *Official Records*, ser. 1, vol. 30, pt. 3 (Mrs. Hunter and her daughter); Kinchen, *Spies for the Blue and Gray*, pp. 139–45, *Official Records*, ser. 2, vol. 5, and ser. 2, vol. 6, and RG 110, Provost Marshal General's Bureau, List of Scouts, Guides, Spies and Detectives, box 3, National Archives, Washington, D.C. (Clara Judd); Schultz, "Women at the Front," p. 302 (Abby Kerr); Underwood, *The Women of the Confederacy*, pp. 192–94 (Nora McCarthy); Simkins and Patton, *The Women of the Confederacy*, p. 78 (Mrs. A. M. Meekins); John Edwin Bakeless, *Spies of the Confederacy* (Philadelphia: J. B. Lippincott, 1970), pp. 197–200 (Mary Overall), 201–3 (Ann and Kate Patterson), and 347 (Bessie Perrine, Carrie Gray); Massey, *Bonnet Brigades*, p. 99, Simkins and Patton, *The Women of the Confederacy*, p. 78, and *Official Records*, ser. 1, vol. 18, p. 801 (Emeline Piggott); Massey, *Bonnet Brigades*, p. 95, and *Official Records*, ser. 2, vol. 2 (Ellie Poole); Simkins and Patton, *The Women of the Confederacy*, p. 76 (Miss Porterfield); Schultz, "Women at the Front," p. 300 (Mary Walker Roberts); Massey, *Bonnet Brigades*, p. 103, and Underwood, *The Women of the Confederacy*, pp. 213–15 (Emma Samsom); Massey, *Bonnet Brigades*, p. 105 (S. Smith); Bakeless, *Spies of the Confederacy*, p. 347 (Molly Tatum).

12. Loretta and William Galbraith, eds., *A Lost Heroine of the Confederacy: The Diaries and Letters of Belle Edmondson* (Jackson: University Press of Mississippi, 1990). This is the main published source for information on Edmondson, whose papers are a part of the Southern Historical Collections at the University of North Carolina, Chapel Hill.

13. Kinchen, *Women Who Spied for the Blue and Gray*, pp. 2–3.

14. C. Vann Woodward and Elisabeth Muhlenfeld, *The Private Mary Chesnut: The Unpublished Civil War Diaries* (New York: Oxford University Press, 1984), p. 145. See also Massey, *Bonnet Brigades*, pp. 105–6; Bell Irvin Wiley, *Confederate Women* (Westport, Conn.: Greenwood Press, 1975), p. 143; Margaret Leech, *Reveille in Washington, 1860–1865* (New York: Harper & Brothers, 1941), p. 271.

15. Galbraith and Galbraith, *A Lost Heroine of the Confederacy*, p. 97.

16. Ibid., pp. 100, 105.

17. Sources for material on Phillips include Nash K. Burger, *Confederate Spy: Rose O'Neale Greenhow* (New York: Franklin Watts, 1967); T. C. De Leon, *Belles, Beaus, and Brains of the 60's* (New York: G. W. Dillingham, 1907); Kinchen, *Women Who Spied for the Blue and Gray*; and Daniel Morgan, "Eugenia Levy Phillips: The Civil War Experiences of a Southern Jewish Woman," in Samuel Proctor and Louis Schmeir, eds., *Jews of the South: Selected Essays from the Southern Jewish Historical Society* (Macon, Ga.: Mercer University Press, 1984). See also Phillips's unpublished memoir of her wartime experiences ("Mrs. Phillips: A Southern Woman's Story of Her Imprisonments"), which she based on a journal she claimed to have kept while in prison ("Journal of Eugenia Yates Levy Phillips"), both of which are in the Phillips Family Papers, Library of Congress, Washington, D.C.

18. "Mrs. Phillips: A Southern Woman's Story of Her Imprisonments," p. 2.

19. See *New York Times*, August 26, 1861; and *New York Herald*, August 26, 1861. For Phillips's denial of this particular charge, see "Mrs. Phillips: A Southern Woman's Story of her Imprisonments," p. 2.

20. "Mrs. Phillips: A Southern Woman's Story of Her Imprisonments," p. 3. A *New York Times* article published shortly after the Phillips women's release suggested that conditions at Fort Greenhow, due not least of all to the dignity and respectability of the First Inmate, were in fact plush, amounting to "two large apartments, cleanly and well furnished," with

beds "furnished with sheets, blankets and pillows by Mrs. Greenhow herself, who, whatever may be her faults in a political point of view, is a lady by birth and education, and of refinement and taste, as every visitor at her house can abundantly testify." The article goes on to say that the Phillips women were treated to all sorts of culinary delicacies during their confinement at Fort Greenhow, and that they had with them three servants, befitting their "station in life" (*New York Times*, September 28, 1861).

A document in the *Official Records* wrongly indicates that the Phillips women were imprisoned at the Old Capitol (see *Official Records*, ser. 2, vol. 2, p. 237).

21. "Journal of Eugenia Levy Phillips," pp. 9, 10. See also ibid., pp. 22, 24.

22. See *Official Records*, ser. 2, vol. 3, pp. 719–20, for a document pertaining to the Phillipses' transfer to the South.

The Phillips women knew the identity and the reputation of their famous "hostess," Rose Greenhow. On September 9 Eugenia Phillips described in her journal a dream that put Greenhow in a most sympathetic light. Phillips also mentioned a farewell embrace from Greenhow at the time the Phillips women were released (see "Journal of Eugenia Yates Levy Phillips," pp. 23, 36).

23. See *Official Records*, ser. 1, vol. 15, pp. 510–11. Butler had already made a name for himself in New Orleans, with his General Orders No. 28, as a man more than willing to punish Confederate women for their lack of discretion in expressing anti-Union sentiments. See, among other things, *Private and Official Correspondence of General Benjamin F. Butler During the Period of the Civil War*, vol. 1, April 1860–June 1862 (Norwood, Mass.: privately issued, 1917), pp. 490, 493, 581–83. See also Mary Ryan's interesting discussion of Butler's Orders No. 28 in Mary Ryan, *Women in Public: Between Banners and Ballots, 1825–1880* (Baltimore: Johns Hopkins University Press, 1990), pp. 130–71.

Two weeks after Butler issued Special Orders No. 150, the *New York Times* published an article describing Lieutenant De Kay's funeral and the disruptive behavior of a number of Southern women on that occasion. The article also commented on Phillips's "flippant and contemptuous manner" during Butler's interrogation of her in the wake of the event. "She was so cool," the article's author wrote, "I found it quite refreshing to sit in her shade" (see *New York Times*, July 14, 1862).

24. "Mrs. Phillips: A Southern Woman's Story of Her Imprisonments," pp. 8, 9. Butler's Orders No. 150 assigned her to "one of the houses for hospital purposes" and granted her a soldier's ration daily (see *Official Records*, ser. 1, vol. 15, p. 511).

25. On the Fidel Keller matter, see, among other things, *Official Records*, ser. 2, vol. 4, pp. 880–81.

26. See ibid., p. 516.

27. Sources for information on Mary Caroline Allan include J. B. Jones, *A Rebel Clerk's Diary* (New York: Sagamore Press, 1958); Massey, *Bonnet Brigades*; and the *Richmond Daily Examiner* from July 20 and 23, 1863, and February 4, 11, 12, 20, and 22, October 28, and December 19, 1864.

I have found no hard evidence that Allan and Van Lew ever met, although one imagines that as active Unionists and members of the Richmond elite, they might well have done so.

28. *Richmond Daily Examiner*, July 20, 1863.

29. Ibid., July 20 and 23, 1863.

30. On Gwin, see *New York Herald*, August 26, 1861, and *New York Times*, August 26, 1861. On Hosler, see *Frank Leslie's Illustrated Newspaper*, June 13, 1863. On Ward, see *Frank Leslie's Illustrated Newspaper*, April 4, 1863. On Jones, see *Frank Leslie's Illustrated Newspaper*, June 4, 1864. On Reynolds, Shuller, and Oliver, see *Vicksburg Daily Herald*, August 20, 1864. See also *Richmond Daily Examiner*, October 31, 1864 (Mary Pitt), and *New York Herald*, July 1, 1862 (Susan Archer Tulley).

31. Needless to say, the *Official Records* also contain information pertaining to Boyd, Greenhow, Phillips, and Van Lew, as well as some of the other women already mentioned in this chapter. See the general index to the series for relevant citations.

Writing in 1972, Oscar Kinchen noted that "the women spies of Civil War times, in common with those of the opposite sex, were expected to secure information about plans and movements of the enemy, ascertain their number and resources, intercept dispatches, convey false information to the enemy and, if need be, tell 'patriotic lies' in defense of the cause they served. Smuggling goods out of enemy territory was looked upon as spying, so was the transmission of secret messages for or against the enemy" (Kinchen, *Women Who Spied for the Blue and Gray*, p. 1).

32. On Corner, see *Official Records*, ser. 1, vol. 12, pt. 3, p. 98. On

Banks, see ser. 1, vol. 32, pt. 2, p. 688. On McCune, see ser. 1, vol. 41, pt. 3, p. 318. On Hodges, see ser. 1, vol. 44, p. 764.

For additional references in the *Official Records* to women of whom we know little more than that they provided welcome reports on military affairs to officials in their respective nations' armies, see: ser. 1, vol. 20, pt. 2, p. 212 (Mrs. B. F. Smith); ser. 1, vol. 23, pt. 2, p. 64 (Mrs. Alcon); ser. 1, vol. 23, pt. 2, p. 723 (Mrs. Ware); ser. 1, vol. 25, pt. 2, p. 79 (Mrs. Catherine Graham); ser. 1, vol. 28, pt. 2, p. 260 (Mrs. Savage); ser. 1, vol. 30, pt. 4, p. 8 (Mrs. James Rhett); ser. 1, vol. 30, pt. 4, p. 13 (Mrs. Filby); ser. 1, vol. 30, pt. 4, p. 459 (Mrs. Casey and Mrs. Gilbreath); ser. 1, vol. 30, pt. 4, pp. 464, 484 (Mrs. Puckett); ser. 1, vol. 30, pt. 4, p. 465 (Mrs. Vinson); ser. 1, vol. 31, pt. 1, pp. 795–96 (Mrs. Whiteburg); ser. 1, vol. 31, pt. 3, pp. 125–26 (Mrs. Varnell); ser. 1, vol. 32, pt. 3, p. 4 (Mrs. Dr. Gordon); ser. 1, vol. 32, pt. 3, p. 149 (Joanna Eastef and Cynthia Brockville); ser. 1, vol. 33, p. 1287 (Mrs. McMullen); ser. 1, vol. 34, pt. 2, p. 1077 (Mrs. Sappington); ser. 1, vol. 34, pt. 4, p. 28 (Mrs. Porter); ser. 1, vol. 35, pt. 1, p. 419 (Mrs. Murry); ser. 1, vol. 37, pt. 1, p. 360 (Mrs. Davis and her daughter); ser. 1, vol. 37, pt. 2, pp. 415–16 (Mrs. Barnes); ser. 1, vol. 38, pt. 5, p. 313 (Mrs. Smith); ser. 1, vol. 38, pt. 5, p. 847 (Mrs. Boddeker); ser. 1, vol. 39, pt. 3, p. 138 (Mrs. House); ser. 1, vol. 39, pt. 3, p. 342 (Mrs. Gill and "a Union woman"); ser. 1, vol. 41, pt. 1, pp. 233, 623 (Mrs. Campbell); ser. 1, vol. 41, pt. 1, p. 283 (Mrs. Jones); ser. 1, vol. 41, pt. 1, p. 893 (Mrs. Phelps); ser. 1, vol. 41, pt. 2, p. 784 (Mrs. Grace); ser. 1, vol. 41, pt. 3, pp. 181–82 (Mrs. Lyle); ser. 1, vol. 41, pt. 3, p. 655 (Mrs. Thompson); ser. 1, vol. 43, pt. 2, p. 718 ("a Union lady"); ser. 1, vol. 45, pt. 2, pp. 290–91 (Mrs. Brown); ser. 1, vol. 46, pt. 2, p. 100 (Mrs. Kittle); ser. 1, vol. 46, pt. 2, pp. 261, 384 (Mrs. White); ser. 1, vol. 47, pt. 2, p. 1087 (Mrs. Mew); ser. 1, vol. 48, pt. 1, p. 1268 (Mrs. Reiley); ser. 1, vol. 48, pt. 2, p. 782 (Mrs. Prince); ser. 1, vol. 49, pt. 2, p. 278 (Mrs. Howell); ser. 1, vol. 51, pt. 1, p. 665 (Miss Anna Taylor); ser. 1, vol. 51, pt. 2, p. 329 ("a lady [perfectly reliable]").

33. On "a negro girl," see ibid., ser. 1, vol. 30, pt. 3, p. 625.

34. On Willard, see ibid., ser. 1, vol. 18, p. 669; on Nottingham, see ser. 1, vol. 33, p. 434; on Wilson, see ser. 1, vol. 25, pt. 2, p. 81. See also ser. 1, vol. 41, pt. 3, pp. 932–33 (Mrs. Bruce).

35. On Baldwin, see ibid., ser. 2, vol. 2, p. 805. See also ser. 2, vol. 4, pp. 508–9 (Miss Walters); ser. 2, vol. 5, p. 464 (Mrs. Emma Moore); ser. 1, vol. 31, pt. 1, p. 192 (Mrs. Ritchie); ser. 1, vol. 32, pt. 2, p. 227 (Miss Kline).

See also ibid., ser. 1, vol. 41, pt. 1, pp. 799–800 (Mrs. Ratliff); ser. 1, vol. 40, pt. 2, pp. 298, 637 (Mrs. Grover); ser. 2, vol. 2, pp. 277, 394 (Mrs. Norris); and ser. 2, vol. 4, p. 66 (Miss Wells).

36. On Kennedy, see ibid., ser. 2, vol. 2, p. 317. On Wood, see ser. 2, vol. 2, p. 344. On Wilcoxen, see ser. 1, vol. 26, pt. 1, p. 40. On Locke and Barnet, see ser. 1, vol. 32, pt. 1, p. 103. On Bowles, see ser. 1, vol. 36, pt. 3, pp. 668, 684. For evidence of the arrests of other women on similar charges, see ibid., ser. 2, vol. 2, p. 328 (Mrs. Rachel Mayer); ser. 2, vol. 2, p. 1032 (Mrs. John Low); ser. 2, vol. 7, p. 236 (Miss Woods and Miss Cassell); ser. 1, vol. 30, pt. 2, p. 703 ("two young ladies, named Badey").

37. On the Gibson women, see ibid, ser. 1, vol. 34, pt. 1, p. 993. On Palmer, see ser. 1, vol. 34, pt. 4, p. 249.

38. On Smith, see ibid., ser. 2, vol. 2, pp. 905, 907. On Mrs. Frost et al., see ser. 2, vol. 5, p. 320. See also ser. 1, vol. 22, pt. 2, pp. 271–72; and ser. 2, vol. 5, p. 685 (Mollie Hyde).

39. Ibid., ser. 1, vol. 49, pt. 1, pp. 856, 862. See also Bakeless, *Spies of the Confederacy*, p. 200.

For discussion of another family, in Louisville, Kentucky, whose womenfolk perpetrated a combination of offenses against the Union in the spring of 1864, see ibid., ser. 2, vol. 7, p. 265ff.

40. *Official Records*, ser. 2, vol. 5, p. 567 (Dora and Julia Dunbar, Elizabeth Phillips, Eliza Hughes, Amanda and Belle Goshorn, Hanna and Joanna Smith); ser. 1, vol. 34, pt. 4, p. 434 (Mrs. S. C. Jones); ser. 1, vol. 43, pt. 2, p. 682 (Mrs. Thomas Carter, Mrs. Charles Clark, Mrs. Whiting, Mrs. Smith, the Misses Bell, Mrs. Mitchell, and Mrs. Richardson); ser. 1, vol. 22, pt. 2, p. 272 (Mrs. McCune); ser. 1, vol. 50, pt. 1, p. 565 (Mrs. Bettis); ser. 1, vol. 16, pt. 2, p. 373 (Mrs. Cross); ser. 2, vol. 7, p. 742 (Mrs. Riggins and Miss Merritt); ser. 2, vol. 5, p. 447 (Mrs. Jeff. Thompson and Mrs. Colhoun); ser. 2, vol. 6, p. 381 (Evaline, Paulina, and Arabella White); ser. 2, vol. 4, p. 482 (Mrs. Peck and daughter); ser. 1, vol. 39, pt. 2, pp. 191–92 (Mary Buckner et al.); ser. 2, vol. 7, p. 567 (Emily Helm); ser. 1, vol. 32, pt. 3, p. 219 (Louisa Phillips); ser. 1, vol. 38, pt. 5, p. 578 (Mrs. Seely).

For B. F. Kelley's August 1862 order, see *Official Records*, ser. 2, vol. 4, p. 482.

41. Ibid., ser. 2, vol. 6, p. 137 (Mrs. Sawyer); ser. 2, vol. 6, p. 776 (Kate Barnett et al.).

42. Michael Fellman, "Women and Guerrilla Warfare," in Catherine Clinton and Nina Silber, eds., *Divided Houses: Gender and the Civil War* (New York: Oxford University Press, 1992), pp. 147–48.

43. *Official Records*, ser. 2, vol. 5, p. 78 (Miss Powell and Miss Creath); ser. 1, vol. 22, pt. 1, p. 588 (Miss Hutchins); ser. 1, vol. 48, pt. 1, p. 724 (Mrs. John Brown et al.).

For examples of other women accused of aiding guerrillas, see *Official Records*, ser. 1, vol. 29, pt. 2, p. 174 (Mrs. Bell); ser. 1, vol. 32, pt. 2, pp. 132–33 (Mrs. McKinney, Mrs. Bryant); ser. 1, vol. 34, pt. 1, pp. 858–59 (Olivia McAdo, Sue Thompson, Jane Elrod, Bethena Wiley, Sarah Miller, Fanny Lee, Mrs. Thomas Glidewell); ser. 1, vol. 49, pt. 1, pp. 38–39 (Mrs. Patterson); ser. 1, vol. 34, pt. 3, pp. 624, 720 (Charlotte and Mary Ann Hopkins); ser. 1, vol. 34, pt. 1, p. 995 (Mrs. Haney, her two daughters, and Miss Williams); ser. 1, vol. 41, pt. 2, pp. 476, 606 (Mrs. Ellis); ser. 1, vol. 41, pt. 1, p. 973 (Mrs. Welsh); ser. 1, vol. 34, pt. 4, pp. 477, 493 (Mrs. John Winston); ser. 1, vol. 48, pt. 1, p. 134 (Miss Hines); ser. 1, vol. 48, pt. 1, pp. 147–48 (Mrs. Demastus, Mrs. Wilhite); and ser. 2, vol. 4, p. 486 (Mrs. Sappington).

A collection of unpublished special orders from the District of South West Missouri during the Civil War, housed at the National Archives, contains numerous references to women whom federal officials deemed worthy of punishment for their collaboration with male guerrillas in the area. See, for example, Special Orders No. 236 (September 2, 1864) and Special Orders No. 238 (September 4, 1864), District of South West Missouri, National Archives, Washington, D.C.

44. Sources for material on Hart include Funderberg, "Women of the Confederacy"; Kinchen, *Women Who Spied for the Blue and Gray*; Simkins and Patton, *The Women of the Confederacy*; Boyd B. Sutler, "Nancy Hart, Lady Bushwhacker," *Civil War Times* 1 (January 1960): p. 7 (I thank Philip A. Gonyar for passing this article on to me); and Francis Trevelyan Miller, ed., *Photographic History of the Civil War*, vol. 8 (New York: Thomas Yoseloff, 1957), p. 287.

45. On Mrs. Cherry, see *Official Records*, ser. 1, vol. 49, pt. 1, p. 7. See also ser. 1, vol. 41, pt. 4, p. 744 (Mrs. White); and ser. 1, vol. 41, pt. 1, p. 994 (Mrs. Winston).

46. Kinchen, *Women Who Spied for the Blue and Gray*, p. 3. On this same theme in the context of World War I, see Julie Wheelwright, *The Fatal*

*Lover: Mata Hari and the Myth of Women in Espionage* (London: Collins & Brown, 1992).

47. Still, Massey noted, the "spirited girls" and "imaginative women" who became Civil War spies, couriers, guides, scouts, saboteurs, smugglers, and informers bravely responded to the call to serve their respective nations, and in later life tended to remember the war years as among the most exciting of their lives (see Massey, *Bonnet Brigades*, pp. 87, 89). See also Schultz, "Women at the Front," p. 293.

48. Richardson Wright, *Forgotten Ladies: Nine Portraits from the American Family Album* (Philadelphia: J. B. Lippincott, 1928), p. 254.

49. *Philadelphia Inquirer*, May 28, 1862, and *New York Herald*, May 28, 1862. See also Edwin C. Fishel, *The Secret War for the Union: The Untold Story of Military Intelligence in the Civil War* (Boston: Houghton Mifflin, 1996), p. 176.

50. See, for example, Kane, *Spies for the Blue and Gray*, p. 130; Leech, *Reveille in Washington, 1860–1865*, pp. 156–57; Leonora Wood, *Belle Boyd: Famous Spy of the Confederate States Army* (Keyser, W.Va.: Mountain Echo, 1940), pp. 2–3.

According to at least one scholar, Boyd herself consciously manipulates this image in her own memoir. See Schultz, "Women at the Front," p. 322. For another close reading of the tone of Boyd's memoir, see Karen Sue Nulton, "The Social Civil War" (Ph.D. diss., Rutgers University, New Brunswick, N.J., 1993).

Some accounts—from her own time and ours—do negatively critique Boyd's physical appearance (see *New York Herald*, August 3, 1862, and July 30, 1865; *Frank Leslie's Illustrated Newspaper*, August 9, 1862; Bakeless, *Spies of the Confederacy*, p. 141; Curtis Carroll Davis, "The Civil War's Most Over-Rated Spy," *West Virginia History* 27 [October 1965]: p. 4; William E. Doster, *Lincoln and Episodes of the Civil War* [New York: G. P. Putnam & Sons, 1915], p. 101; Ruth Scarborough, *Belle Boyd: Siren of the South* [Macon, Ga.: Mercer University Press, 1983], p. xiv). But even these accounts insist that Boyd's strength as a spy derived in large part from her skills as a seductress of men.

51. *Official Records*, ser. 2, vol. 2, pp. 567–68. See also William Gilmore Beymer, *On Hazardous Service: Scouts and Spies of the North and South* (New York: Harper & Brothers, 1912), p. 179; Burger, *Confederate Spy*, pp. 1, 4–5, 47; Leech, *Reveille in Washington*, p. 19; and Ishbel Ross,

*Rebel Rose: Life of Rose O'Neal Greenhow, Confederate Spy* (New York: Harper & Brothers, 1954), p. 4.

Greenhow's self-representation was somewhat different: in her memoir, *My Imprisonment*, Greenhow portrayed herself not as an irresistible seductress but rather as an essentially weak woman who nevertheless (and inexplicably) had the ability to confound her enemies and thwart their plans on a regular basis. Indeed, Greenhow simultaneously mocked and derived evident pleasure from such characterizations of herself as that found in Pinkerton's report. See Rose O'Neal Greenhow, *My Imprisonment, and the First Year of Aboliton Rule at Washington* (London: Richard Bentley, 1863), pp. 6, 7, 93–94, 40. See also Schultz, "Women at the Front, pp. 312–13.

52. Kinchen, *Women Who Spied for the Blue and Gray*, p. 43. There are numerous accounts from her own time that portray Ford as an "innocent," but as one might expect, the authors of such accounts are almost uniformly Southern and supportive of her activities on behalf of the Confederacy. See, for example, the notes of Mrs. Thomas Mason, quoting page 52 of *Partison* [sic] *Life with Colonel John S. Mosby*, in the Antonia Ford Willard Papers, Willard Family Papers, Library of Congress, Washington, D.C. See also Obituary in the Antonia Ford Willard Papers (this obituary failed to implicate Ford in any crimes against the Union, or even to mention her arrest and imprisonment); John Esten Cooke, article on Antonia Ford, *Southern Illustrated News*, August 15, 1863, in the Antonia Ford Willard Papers.

53. Kane, *Spies for the Blue and Gray*, pp. 177–78. See also Irwin Richman, "Pauline Cushman: She Was a Heroine but Not a Lady," *Civil War Times Illustrated* 7 (February 1969): pp. 38–44.

Cushman's initial biographer, F. L. Sarmiento—who devoted himself to the preservation of her reputation—himself stressed his subject's virtue, despite her great beauty and her ability to set the hearts of men aflutter. She was *"born* a heroine," he wrote, adding that "since the days of the Maid of Saragossa no woman has ever lived who has so completely come up to the ideal of a heroine, as Miss Pauline Cushman" (F. L. Sarmiento, *Life of Pauline Cushman, the Celebrated Union Spy and Scout* (Philadelphia: John E. Potter, 1865), p. 13).

54. Kane, *Spies for the Blue and Gray*, p. 232.

55. Charles Wesley Alexander, *Pauline of the Potomac; or, General McClellan's Spy* (Philadelphia: Barclay, 1862), pp. 66, 53, 70, 28; *Maud of*

the Mississippi: *General Grant's Daring Spy* (Philadelphia: C. W. Alexander, 1863), pp. 42, 86, 87, 28, 29; *General Sherman's Indian Spy* (Philadelphia: C. W. Alexander, 1865), pp. 52, 19; *The Picket Slayer* (Philadelphia: C. W. Alexander, 1863), pp. 64–65.

## Chapter Three

1. Mary Livermore, *My Story of the War* (Hartford, Conn.: A. D. Worthington, 1889), p. 119.

2. Jane Ellen Schultz, "Women at the Front: Gender and Genre in Literature of the American Civil War" (Ph.D. diss., University of Michigan, Ann Arbor, 1988), p. 182; Agatha Young, *The Women and the Crisis: Women of the North in the Civil War* (New York: McDowell, Obolensky, 1959), p. 96. See also Richard C. Hall, *Patriots in Disguise: Women Warriors of the Civil War* (New York: Paragon House, 1993); and Mary Elizabeth Massey, *Bonnet Brigades* (New York: Alfred A. Knopf, 1966).

For a critique of the traditional use of the term "camp follower," see Schultz, "Women at the Front," pp. 189–92. See also Barton C. Hacker, "Women and Military Institutions in Early Modern Europe: A Reconnaissance," *Signs* 6 (Summer 1981): pp. 651–52; Linda Grant De Pauw, "Women in Combat: The Revolutionary War Experience," *Armed Forces and Society* 7 (Winter 1981): p. 210.

3. Hacker, "Women and Military Institutions in Early Modern Europe," pp. 643–71; H. Sinclair Mills, *The Vivandière: History, Tradition, Uniform and Service* (Collinswood, N.J.: C. W. Historicals, 1988), pp. 1–3. According to Mills, an 1865 French army regulation fixed army women's numbers at "one per infantry battalion, two per light infantry battalion, two per cavalry squadron, and four per artillery or engineer regiment" (Mills, *The Vivandière*, p. 3).

4. Hacker, "Women and Military Institutions in Early Modern Europe," pp. 664–65. The specific act to which Hacker refers can be found in the records of the Seventh Congress, 1st sess., 1802, chap. 9, sec. 5. I thank Peggy Menchen for locating this document for me.

5. Jeanne Holmes, *Women in the Military* (Novato, Calif.: Presidio Press, 1982), p. 4.

6. De Pauw, "Women in Combat," p. 209ff. See also Linda Grant De

Pauw, writing to the MINERVA list, September 17, 1995; and Walter Hart Blumenthal's not entirely accurate but nevertheless useful *Women Camp Followers of the American Revolution* (Philadelphia: George S. MacManus, 1952).

Women who served with the British regular army during the American Revolution numbered between five and seven per company, received half a soldier's pay and half a soldier's rations, were permitted transport on ships and in provision wagons when space was available, and were subject to military regulations and punishments (see De Pauw, "Women in Combat," p. 212; and Jay Callaham, writing to the MINERVA list, September 15, 1995).

7. Sources for information on Corbin include J. Clement, ed., *Noble Deeds of American Women; with Biographical Sketches of Some of the More Prominent* (New York: George H. Derby, 1851; reprint, Williamstown, Mass.: Corner House Publishers, 1975); William Henry Egle, *Some Pennsylvania Women During the War of the Revolution* (Harrisburg, Pa.: Harrisburg Publishing, 1898); Edward Hagaman Hall, *Margaret Corbin: Heroine of the Battle of Fort Washington, 16 November 1776* (New York: American Scenic and Historic Preservation Society, 1932); Carol Klaver, "An Introduction to the Legend of Molly Pitcher," *MINERVA: Quarterly Report on Women and the Military* 12 (Summer 1994): pp. 36–61; Randolph Klein, "Heroines of the Revolution: Mary Ludwig Hays, the Heroine of Monmouth, and Margaret Cochran Corbin, the Heroine of Fort Washington," *Journal of American History* 16 (January 1922): pp. 31–35; Robert H. Land, "Margaret Cochran Corbin," in Edward T. James and Janet W. James, eds., *Notable American Women, 1607–1950: A Biographical Dictionary* (Cambridge, Mass.: Belknap Press, 1971), vol. 1, pp. 385–86; and William S. Stryker, *The Battle of Monmouth* (Princeton, N.J.: Princeton University Press, 1927).

8. Hall, *Margaret Corbin*, p. 24.

9. Ibid., pp. 26–27.

10. Sources for material on McCauley include the *Acts of the General Assembly of the Commonwealth of Pennsylvania, 1821–1822*; Edward W. Biddle, "Historical Address at the Unveiling of Molly Pitcher Monument in Carlisle, Pennsylvania, June 28, 1916" (Carlisle, Pa.: Hamilton Library Association, 1916); Elizabeth Cometti, "Mary Ludwig Hays McCauley," in James and James, *Notable American Women*, vol. 2, p. 448; Egle, *Some*

*Pennsylvania Women During the War of the Revolution*; Klaver, "An Introduction to the Legend of Molly Pitcher," pp. 36–61; Klein, "Heroines of the Revolution," pp. 31–35; John Landis, *A Short History of Molly Pitcher: The Heroine of the Battle of Monmouth* (Carlisle, Pa.: The Corman Printing, 1905); and Stryker, *The Battle of Monmouth*.

11. Stryker, *The Battle of Monmouth*, pp. 191–92.

12. Biddle, "Historical Address," pp. 9–10. See also Landis, *A Short History of Molly Pitcher*, p. 20.

13. If Linda Grant De Pauw is correct, the Revolutionary War involved "tens of thousands of women" in "active combat." According to De Pauw, these women fall into three categories: army women such as McCauley and Corbin; women who remained in their communities but were affiliated with the militia or with committees of safety established to safeguard individual communities; and women who disguised themselves as men and enlisted as soldiers (De Pauw, "Women in Combat," p. 209).

14. Sources for material on Etheridge include Linus P. Brockett and Mary C. Vaughan, *Woman's Work in the Civil War: A Record of Heroism, Patriotism, and Patience* (Philadelphia: Zeigler, McCurdy, 1867); A. Mulholland St. Clair, *The Story of the 116th Regiment, Pennsylvania Infantry* (Philadelphia: F. McManus, Jr., 1899); Eileen F. Conklin, *Women at Gettysburg, 1863* (Gettysburg, Pa.: Thomas Publications, 1993); Daniel G. Crotty, *Four Years Campaigning in the Army of the Potomac* (Grand Rapids, Mich.: Dygert Brothers, 1874); *Detroit Advertiser and Tribune*, February 16, 1863; *Michigan Women in the Civil War* (Lansing: Michigan Civil War Centennial Observance Commission, 1863); Frank Moore, *Women of the War: Their Heroism and Self-Sacrifice* (Hartford, Conn.: S. S. Scranton, 1866); Philip N. Racine, ed., *"Unspoiled Heart": The Journal of Charles Mattocks of the 17th Maine* (Knoxville: University of Tennessee Press, 1994); Schultz, "Women at the Front"; Ruth L. Silliker, ed., *The Rebel Yell & the Yankee Hurrah: The Civil War Journal of a Maine Volunteer* (Camden, Maine: Down East Books, 1985); Young, *The Women and the Crisis*; and various documents in the pension record of her third husband, Charles Hooks: RG 15, Records of the Veterans Administration, Charles E. Hooks Pension File, application #40925, certificate #25505, National Archives, Washington D.C. (hereafter cited as Charles E. Hooks Pension File); and a letter from Mary Morris Husband to Frank Moore dated January 30, 1866, in the Frank Moore Papers, William R. Perkins Library, Duke University, Durham, N.C.

15. Evidence suggests that Annie had already been married once before, to a David Kellogg. Nothing is known about what became of Kellogg or how their marriage ended, but given the difficulty of obtaining a divorce in mid-century America, one presumes that Kellogg died soon after their marriage, leaving open the possibility for Annie's remarriage to Etheridge.

16. *Detroit Advertiser and Tribune*, February 16, 1863.

17. Silliker, *The Rebel Yell & the Yankee Hurrah*, pp. 78–79.

18. Racine, *"Unspoiled Heart,"* p. 30. See also Edwin B. Houghton, *The Campaigns of the Seventeenth Maine* (Portland, Maine: Short & Loring, 1866), pp. 62–64, 70; and Robert Goldthwaite Carter, *Four Brothers in Blue* (1913; reprint, Austin: University of Texas Press, 1978) pp. 248, 251–52.

19. Mary Morris Husband to Frank Moore, January 30, 1866, in the Frank Moore Papers.

20. *Michigan Women in the War*, p. 25. See also Schultz, "Women at the Front," p. 241.

21. Crotty, *Four Years Campaigning in the Army of the Potomac*, pp. 148–49.

22. *The War of the Rebellion: The Official Records of the Union and Confederate Armies* (Washington, D.C.: Government Printing Office, 1881–1902), ser. 1, vol. 51, pt. 1, pp. 1275–76 (hereafter cited as Official Records).

23. G. W. Holmes to "Major," in file #1122, RG 94, Records of the Adjutant General's Office, Administrative Precedent File ("Frech File") #3H35, National Archives, Washington, D.C.

24. Frank Moore, *Women of the War*, p. 513.

25. Livermore, *My Story of the War*, p. 116; Moore, *Women of the War*, pp. 517–18; Crotty, *Four Years Campaigning in the Army of the Potomac*, pp. 57–58.

26. Crotty, *Four Years Campaigning in the Army of the Potomac*, p. 204.

27. What happened to James Etheridge after he deserted the army early in the war is unclear. See Conklin, *Women at Gettysburg*, p. 385, for some general speculations on the matter.

28. C. S. Shepherd to Frank Moore, February 22, 1866, in the Frank Moore Papers; Mary Morris Husband to Frank Moore, January 30, 1866, in the Frank Moore Papers; Brockett and Vaughan, *Woman's Work in the Civil War*, p. 753; Schultz, "Women at the Front," p. 240; John T. Huddle

to "To Whom It May Concern," January 27, 1911, in the Charles E. Hooks Pension File; Letter to the Commissioner of Pensions, May 18, 1911, and Declaration of a Widow for Accrued Pension, January 12, 1911, in the Charles E. Hooks Pension File; *Michigan Women in the Civil War*, p. 25; and Conklin, *Women at Gettysburg*, p. 104.

Evidence suggests that Etheridge was somewhat bitter about her financial struggle in her later years. Conklin quotes a document from Etheridge's pension file in which the former daughter of the regiment, in connection with her 1886 application for a pension, described her service to the army and then made pointed reference to the fact that she had "received no compensation whatever during the war for any services . . . not even what the soldiers received. . . ." Rather, she noted, she was "obliged to expend for personal expenses in living—clothing, some even in transportation though *that* it was expected I would be furnished . . ." (Conklin, *Women at Gettysburg*, p. 104).

29. Sources for material on Kady Brownell include Brockett and Vaughan, *Woman's Work in the Civil War*; Margaret Leech, *Reveille in Washington: 1860–1865* (New York: Harper & Brothers, 1941); Livermore, *My Story of the War*; Moore, *Women of the War*; Schultz, "Women at the Front"; Young, *The Women and the Crisis*; "The Heroine of Newbern," *The Sibyl* 7 (August 1862): p. 1070; *New York Times*, February 16, 1913; "Woman Soldier Now a Veteran," *New York Herald* (1895), in RG 94, Records of the Adjutant General's Office, Administrative Precedent File ("Frech File") #3H36, National Archives, Washington, D.C.; *New York Herald*, April 25, 1861; RG 15, Records of the Veterans Administration, Robert S. Brownell Pension File, application #6135, certificate #23495, National Archives, Washington, D.C. (hereafter cited as Robert S. Brownell Pension File); and RG 15, Records of the Veterans Administration, Kady Brownell Pension File, certificate #279843, National Archives, Washington, D.C. (hereafter cited as Kady Brownell Pension File).

30. *New York Times*, February 16, 1913. A Washington *Star* reporter, when he described the arrival of the 1st Rhode Island in the federal capital, noted that the regiment had brought along with it four women, including "a laundress and three [soldiers'] relatives" who had "utterly refused to be left at home" (see Leech, *Reveille in Washington*, p. 69. See also *New York Herald*, April 25, 1861).

31. See Gerald F. Linderman, *Embattled Courage: The Experience of Combat in the American Civil War* (New York: Free Press, 1987), p. 157.

32. "Woman Soldier Now a Veteran." See also Livermore, *My Story of the War*, p. 119; Moore, *Women of the War*, p. 56; and *New York Times*, February 16, 1913.

Moore describes one perhaps apocryphal incident during Brownell's army career in which she almost lost control of herself with weapon in hand. Having tended to the wounds of a rebel soldier, Brownell was caught off guard by the soldier's sudden and vehement announcement of his intention to take revenge on the Yankees by killing her. In response, Moore wrote, Brownell "snatched a musket with bayonet fixed, that lay close by, and an instant more and his profane and indecent tongue would have been hushed forever." Just as Brownell was about to drive the bayonet into the rebel soldier's chest, however, a wounded Union soldier lying nearby caught hold of it and persuaded her not to kill an already wounded man. (Moore, *Women of the War*, pp. 61–62.)

33. Declaration for Original Invalid Pension, in the Kady Brownell Pension File. See also Young, *The Women and the Crisis*, pp. 121, 125; and "Woman Soldier Now a Veteran."

34. Moore, *Women of the War*, pp. 56–57.

35. *New York Times*, February 16, 1913.

36. "The Heroine of Newbern," p. 1070. See also Young, *The Women and the Crisis*, p. 308; *New York Times*, February 16 , 1913.

Sources disagree as to whether Kady Brownell was wounded at New Bern or Bull Run, or at all. See "Woman Soldier Now a Veteran"; Report No. 524 (to accompany S. 773), 48th Cong., 1st sess., in the Kady Brownell Pension File. Brownell's original pension claim, dated 1884, included a declaration signed by her in which mention of a leg wound appears but no battle is named (see Declaration for Original Invalid Pension, in the Kady Brownell Pension File). Moore and Brockett and Vaughan do not mention her receiving a wound at either battle.

37. George W. Tew to Frank Moore, January 26, 1865 [should be 1866], in the Frank Moore Papers; Job Arnold to Frank Moore, February 2, 1866, in the Frank Moore Papers; J. M. Wheeler to Frank Moore, February 24, 1866, in the Frank Moore Papers.

38. See Francis Trevelyan Miller, ed., *Photographic History of the Civil War* (New York: Thomas Yoseloff, 1957), vol. 9, pp. 68–70.

39. Report No. 524 (to accompany S. 773), 48th Cong., 1st sess. (1884), in the Kady Brownell Pension File.

40. Livermore, *My Story of the War*, p. 119.

41. *New York Times*, February 16, 1913.

42. Sources for material on Bridget Divers include Brockett and Vaughan, *Woman's Work in the Civil War*; Conklin, *Women at Gettysburg*; Hall, *Patriots in Disguise*; Livermore, *My Story of the War*; Moore, *Women of the War*; *Michigan Women in the Civil War*; Schultz, "Women at the Front"; Young, *The Women and the Crisis*; J. R. Miller to Frank Moore, March 5, 1866, in the Frank Moore Papers; Edward P. Smith to Frank Moore, January 29, 1866, in the Frank Moore Papers; G. Foster White to Frank Moore, August 29, 1866, in the Frank Moore Papers; and Rebecca Usher to "Ellen," April 7, 1865, in the Rebecca Usher Papers, Maine Historical Society, Portland, Maine (hereafter cited as Rebecca Usher Papers).

43. Rebecca Usher to "Ellen," April 7, 1865, in the Rebecca Usher Papers. See also Moore, *Women of the War*, p. 462; Brockett and Vaughan, *Woman's Work in the Civil War*, p. 772.

44. Charlotte E. McKay, quoted in *Michigan Women in the Civil War*, p. 30. See also Schultz, "Women at the Front," pp. 242–43.

45. G. Foster White to Frank Moore, August 29, 1866, in the Frank Moore Papers.

46. J. R. Miller to Frank Moore, March 5, 1866, in the Frank Moore Papers. See also Schultz, "Women at the Front," p. 244.

47. Sources for material on Belle Reynolds include Moore, *Women of the War*; pp. 254–77; Young, *The Women and the Crisis*; pp. 159–67; and Schultz, "Women at the Front," pp. 243–45. See also "Only Woman Officer," *Washington Post*, June 12, 1898, in RG 94, Records of the Adjutant General's Office, Administrative Precedent File ("Frech File") #3H36, National Archives, Washington, D.C.; and *The Sibyl* 7 (August 1862), p. 1070.

48. "Only Woman Officer."

49. Moore, *Women of the War*, p. 256.

50. Young, *The Women and the Crisis*, p. 160.

51. Moore, *Women of the War*, p. 262.

52. Not all women designated "daughter of the regiment" received such formal documentation of their status. Indeed, Reynolds's case seems to be the exception. For other women, it appears that the honorary title was

conferred verbally, or was simply a matter of regimental consensus and understanding. Such an "unofficial" designation does not seem to have been in any way less meaningful, however, as we know from the fact that Kady Brownell was able to apply successfully for a pension after the war on the basis of her wartime status as a daughter of the regiment, even without having in hand—apparently—any official paperwork to that effect.

53. "Only Woman Officer."

54. Ibid.

55. Ibid.

56. Sources on Nadine Turchin include Brockett and Vaughan, *Woman's Work in the Civil War*; J. Henry Haynie, *The Nineteenth Illinois* (Chicago: M. A. Donohue, 1912); Livermore, *My Story of the* War; Mary Ellen McElligott, ed., "'A Monotony Full of Sadness': The Diary of Nadine Turchin, May, 1863–April, 1864," *Journal of the Illinois State Historical Society* 70 (1977): pp. 27–89; Schultz, "Women at the Front"; Young, *The Women and the Crisis*; and RG 15, Records of the Veterans Administration, John B. Turchin Pension File, application #744629, certificate #532315, National Archives, Washington, D.C. (hereafter cited as John B. Turchin Pension File).

57. Although McClellan was probably instrumental in her husband's appointment as a Union army officer, Nadine Turchin did not respect him as a military man. Two years into the war, she described him as a "mediocre personage who has had the impudence to maneuver for two years and a half the armies . . ." (McElligott, "'A Monotony Full of Sadness,'" p. 31).

58. Haynie, *The Nineteenth Illinois*, p. 132.

59. J. B. Foraker to H. Clay Evans, November 9, 1901, in the John B. Turchin Pension File. See also Haynie, *The Nineteenth Illinois*, p. 132.

60. S. T. Carrico to "Mr. President," February 1, 1902, in the John B. Turchin Pension File.

61. Brockett and Vaughan, *Woman's Work in the Civil War*, p. 771.

62. Livermore, *My Story of the War*, p. 115.

63. "A Famous Woman in Straits," from the Chicago *Record-Herald*, in the John B. Turchin Pension File.

64. McElligott, "'A Monotony Full of Sadness,'" pp. 67, 76.

65. S. T. Carrico to "Mr. President," February 1, 1902, in the John B. Turchin Pension File; Louis Krughoff et al. to J. B. Foraker, October 17, 1901, in the John B. Turchin Pension File.

66. See Official Copy of the Proceeds of the Court Martial against John Turchin, Headquarters Army of Ohio, in camp, Huntsville, Ala., August 6, 1862, furnished to the Commissioner of Pensions on November 22, 1898, in the John B. Turchin Pension File. See also Proceeds of the Court Martial against Turchin, in the John B. Turchin Pension File; and various references to the case in the *Official Records*: ser. 1, vol. 16, pt. 2, pp. 273–78; ser. 1, vol. 16, pt. 2, p. 99; ser. 1, vol. 10, pt. 2, pp. 294–95; ser. 1, vol. 16, pt. 2, p. 80; ser. 2, vol. 1, pp. 186–87; ser. 2, vol. 1, p. 774; and ser. 4, vol. 2, p. 1047.

67. Some postwar sources suggested that Nadine herself had a strong hand in Lincoln's decision making (see Brockett and Vaughan, *Woman's Work in the Civil War*, p. 771; Livermore, *My Story of the War*, pp. 115–16; Schultz, "Women at the Front," p. 187); others suggest that her involvement was limited to delivering the news to Turchin after she received it in Chicago (see Louis Krughoff et al. to J. B. Foraker, October 17, 1901, in the John B. Turchin File).

68. McElligott, "'A Monotony Full of Sadness,'" p. 28; Report No. 484 (to accompany S. 3518), 57th Cong., 1st sess., February 17, 1902, in the John B. Turchin Pension File; Records and Pension Office War Department Document dated March 12, 1898, in the John B. Turchin Pension File.

69. See the various references to Turchin's service in the *Official Records*: ser. 1, vol. 7, p. 460; ser. 1, vol. 10, pt. 2, pp. 85, 149; ser. 1, vol. 16, pt. 2, pp. 5–6; ser. 1, vol. 16, pt. 2, p. 92; ser. 1, vol. 23, pt. 1, p. 410; ser. 1, vol. 23, pt. 2, p. 246; ser. 1, vol. 30, pt. 1, p. 40; ser. 1, vol. 32, pt. 2, p. 289; ser. 1, vol. 32, pt. 3, p. 554; ser. 1, vol. 38, pt. 1, p. 96.

70. McElligott, "'A Monotony Full of Sadness,'" pp. 33, 55.

71. Ibid., pp. 30, 37, 40, 41, 43, 53, 55, 56, 65–69, 74, 75, 81.

72. Ibid., pp. 33, 34, 37, 40, 43.

73. Ibid., pp. 37, 39, 47, 63, 64–65, 66–69, 77.

74. Ibid., pp. 48, 65, 67.

75. Ibid., pp. 29, 37, 38, 41, 44, 46, 57, 60, 61, 63, 75, 89.

76. There were several people who considered the pension she received in 1902 small recompense for Turchin's devotion to the army and to her husband during the Civil War. Some were particularly resentful that the pension was granted only after a period of bureaucratic resistance. See S. T. Carrico to "Mr. President," February 1, 1902, in the John

B. Turchin Pension File. See also J. B. Foraker to H. Clay Evans, November 9, 1901, in the John B. Turchin Pension File.

### Chapter Four

1. Jane Goodwin Austin, *Dora Darling: The Daughter of the Regiment* (Boston: J. E. Tilton, 1865), p. 78.

2. *Frank Leslie's Illustrated Newspaper*, December 7, 1861; Ethel Alice Hurn, *Wisconsin Women in the War Between the States* (Madison: Wisconsin Historical Commission, 1911), p. 102. See also Richard C. Hall, *Patriots in Disguise: Women Warriors of the Civil War* (New York: Paragon House, 1993), p. 18.

3. John Chaplain Hanson, *Historical Sketch of the Old Sixth Regiment of Massachusetts Volunteers During Its Three Campaigns in 1861, 1862, 1863 & 1864* (Boston: Lee & Shepard, 1866), pp. 18, 66; H. Sinclair Mills, *The Vivandière: History, Tradition, Uniform and Service* (Collinswood, N.J.: C. W. Historicals, 1988), pp. 15, 16; Jane Ellen Schultz, "Women at the Front: Gender and Genre in Literature of the American Civil War" (Ph.D. diss., University of Michigan, Ann Arbor, 1988), pp. 184–85.

On Jones, see also Mills, *The Vivandière*, p. 15; Hall, *Patriots in Disguise*, pp. 17–18; Agatha Young, *The Women and the Crisis: Women of the North in the Civil War* (New York: McDowell, Obolensky, 1959), p. 95. On the women of the 39th New York, see also Hall, *Patriots in Disguise*, p. 17. On Taylor, see also John Laffin, *Women in Battle* (New York: Abelard-Schuman, 1967), p. 51; Mary Elizabeth Massey, *Bonnet Brigades* (New York: Alfred A. Knopf, 1966), p. 85.

4. Massey, *Bonnet Brigades*, p. 85.

5. J. L. Underwood, *The Women of the Confederacy* (New York: Neale Publishing, 1906), p. 100. See also Massey, *Bonnet Brigades*, p. 85.

6. On the laundress with the Irish Brigade, see Bell Irvin Wiley, *The Life of Billy Yank: The Common Soldier of the Union* (Baton Rouge: Louisiana State University Press, 1952, 1971), p. 339. On Finnan, see Schultz, "Women at the Front," p. 188. On Rooney, see Francis Butler Simkins and James Welch Patton, *The Women of the Confederacy* (New York: Garrett & Massie, 1936; reprint, St. Clair Shores, Mich.: Scholarly Press, 1976), p. 75; Fannie A. Beers, *Memories: A Record of Personal Experience and Adventure During Four Years of War* (Philadelphia: J. B. Lippincott, 1888),

pp. 217–20; Eileen F. Conklin, *Women at Gettysburg, 1863* (Gettysburg, Pa.: Thomas Publications, 1993), pp. 111–16; and the New Orleans *Times Picayune*, February 5, 1893, and March 1, 1895. For information on the Irish Brigade, see Hall, *Patriots in Disguise*, p. 17.

7. On Sullivan, see Simkins and Patton, *Women of the Confederacy*, p. 75. On Mrs. Bahr, see Mills, *The Vivandière*, p. 16. On Goodridge, see Frank Moore, *Women of the War: Their Heroism and Self-Sacrifice* (Hartford, Conn.: S. S. Scranton, 1866), pp. 532–33; Hall, *Patriots in Disguise*, p. 18; and Massey, *Bonnet Brigades*, p. 80. On Dutch Mary, see Ruth L. Silliker, ed., *The Rebel Yell & the Yankee Hurrah: The Civil War Journal of a Maine Volunteer* (Camden, Maine: Down East Books, 1985), p. 64; and Hall, *Patriots in Disguise*, p. 17.

8. Bradley T. Johnson, "Memoir of Jane Claudia Johnson," *Southern Historical Society Papers* 29 (1901): pp. 33–42. See also Simkins and Patton, *Women of the Confederacy*, p. 75.

9. On Tepe, see Robert Goldthwaite Carter, *Four Brothers in Blue* (1913; reprint, Austin: University of Texas Press, 1978), pp. 281–83; Conklin, *Women at Gettysburg*, pp. 105–10; Mills, *The Vivandière*, pp. 6–7; Hall, *Patriots in Disguise*, pp. 7–8; *The War of the Rebellion: The Official Records of the Union and Confederate Armies* (Washington, D.C.: Government Printing Office, 1881–1902), ser. 1, vol. 51, pt. 1, pp. 1275–76.

10. On Wilson, see Hurn, *Wisconsin Women in the War*, pp. 100–101; Hall, *Patriots in Disguise*, p. 18; Massey, *Bonnet Brigades*, p. 85; and *Frank Leslie's Illustrated Newspaper*, August 17, 1861.

One observer described Wilson's uniform as resembling modified women's reform dress of the period or "the Turkish costume," all in brown and composed of a shortened dress with a gathered waist and wide sleeves, wide pants gathered at the ankles, a black hat with a feather, and boots (Hurn, *Wisconsin Women in the War*, p. 101).

11. Susie King Taylor, *A Black Woman's Civil War Memoirs: Reminiscences of My Life in Camp with the 33rd U.S. Colored Troops, Late 1st South Carolina Volunteers* (New York: Markus Wiener Publishing, 1988).

12. Ibid., p. 61.

13. Ibid., p. 133.

14. See, among others, Elizabeth D. Leonard, *Yankee Women: Gender Battles in the Civil War* (New York: W. W. Norton, 1994).

15. See Jane Ellen Schultz, *Women at the Front* (Chapel Hill: University

of North Carolina Press, forthcoming); and Jane Ellen Schultz, "The Inhospitable Hospital: Gender and Professionalism in Civil War Medicine," *Signs* 17 (Winter 1992): pp. 363–92.

16. Moore, *Women of the War*, p. 109.

17. Brockett and Vaughan, *Woman's Work in the Civil War*, p. 774. See also Schultz, "Women at the Front," pp. 183–84, 228, 239, for a discussion of postwar writers' discomfort with the lower-class roots of the army women they otherwise celebrated.

18. Edward W. Biddle, "Historical Address at the Unveiling of Molly Pitcher Monument in Carlisle, Pennsylvania, June 28, 1916" (Carlisle, Pa.: Hamilton Library Association), p. 11.

Frank Moore in particular made the explicit connection between Civil War army women and the legend of Molly Pitcher in his introductory comments to his chapter on Kady Brownell. See Moore, *Women of the War*, p. 54.

On the Molly Pitcher legend and its development, see Linda Grant De Pauw, "Women in Combat: The Revolutionary War Experience," *Armed Forces and Society* 7 (Winter 1991): p. 215; Joseph Plumb Martin, *Private Yankee Doodle: Being a Narrative of Some of the Adventures, Dangers and Sufferings of a Revolutionary Soldier* (New York: Eastern Acorn Press, 1979), pp. 132–33; William S. Stryker, *The Battle of Monmouth* (Princeton, N.J.: Princeton University Press, 1927), p. 189; J. Clement, ed., *Noble Deeds of American Women; with Biographical Sketches of Some of the More Prominent* (New York: George H. Derby, 1851; reprint, Williamstown, Mass.: Corner House Publishers, 1975), p. 237; B. J. Lossing, *Pictorial Field Book of the Revolution* (New York: Harper & Brothers, 1860), vol. 1, p. 732, and vol. 2, pp. 155–56n; John W. Barber, *Historical Collections of New Jersey: Past and Present* (New Haven, Conn.: John W. Barber, 1868), p. 342; Reverend C. P. Wing to Editor, June 15, 1878, in the *Pennsylvania Magazine of History and Biography* 3 (1879): p. 109; Biddle, "Historical Address," p. 11; John Landis, *A Short History of Molly Pitcher: The Heroine of the Battle of Monmouth* (Carlisle, Pa.: Corman Printing, 1905); William Henry Egle, *Some Pennsylvania Women During the War of the Revolution* (Harrisburg, Pa.: Harrisburg Publishing, 1898), pp. 53–54; Edward Hagaman Hall, *Margaret Corbin: Heroine of the Battle of Fort Washington, 16 November 1776* (New York: American Scenic and Historic Preservation Society, 1932).

Given the obvious parallels between the Molly Pitcher myth and the documented details of Corbin's and McCauley's Continental army careers, it is probably not surprising that we can uncover without too much difficulty separate efforts in the nineteenth and twentieth centuries to elevate both the historical McCauley and the historical Corbin to the status of the "true Molly Pitcher." See Egle, *Some Pennsylvania Women During the War of the Revolution*, p. 85; Landis, *A Short History of Molly Pitcher*, pp. 13–14; *New York Times*, January 28, March 17, and April 15, 1926, and May 1, 1902.

19. Even today the United States Army's Field Artillery Association grants an award called the "Order of Molly Pitcher." There is some dispute—aired in a recent Internet debate on the award—as to how recipients are chosen. According to Gene Moser, the Order of Molly Pitcher is given to "females (non artillery types) who have rendered distinguished service to the artillery." According to Eloise Prendergast, "The only ones I saw receive the Molly Pitcher [while in the service] were the die-hard [artillery] wives that tolerated a lot of crap." According to Joan Biddle, the Order of Molly Pitcher "is an award which is highly valued by the Artillery community, for the service to the community and to the husbands. (One must be nominated by one's husband, and rest assured, not all husbands consider their wives for the Molly Pitcher award. Again—it isn't just handed out to any live and breathing body.)" (See contributions to the MINERVA list on this topic, November 9–11, 1996.)

20. Clement, *Noble Deeds of American Women*, p. 238; Landis, *A Short History of Molly Pitcher*, p. 16; C. P. Wing to Editor, June 15, 1878, in the *Pennsylvania Magazine of History and Biography* 3 (1879): p. 109; Stryker, *The Battle of Monmouth*, p. 192, n. 19; Hall, *Margaret Corbin*, p. 31; Lossing, *Pictorial Field Book of the Revolution*, vol. 1, p. 732.

21. Joseph Hodgson, *The Confederate Vivandière; or, The Battle of Leesburg* (Montgomery, Ala.: John M. Floyd, Book and Job Printer, 1862); Jane Goodwin Austin, *Dora Darling*, 1865.

22. Hodgson, *The Confederate Vivandière*, p. 17.

23. Austin, *Dora Darling*, p. 147.

24. Ibid., pp. 165.

25. Ibid., p. 234.

26. Mentioned at least a couple of times in *Dora Darling* is the Italian composer Gaetano Donizetti's opera *La Fille du Régiment*. First produced

in Paris in 1849, *La Fille du Regiment* tells the story of Marie, the daughter of a regiment in the French army, and her ultimately successful attempt to be united in marriage with her beloved Tonio, a Tyrolean soldier. Like Clara, Marie has grown up in the army and has, the audience soon discovers, learned to be "as brave as a soldier" and to "prefer to all else the sound of the drum."

27. Hodgson, *The Confederate Vivandière*, p. 17.

## Chapter Five

1. Comment of Captain William R. Morse, describing Civil War woman soldier Sarah Emma Edmonds, in Report No. 929 (to accompany H.R. 1172), 49th Cong., 1st sess., 1885, p. 9.

2. There has been considerable debate over the question of how many women served as soldiers in the armies of the Union and the Confederacy. In 1889 Mary Livermore offered what has become the most frequently quoted estimate—400—of "women who actually bore arms and served in the ranks" of the Union army. But even Livermore believed that estimate to be too low. In 1906 Adjutant General F. C. Ainsworth of the Records and Pension Office in Washington, D.C., flatly wrote to an inquirer that "nothing has been found of record to show the enlistment and service of a woman soldier or officer in the civil war." However, since 1906 researchers have collectively proved Ainsworth's conclusion misleading at best. In 1959 Agatha Young reconsidered Livermore's basic estimate and persuasively argued that "if the astonishing figure of four hundred is correct, that is [only] the number of women who were discovered. . . . How many more there may have been we do not know." Likewise, in 1988 Jane Schultz noted her own inclination to believe the estimate of 400 to be "arbitrarily low": "My own cursory search for soldiers *in cognito*," wrote Schultz, "has uncovered fifty without much digging." In 1993 military archivist and historian DeAnne Blanton noted that to Livermore's standard estimate for the Union's women soldiers, a further estimate of approximately 250 women in the Confederate army must be added. In 1994 Thomas Lowry roughly figured the total number of women soldiers on both sides at "probably between 500 and 1,000." Although the most thorough count of documented women soldiers by 1994 stood at just over 130, I accept Lowry's estimate as the most persuasive. (See Mary Livermore, *My Story of the War*

[Hartford, Conn.: A. D. Worthington, 1889], pp. 116, 119–20; RG 94, Records of the Adjutant General's Office, Records and Pension Office Record Cards, card #1183893, National Archives, Washington, D.C.; Agatha Young, *The Women and the Crisis: Women of the North in the Civil War* [New York: McDowell, Obolensky, 1959], pp. 96–97; Jane Ellen Schultz, "Women at the Front: Gender and Genre in Literature of the American Civil War" [Ph.D. diss., University of Michigan, Ann Arbor, 1988], p. 273; DeAnne Blanton, "Women Soldiers of the Civil War," *Prologue* 25 [Spring 1993]: p. 27; Thomas Lowry, *The Story the Soldiers Wouldn't Tell: Sex in the Civil War* [Mechanicsburg, Pa.: Stackpole Books, 1994], p. 118; Lauren Cook Burgess, ed., *An Uncommon Soldier: The Civil War Letters of Sarah Rosetta Wakeman, Alias Pvt. Lyons Wakeman, 153rd Regiment, New York State Volunteers, 1862–1864* [Pasadena, Md.: MINERVA Center, 1994], p. xii.)

3. Indeed, scholars and others have unearthed a substantial amount of material to indicate that Civil War women soldiers participated in traditions that were not only American but also international in scope. See, among others, Ellen C. Clayton, *Female Warriors: Memorials of Female Valour and Heroism, from the Mythological Ages to the Present Era* (London: Tinsley Brothers, 1879); Margaret S. Creighton and Lisa Norling, *Iron Men, Wooden Women: Gender and Seafaring in the Atlantic World, 1700–1920* (Baltimore: Johns Hopkins University Press, 1996); Rudolf M. Dekker and Lotte C. van de Pol, *The Tradition of Female Transvestism in Early Modern Europe* (New York: St. Martin's Press, 1989); Catalina de Erauso, *Lieutenant Nun: Memoir of a Basque Transvestite in the New World* (Boston: Beacon Press, 1996); Elizabeth Ewing, *Women in Uniform Through the Centuries* (London: B. T. Batsford, 1975); Barton C. Hacker, "Women and Military Institutions in Early Modern Europe: A Reconnaissance," *Signs* 6 (Summer 1981): pp. 643–71; John Laffin, *Women in Battle* (New York: Abelard-Schuman, 1967); Jessica Amanda Salmonson, *The Encyclopedia of Amazons: Women Warriors from Antiquity to the Modern Era* (New York: Paragon House, 1991); Jo Stanley, ed., *Bold in Her Breeches: Women Pirates Across the Ages* (London: Pandora Press, 1995); Suzanne J. Stark, *Female Tars: Women Aboard Ship in the Age of Sail* (Annapolis, Md.: Naval Institute Press, 1996) (I thank Warren B. Randall of Brunswick, Maine, for drawing this book to my attention); Julie Wheelwright, *Amazons and Military Maids: Women Who Dressed as Men in the Pursuit of Life, Liberty and Happiness* (London: Pandora Press, 1989).

312 Notes to page 166

4. Sources for material on Sampson include J. Clement, ed., *Noble Deeds of American Women; with Biographical Sketches of Some of the More Prominent* (New York: George H. Derby, 1851; reprint, Williamstown, Mass.: Corner House Publishers, 1975); Elizabeth F. Ellet, *Women of the American Revolution*, 2 vols. (Philadelphia: George W. Jacobs, 1900); Lucy Freeman and Alma Halbert Bond, *America's First Woman Warrior: The Courage of Deborah Sampson* (New York: Paragon House, 1992); Herman Mann, *The Female Review: Life of Deborah Sampson* (Boston: J. K. Wiggin & Wm. Parsons Lunt, 1866; reprint, New York: Arno Press, 1972); Pauline Moody, "Massachusetts's Deborah Sampson" (Sharon, Mass.: privately printed, 1975); Julia Ward Stickley, "The Records of Deborah Sampson Gannett, Woman Soldier of the Revolution," *Prologue* 4 (Winter 1972): pp. 233–41; Julia Ward Stickley Files on Deborah Sampson Gannett, 1786–1990, Massachusetts State Archives, Boston (hereafter cited as Julia Ward Stickley Files); Deborah Sampson Gannett deposition, September 14, 1918, Sharon Public Library, Sharon, Mass.; Deborah Sampson Gannett Diary (1802), Sharon Public Library, Sharon, Mass. (hereafter cited as Sampson Diary); Deborah Sampson Gannett, "An Address Delivered in 1802 in Various Towns in Massachusetts, Rhode Island and New York," Sharon Public Library, Sharon, Mass.; RG 15, Records of the Veterans Administration, Deborah Sampson Gannett Pension File, certificate #32722, National Archives, Washington, D.C. (hereafter cited as Deborah Sampson Pension File); RG 15, Records of the Veterans Administration, Ephraim Sampson Pension File, certificate #W11053, National Archives, Washington, D.C. (hereafter cited as Ephraim Sampson Pension File); and John A. Vinton Papers, New Hampshire Antiquarian Society, Hopkinton, N.H.

According to historian Linda Grant De Pauw, perhaps as many as a few hundred other women joined Sampson in uniform in the Continental army. Among these women De Pauw has identified four, apparently without much effort: Sally St. Clair, whose sex was discovered only when she was killed at the battle of Savannah; Elizabeth Gilmore of Pennsylvania, for whom the evidence in the Pennsylvania state archives and on the plaque posted on her grave indicates that she drew a private's pay while in the Continental army, married a fellow soldier in 1780, and continued to serve until the end of the war in the same company with him; Anna Maria Lane of Virginia, whom the Virginia state legislature in

1807–8 noted had "been disabled by a severe wound which she received while fighting as a common soldier in one of our Revolutionary battles"; and a woman posing as "Corporal Samuel Gay" with the 1st Massachusetts Regiment, whose service records at the National Archives conclude that "he" was "discharged, being a woman, dressed in men[']s clothes. Augt. 1777." Of the four, to date only "Samuel Gay" has been the subject of more extensive research. Patrick J. Leonard writes that "Samuel Gay" served with the Continental army for only about three weeks before being discovered to be a woman whose real name was either Nancy or Ann Bailey. Leonard cites a March 1777 edict from the state of Massachusetts relating to her military service which accused Bailey of trying to defraud the state of fifteen pounds, ten shillings in bounty money and demanded that she appear before the court in April to respond to the charge of having posed as a man. Leonard also cites an August 1777 document that recapped the charges against Bailey and recorded both her admission of guilt and the final disposition in her case, namely, that she must spend two months in jail and pay to the state a fine of sixteen pounds as well the costs of prosecuting her case (she would have to remain in jail until she covered her debts). Comments Leonard: "Presumably young Ann Bailey . . . suffered her two months imprisonment, paid the fine of 16 pounds, and then as far as can be determined, faded into obscurity." See Patrick J. Leonard, "Ann Bailey: Mystery Woman Warrior of 1777," *MINERVA: Quarterly Report of Women and the Military* 11 (Fall/Winter 1993): pp. 1–4. See also Linda Grant De Pauw, "Women in Combat: The Revolutionary War Experience," *Armed Forces and Society* 7 (Winter 1981): p. 210, 217, 226.

There is also evidence of women serving in disguise as soldiers during the American war with Mexico, 1846–48. The individual most frequently mentioned in this context is Sarah Borginis, about whose experiences I have been unable to locate sufficient evidence to include more than her name here.

5. Mann, *The Female Review*, p. 75.

6. *The Female Review* indicates that Sampson made her decision in the spring of 1781 (p. 116), and in 1818 Sampson herself claimed to have enlisted at that time (see her September 14, 1818, petition for a federal pension, in the Deborah Sampson Pension File). However, other sources more credibly pinpoint the following year. See Sampson's mustering-in

certificate, in the Julia Ward Stickley Files, and Sampson's 1792 petition to the Massachusetts General Court for back pay for her services as a soldier, cited in Mann, *The Female Review*, p. xxiv. (The petition appears not in Mann's original version of the biography but in John Adams Vinton's edited version, published in 1866.)

7. See Mann, *The Female Review*, pp. 134, 227, 229; Ellet, *Women of the American Revolution*, vol. 2, pp. 149–50; Freeman and Bond, *America's First Woman Warrior*, pp. 2–3.

8. Article in *Niles's Weekly Register*, cited in Mann, *The Female Review*, p. 231.

9. See Resolve of the General Court of Massachusetts, January 20, 1792, in the Deborah Sampson Pension File.

10. In 1797 Harrison Gray Otis introduced a claim in the United States Congress for a veteran's pension for Sampson, a claim behind which the poet Philip Freneau threw his literary weight in the form of an ode to Sampson that he published in a magazine called the *Time-Piece* (Moody, "Massachusetts's Deborah Sampson," pp. 23–24). It is not clear whether Otis's petition, bolstered by Freneau's poem, was a success. If it was not, however, Herman Mann's biography of Sampson appeared the same year and all fifteen hundred copies of the book were sold, undoubtedly providing a source of income for Sampson and her family even if Mann kept a portion of the proceeds. In 1802 Sampson embarked on a lecture tour through Massachusetts, Rhode Island, and New York. At each site Sampson delivered, for a set fee, a narrative about her military service for which she typically dressed in uniform and performed an exhibition of her skills in military drill (see Sampson Diary, unnumbered pages). In 1804 Sampson again applied to the federal government for assistance, this time in the form of an invalid pension. Her request was granted on March 11, 1805, laying the groundwork for her to receive until 1818 a pension of four dollars per month retroactive to January 1, 1803. In 1818 Congress's passage of the "Act to Provide for Certain Persons Engaged in the Land and Naval Service of the United States, in the Revolutionary War" led Sampson to seek from the federal government not just an invalid pension but the full pension of a former soldier. In line with her obvious indigence—a schedule of property Sampson filed with this petition lists as her only property clothing valued at twenty dollars—the committee determined to grant

Sampson a standard veteran's pension of eight dollars per month, which she received until she died in 1827. A decade after Sampson's death, Benjamin Gannett submitted his own unprecedented claim to her veteran's pension, citing himself as the widower of a Revolutionary War soldier. Eighty-three and quite infirm himself when he applied to the federal government, Benjamin Gannett did not live long enough to see the pension committee determine, in July 1838, to grant him relief under an 1836 "Act Granting Half Pay to Widows or Orphans Where Their Husbands or Fathers Have Died of Woundes Received in the Military Service of the United States in Certain Cases, and for Other Purposes." The committee's decision came too late for Benjamin, who had died eighteen months earlier, but not too late for the Gannetts' children and grandchildren. A lump sum of $466.66 was distributed to the Gannetts' heirs, representing an eighty-dollar-per-year disbursement retroactive to 1831 and extending to the date of Benjamin's death on January 4, 1837.

11. Sources for material on Edmonds include Linus P. Brockett, *The Camp, the Battlefield, and the Hospital; or, Light and Shadows of the Great Rebellion* (Philadelphia: National Publishing, 1866), pp. 67–72; Sylvia G. L. Dannett, *She Rode with the Generals: The True and Incredible Story of Sarah Emma Seelye, Alias Franklin Thompson* (New York: Thomas Nelson & Sons, 1960); Kathleen De Grave, *Swindler, Spy, Rebel: The Confidence Woman in Nineteenth Century America* (Columbia, Mo.: University of Missouri Press, 1995); Sarah Emma Edmonds, *Nurse and Spy in the Union Army: Comprising the Adventures and Experiences of a Woman in Hospitals, Camps, and Battle-Fields* (Hartford, Conn.: W. S. Williams, 1865); Betty L. Fladeland, "New Light on Sarah Emma Edmonds Alias Franklin Thompson," *Michigan History* 47 (1963): p. 358; Betty L. Fladeland, "Sarah Emma Evelyn Edmonds," in Edward T. James and Janet W. James, eds., *Notable American Women, 1607–1950: A Biographical Dictionary* (Cambridge: Belknap Press, 1971), vol. 1, pp. 561–62; Earl W. Fornell, "A Woman in the Union Army," *American-German Review* 26–27 (February–March 1961), pp. 13–15; *Michigan Women in the Civil War* (Lansing: Michigan Civil War Centennial Observance Commission, 1963); John Robertson, *Michigan in the War* (Lansing, Mich.: W. S. George, State Printers, 1882), p. 205; Schultz, "Women at the Front"; Marian Talmadge and Iris Gilmore, *Emma Edmonds: Nurse and Spy* (New York: G. P. Putnam's Sons, 1970); Wheelwright, *Amazons and Military Maids*; Jerome John Robbins Diary,

Jerome John Robbins Papers, Michigan Historical Collections, Bentley Historical Library, University of Michigan, Ann Arbor (hereafter cited as Robbins Diary); Military Service Records of Franklin Thompson, Co. F. 2nd Michigan Infantry, in RG 94, Records of the Adjutant General's Office, Compiled Military Service Records, National Archives, Washington, D.C.; and RG 15, Records of the Veterans Administration, Sarah Emma Edmonds Seelye Pension File, application #526889, certificate #232136, National Archives, Washington, D.C. (hereafter cited as Sarah Edmonds Pension File).

12. Bell Irvin Wiley, *The Life of Billy Yank: The Common Soldier of the Union* (Baton Rouge: Louisiana State University Press, 1952, 1971), pp. 45–47.

13. Military Service Records of Franklin Thompson; Report No. 939, 49th Cong., 1st sess. (to accompany H.R. 1172), pp. 9–10, in the Sarah Edmonds Pension File.

14. Report No. 820, 48th Cong., 1st sess. (to accompany H.R. 5334), p. 2, in the Sarah Edmonds Pension File. The description of Edmonds as "effeminate" contrasts considerably with the description of her that appeared in an obituary claiming that she was a "tall, raw-boned [woman], with a harsh voice, and masculine features . . . [who] appeared in many respects more like a man. . . ." See undated, unidentified newspaper obituary in the Jerome John Robbins Papers, Michigan Historical Collections, Bentley Historical Library, University of Michigan, Ann Arbor.

15. Fladeland, "Sarah Emma Evelyn Edmonds," p. 561. Fladeland here quotes an army acquaintance of Edmonds's, speaking in 1900 to a journalist for the *Lansing State Republican*.

16. Report No. 836, 48th Cong., 1st sess. (to accompany H.R. 5335), p. 1, in the Sarah Edmonds Pension File. See also the individual testimony of various former soldiers in Report No. 820, 28th Cong., 1st sess. (to accompany H.R. 5334), pp. 4–7, also in the Sarah Edmonds Pension File.

17. Robbins Diary.

18. Ibid. See also Fladeland, "New Light on Sarah Emma Edmonds," for her discussion of the relationship between Robbins and Edmonds and Robbins's response to Edmonds's confession.

19. Robbins Diary.

20. Ibid.

21. Sarah Emma Edmonds to Jerome John Robbins, January 16, 1863, in the Jerome John Robbins Papers.

22. Robbins Diary.

23. Ibid.

24. Report No. 820, 48th Cong., 1st sess. (to accompany H.R. 5334), pp. 5–9, in the Sarah Edmonds Pension File; Robertson, *Michigan in the War*, p. 205.

25. See William Boston Diary, April 23, 1863, in the Michigan Historical Collections, Bentley Historical Library, Ann Arbor.

26. S. Emma E. Edmonds, *Unsexed; or, The Female Soldier: The Thrilling Adventures, Experiences and Escapes of a Woman, as Nurse, Spy, and Scout, in Hospitals, Camp and Battlefields* (Philadelphia: Philadelphia Publishing, 1864), p. 6.

27. Sources for material on Pitman include RG 110, Provost Marshal General's Bureau, List of Scouts, Guides, Spies and Detectives, National Archives, Washington, D.C.; RG 109, Union Provost Marshal's File of Two- or More-Named Papers Relating to Citizens, file #7656, National Archives, Washington, D.C.; *The War of the Rebellion: The Official Records of the Union and Confederate Armies* (Washington, D.C.: Government Printing Office, 1881–1902), ser. 2, vol. 7, pp. 314–17, 345–55, 930–53; and Michael Fellman, "Women and Guerrilla Warfare," pp. 147–65, in Catherine Clinton and Nina Silber, eds., *Divided Houses: Gender and the Civil War* (New York: Oxford University Press, 1992).

28. Robertson, *Michigan in the War*, p. 205. See also an undated, unidentified newspaper obituary of Edmonds in the Jerome John Robbins Papers; Brockett, *The Camp, the Battlefield, and the Hospital*, pp. 67–72; and George Barton, *The World's Greatest Military Spies and Secret Service Agents* (Boston: Page, 1918), pp. 223–40.

29. Report No. 820, 48th Cong., 1st sess. (to accompany H.R. 5334), pp. 3, 9, in the Sarah Edmonds Pension File. See also Dannett, *She Rode with the Generals*, p. 235; Fladeland, "Sarah Emma Evelyn Edmonds," p. 562; Fornell, "A Woman in the Union Army," p. 14.

30. Wheelwright, *Amazons and Military Maids*, pp. 100, 138; Dannett, *She Rode with the Generals*, p. 221.

31. Report No. 820, 48th Cong., 1st sess. (to accompany H.R. 5334), p. 3, in the Sarah Edmonds Pension File.

32. See chapter 7 for Emma Porch's story.

33. See Statutes of the United States, 48th Cong., 1st sess., chap. 298 (July 5, 1884); H.R. 5335, dated February 25, 1884; H.R. 5334, 48th Cong., 1st sess.; Pat Lammers and Amy Boyce, "A Female in the Ranks," *Civil War Times Illustrated* 22 (January 1984): p. 30; Fornell, "A Woman in the Union Army," p. 13; *Houston Daily Post*, June 2, 1901.

34. Sources for material on Hodgers include Gerhard Clausius, "The Little Soldier of the 95th: Albert D. J. Cashier," *Journal of the Illinois State Historical Society* 51 (Winter 1958): pp. 380–87; Schultz, "Women at the Front"; Wheelwright, *Amazons and Military Maids*; and RG 15, Records of the Veterans Administration, Albert D. J. Cashier Pension File, application #755646, certificate #1001132, National Archives, Washington, D.C. (hereafter cited as Albert Cashier Pension File); Medical Records of Albert Cashier, in RG 94, Records of the Adjutant General's Office, Carded Medical Records, Mexican and Civil Wars, National Archives, Washington, D.C.; and Military Service Records of Albert D. J. Cashier, 95th Illinois Infantry, in RG 94, Records of the Adjutant General's Office, Compiled Military Service Records, National Archives, Washington, D.C.

Many thanks also to Philip A. Gonyar of Waterville, Maine, and Anthony Thorsen of the Dwight Historical Society in Dwight, Illinois, for sending me numerous clippings and other documents relating to Hodgers's story.

35. James M. McPherson, *Ordeal by Fire: The Civil War and Reconstruction* (New York: Alfred A. Knopf, 1982), p. 383; Burgess, *An Uncommon Soldier*, p. 82.

36. Clausius, "The Little Soldier of the 95th," p. 381; "Sketch of the 95th Illinois from the Department of the Interior," dated November 12, 1913, in the Albert Cashier Pension File.

37. See the depositions of Charles W. Ives (January 9, 1915), Joy Saxton (December 1, 1914), Eli Brainerd (December 1, 1914), Robert Horan (December 1, 1914), and Robert D. Hannah (January 24, 1915), and Robert D. Hannah's response to a questionnaire sent out by the Bureau of Pensions, dated January 6, 1915, all in the Albert Cashier Pension File.

38. There is some evidence to suggest that a couple of townsfolk had become aware of Hodgers's sex a year earlier. According to one source, "Cashier" became ill in 1910 and her neighbor, a Mrs. Lannon, sent a nurse to attend to her. "It wasn't long," the source claims, "before the nurse ran back exclaiming 'My Lord, Mrs. Lannon, he's a full-fledged

woman!'" (see Sue Cummings, "Cashier Battled Confederates; Then She Fought Social Rules," in the Albert D. J. Cashier Papers, Dwight Historical Society, Dwight, Ill.).

39. Jody Bourne, "Woman Recalls Saunemin's Best-Known Civil War Vet," *Dwight* (Illinois) *Star and Herald*, March 21, 1991. Born in 1904, Morehart recalled that Hodgers "used to take a stepladder around town and turn the street lights on. A few hours later, he would go around and turn them off again." Morehart also noted that Hodgers, who functioned among other things as a local church caretaker, taught her how to ring the church bells and would occasionally come to her house to comfort her and her siblings on stormy evenings when their own father, a night watchman, was at work (ibid.).

40. Board of Review Report, dated February 3, 1915, from the Bureau of Pensions, in the Albert Cashier Pension File.

41. Cummings, "Cashier Battled Confederates."

42. Clausius, "The Little Soldier of the 95th," p. 386; depositions of Charles W. Ives and Leroy S. Scott in the Albert Cashier Pension File.

43. Deposition of Nettie Chesbro Rose in the Albert Cashier Pension File.

44. Sources for material on Wakeman include Burgess, *An Uncommon Soldier*; Military Service Record of Lyons Wakeman, in RG 94, Records of the Adjutant General's Office, Compiled Military Service Records, National Archives, Washington, D.C.; Medical Record of Lyons Wakeman, in RG 94, Records of the Adjutant General's Office, Carded Medical Records, Mexican and Civil Wars, National Archives, Washington, D.C.

45. Burgess, *An Uncommon Soldier*, pp. 31, 18, 21.

46. Ibid., p. 18.

47. Ibid., pp. 21–22.

48. Ibid., pp. 22, 23. See also card #2, Medical Record of Lyons Wakeman, in RG 94, Records of the Adjutant General's Office, Carded Medical Records, Mexican and Civil Wars, National Archives, Washington, D.C.

49. Burgess, *An Uncommon Soldier*, pp. 25–27, 31, 40, 48, 58.

50. Ibid., pp. 25, 54, 58.

51. Ibid., pp. 28, 42, 53, 60.

52. Ibid., p. 52.

53. Ibid., pp. 55, 64, 65.

54. Ibid., p. 71.

55. Military Service Record of Lyons Wakeman, in RG 94, Records of the Adjutant General's Office, Compiled Military Service Records, National Archives, Washington, D.C. See also card #3, Medical Record of Lyons Wakeman, in RG 94, Records of the Adjutant General's Office, Carded Medical Records, Mexican and Civil Wars, National Archives, Washington, D.C.

## Chapter Six

1. Quote from the diary of Confederate enthusiast Sarah Morgan, who yearned to go to war as a soldier, in Francis Butler Simkins and James Welch Patton, *The Women of the Confederacy* (New York: Garrett & Massie, 1936; reprint, St. Clair Shores, Mich.: Scholarly Press, 1976), p. 74.

2. Irene Bell, Annie Samuels, et al. to "J. E. [*sic*] Seddon," December 2, 1864, in RG 109, Letters Received by the Confederate Secretary of War, 1861–1865, National Archives, Washington, D.C. See also New York *Evening Express*, May 29, 1861; and *Frank Leslie's Illustrated Newspaper*, April 30, 1861.

3. James B. Kennedy to the MINERVA list, September 29, 1995; Simkins and Patton, *The Women of the Confederacy*, p. 74.

4. Rose Greenhow, *My Imprisonment, and the First Year of Abolition Rule at Washington* (London: Richard Bentley, 1863), pp. 258–59. See also *The War of the Rebellion: The Official Records of the Union and Confederate Armies* (Washington, D.C.: Government Printing Office, 1881–1902), ser. 2, vol. 2, p. 272 (hereafter cited as *Official Records*).

Not all such impostors were equally successful in turning their masquerades as men or as soldiers into tools of effective espionage, and needless to say, in such cases, disclosure of a woman's identity could bring with it a great deal of ridicule. See the story of Sarah E. Mitchel, alias "Charles Wilson," in the *New York Herald*, August 19, 1864.

5. George Worthington Adams, *Doctors in Blue: The Medical History of the Union Army in the Civil War* (New York: Henry Schuman, 1952), p. 12.

6. Lauren Cook Burgess, ed., *An Uncommon Soldier: The Civil War Letters of Sarah Rosetta Wakeman, Alias Pvt. Lyons Wakeman, 153rd Regiment, New York State Volunteers, 1862–1864* (Pasadena, Md.: MINERVA Center,

1994), p. 203; Bell Irvin Wiley, *The Life of Billy Yank: The Common Soldier of the Union* (Baton Rouge: Louisiana State University Press, 1952, 1971), pp. 23, 125; Adams, *Doctors in Blue*, p. 12.

With considerable crudeness, Henry Schelling of Company F of the 64th Illinois Infantry reportedly wrote to a friend on November 21, 1863, of a new recruit who had joined the regiment while it was on its way to Eastport, Tennessee, and who had failed to overcome the obstacle of the physical. "On examination," Schelling wrote, "he proved to have a Cunt so he was discharged. I was sorry for it, for I wanted him for a Bedfellow" (Thomas P. Lowry, *The Story the Soldiers Wouldn't Tell: Sex in the Civil War* [Mechanicsburg, Pa.: Stackpole Books, 1994], p. 35).

7. Wiley, *The Life of Billy Yank*, pp. 54, 49, 64. See also Burgess, *An Uncommon Soldier*, p. 3.

8. Burgess, *An Uncommon Soldier*, p. 3. See also Sylvia G. L. Dannett, *She Rode with the Generals: The True and Incredible Story of Sarah Emma Seelye, Alias Franklin Thompson* (New York: Thomas Nelson & Sons, 1960), pp. 56–57.

9. I thank Judith Bielecki, who reenacts as a private in the 20th Maine Infantry, for her comments on this question. On the nature of Civil War soldiers' uniforms, see Wiley, *The Life of Billy Yank*, pp. 58–65.

10. Burgess, *An Uncommon Soldier*, p. 4; Wiley, *The Life of Billy Yank*, pp. 298–300.

11. Burgess, *An Uncommon Soldier*, p. 3; Lauren Cook Burgess, "Typical Soldier May Have Been Red-blooded American Woman," *Washington Times*, October 5, 1991.

12. Report No. 929, 49th Cong., 1st sess. (to accompany H.R. 1172), p. 10; Burgess, *An Uncommon Soldier*, p. 3.

13. Burgess, *An Uncommon Soldier*, p. 3.

14. "The Dead Soldier Was a Woman," in RG 94, Records of the Adjutant General's Office, Administrative Precedent File ("Frech File") #3H36, National Archives, Washington, D.C.

15. Card #429572, Records and Pension Office Record Cards, in RG 94, Records of the Adjutant General's Office, National Archives, Washington, D.C.

16. Raymond J. Herek, "A Woman in Regimentals," *Civil War Times Illustrated* 22 (January 1984): p. 31.

17. Wiley, *The Life of Billy Yank*, p. 339.

18. Owensburg, Kentucky, *Monitor*, August 20, 1862; *Frank Leslie's Illustrated Newspaper*, July 19, 1862 (see also Jane Ellen Schultz, "Women at the Front: Gender and Genre in Literature of the American Civil War" [Ph.D. diss., University of Michigan, Ann Arbor, 1988], pp. 290–91).

19. Detroit *Advertiser and Tribune*, February 25, 1863 (see also Mary Elizabeth Massey, *Bonnet Brigades* [New York: Alfred A. Knopf, 1966], p. 80); Webb Garrison, "Southern Women Helped Soldiers in Gray," *Atlanta Constitution*, November 26, 1989; Schultz, "Women at the Front," pp. 284–85.

20. Ethel Alice Hurn, *Wisconsin Women in the War Between the States* (Madison: Wisconsin History Commission, 1911), p. 103 (see also Massey, *Bonnet Brigades*, p. 80; and Richard C. Hall, *Patriots in Disguise: Women Warriors of the Civil War* [New York: Paragon House, 1993], p. 19); Maysville, Kentucky, *Dollar Weekly Bulletin*, November 27, 1862; Albert D. Richardson, *The Secret Service: The Field, the Dungeon, and the Escape* (Hartford, Conn.: American Publishing, 1865), p. 175; "Hid Sex in the Army," in RG 94, Records of the Adjutant General's Office, Administrative Precedent File ("Frech File") #3H36, National Archives, Washington, D.C. (see also *New York Times*, April 4, 1915; and Schultz, "Women at the Front," p. 285).

21. Mary A. Livermore, *My Story of the War* (Hartford, Conn.: A. D. Worthington, 1889), pp. 113–14. See also Massey, *Bonnet Brigades*, p. 80.

22. "Sarah E. E. Seelye Fought in the Civil War," in RG 94, Records of the Adjutant General's Office, Administrative Precedent File ("Frech File") #3H36, National Archives, Washington, D.C.; War Department Memorandum dated January 14, 1892, in RG 94, Records of the Adjutant General's Office, Administrative Precedent File ("Frech File") #3H36, National Archives, Washington, D.C.; Medical Record of Charles Freeman, in RG 94, Records of the Adjutant General's Office, Carded Medical Records, Mexican and Civil Wars, National Archives, Washington, D.C.; and Kentucky reg. #121 and Kentucky reg. #394, in RG 94, Records of the Adjutant General's Office, Hospital Registers, Civil War, National Archives, Washington, D.C.; "A Heroine," *The Sibyl* 8 (July 1863): p. 1157; *The Sibyl* 9 (January 1864): p. 1.

23. "A Romantic History: The Story of a Female Soldier," *The Sibyl* 7 (June 1863): p. 1150. See also "Charlie" to "Dear father," May 1, 1863, in the David O. Woodruff Papers, Bentley Historical Library, University of

Michigan, Ann Arbor; Schultz, "Women at the Front," p. 280; and Hall, *Patriots in Disguise*, pp. 26–27.

24. *Frank Leslie's Illustrated Newspaper*, October 31, 1863; *New York Times*, April 4, 1915; *New York Herald*, August 12, 1864. See also Massey, *Bonnet Brigades*, p. 80; Schultz, "Women at the Front," p. 285; *New York Times*, April 4, 1915); *New York Herald*, August 14, 1864; and John Laffin, *Women in Battle* (New York: Abelard-Schuman, 1967), p. 52.

25. Wellsburg, West Virginia, *Weekly Herald*, October 9, 1863; *Frank Leslie's Illustrated Newspaper*, October 31, 1863. See also Hall, *Patriots in Disguise*, pp. 27–28; Schultz, "Women at the Front," p. 290; and Massey, *Bonnet Brigades*, p. 80.

26. Jackson *Mississippian*, December 30, 1862. See also Simkins and Patton, *The Women of the Confederacy*, p. 80; Lowry, *The Story the Soldiers Wouldn't Tell*, p. 122; Schultz, "Women at the Front," pp. 289–90; and Massey, *Bonnet Brigades*, p. 81.

27. Cairo, Illinois, *City Gazette*, December 25, 1862; Massey, *Bonnet Brigades*, p. 81; Robert Hodges to "My Dear Father," August 7, 1863, quoted in *East Texas Historical Journal* 9 (1971): pp. 37–38.

28. Schultz, "Women at the Front," p. 288; Massey, *Bonnet Brigades*, p. 84; Agatha Young, *The Women and the Crisis: Women of the North in the Civil War* (New York: McDowell, Obolensky, 1959), p. 97; *New York Times*, May 27, 1934; DeAnne Blanton, "Women Soldiers of the Civil War," *Prologue* 25 (Spring 1993): p. 32; Schultz, "Women at the Front," p. 288.

29. "A Gallant Female Soldier—Romantic History," *The Sibyl* 8 (April 1864): p. 1231. See also *New York Times*, April 4, 1915; card #2, AGO Document File Record Cards #1502399, in RG 94, Records of the Adjutant General's Office, National Archives, Washington, D.C.; Tennessee reg. #363 and Tennessee reg. #412, in RG 94, Records of the Adjutant General's Office, Hospital Registers, Civil War, National Archives, Washington, D.C.; and "Hid Sex in the Army," in RG 94, Records of the Adjutant General's Office, Administrative Precedent File ("Frech File") #3H35, National Archives, Washington, D.C.

At least one modern source confuses Frances Hook with a woman who served with the 25th Michigan under the alias "Frank Martin" (apparently a common alias). See Hall, *Patriots in Disguise*, pp. 26–27. A 1915 *New York Times* article discusses a woman who supposedly served as "Frank Henderson" in the 19th Illinois. But "Henderson"'s story sounds

# Notes to pages 217–21

much like the story of Frances Hook, and I believe the *Times* article is in error.

30. Sources for material on Blalock include Greg Mast, "'Sam' Blaylock, 26th North Carolina Troops," *Military Images* 11 (July–August 1989): p. 10; Bell Irvin Wiley, *The Life of Johnny Reb: The Common Soldier of the Confederacy* (Baton Rouge: Louisiana State University Press, 1943, 1970, 1978), p. 334; Massey, *Bonnet Brigades*, p. 81; Simkins and Patton, *The Women of the Confederacy*, p. 80; Lowry, *The Story the Soldiers Wouldn't Tell*, p. 122; Garrison, "Southern Women Helped Soldiers in Gray"; John A. Wyeth to "My dear Doctor," April 1, 1909, in file #1507832, in RG 94, Records of the Adjutant General's Office, Records and Pension Office Document File #184934, National Archives, Washington, D.C.; Military Service Record of S. M. Blaylock, in RG 109, War Department Collection of Confederate Records, Compiled Military Service Records, National Archives, Washington, D.C.

31. Sandusky, Ohio, *Commercial Register*, December 12, 1864. See also Burgess, *An Uncommon Soldier*, pp. 4–5; and Bell Irvin Wiley, *Confederate Women* (Westport, Conn.: Greenwood Press, 1975), p. 142.

32. Massey, *Bonnet Brigades*, p. 84; Paul H. Haas, "A Volunteer Nurse in the Civil War: The Diary of Harriet Douglas Whetten," *Wisconsin Magazine of History* 48 (Winter 1964–65): p. 217.

33. Burgess, *An Uncommon Soldier*, pp. 4–5. See also ibid., p. xii.

34. W. E. Beard to General Marcus J. Wright, January 1, 1920, in RG 94, Records of the Adjutant General's Office, Administrative Precedent File ("Frech File") #3H36, National Archives, Washington, D.C.; Fred Brooks, "Shiloh Mystery Woman," *Civil War Times Illustrated* 17 (August 1978): p. 29. See also *Official Records*, ser. 1, vol. 27, pt. 1, p. 378.

35. Ted Alexander, ed., *The 126th Pennsylvania* (Shippensburg, Pa.: Beidel Printing House, 1984), pp. 20, 40; Military Service Record of Frank Mayne, in RG 94, Records of the Adjutant General's Office, Compiled Military Service Records, National Archives, Washington, D.C. See also Hall, *Patriots in Disguise*, p. 20.

36. Military Service Record of John Williams, in RG 94, Records of the Adjutant General's Office, Compiled Military Service Records, National Archives, Washington, D.C.; Military Service Record of William Bradley, in RG 109, War Department Collection of Confederate Records, Compiled Military Service Records, National Archives, Washington,

D.C.; *Frank Leslie's Illustrated Newspaper*, July 19, 1862 (see also Schultz, "Women at the Front," pp. 290–91).

37. Livermore, *My Story of the War*, p. 119. See also Hall, *Patriots in Disguise*, p. 18; Hurn, *Wisconsin Women in the War Between the States*, p. 103; and Massey, *Bonnet Brigades*, p. 80.

38. *Richmond Daily Examiner*, September 3, 1864. See also Schultz, "Women at the Front," p. 287.

39. *Richmond Whig*, February 20, 1865. In his science fiction novel about the Civil War, *Guns of the South*, Harry Turtledove uses the 47th North Carolina as his focus, and he includes a fictionalized Mollie Bean in the regiment. In the "Historical Notes" he appended to the novel, Turtledove admits to having "taken a novelist's liberty in imagining why Bean joined the 47th in the first place" (Harry Turtledove, *Guns of the South* [New York: Ballantine Books, 1992], p. 559). Turtledove casts Bean as a former prostitute who enlists and fights with her regiment, but whose identity is known by at least some of the men. Turtledove's Bean continues to have paid sex with several of her fellow soldiers, although there is no reason to assume that the historical Bean did so (see chapter 7). I am grateful to James M. McPherson for bringing Turtledove's novel to my attention.

40. "Served by Her Lover's Side," in RG 94, Records of the Adjutant General's Office, Administrative Precedent File ("Frech File") #3H36, National Archives, Washington, D.C. See also Betty Ingraham, "And of Mary Owen[s] Jenkins," *Civil War Times*, June 1959, p. 7 (I thank Philip A. Gonyar of Waterville, Maine, for sending me this article); and Lowry, *The Story the Soldiers Wouldn't Tell*, p. 121; Blanton, "Women Soldiers of the Civil War," p. 28; Massey, *Bonnet Brigades*, p. 80; Schultz, "Women at the Front," p. 290; *New York Times*, April 4, 1915.

41. Charlestown, West Virginia, *Farmer's Advocate*, July 30, 1898 (see also Schultz, "Women at the Front," p. 292); *New York Times*, April 4, 1915; "Woman Who Fought in Civil War Beside Hubby Dies, Aged Ninety-two," in RG 94, Records of the Adjutant General's Office, Administrative Precedent File ("Frech File") #3H36, National Archives, Washington, D.C. (see also Lowry, *The Story the Soldiers Wouldn't Tell*, pp. 121–22).

42. On Compton, see Massey, *Bonnet Brigades*, p. 80, and Lowry, *The Story the Soldiers Wouldn't Tell*, p. 122; on Henry and Wright, see Massey,

*Bonnet Brigades*, and Schultz, "Women at the Front," p. 288; on Davidson, see Schultz, "Women at the Front," p. 290; on Hunt, see Blanton, "Women Soldiers of the Civil War," p. 28; on Lillybridge, see *New York Times*, April 4, 1915, and Laffin, *Women in Battle*, p. 51;

For additional accounts, see Schultz, "Women at the Front," pp. 288, 286; and Laffin, *Women in Battle*, pp. 51–52.

## Chapter Seven

1. Curtis Carroll Davis, "Effie Goldsborough: Confederate Courier," *Civil War Times Illustrated* 7 (April 1968): p. 30.

2. Charles Welsey Alexander, *Pauline of the Potomac; or, General McClellan's Spy* (Philadelphia: Barclay, 1862), pp. 26, 33.

3. Charles Welsey Alexander, *General Sherman's Indian Spy* (Philadelphia: C. W. Alexander, 1865), pp. 20–21, 59.

4. Charles Wesley Alexander, *The Picket Slayer* (Philadelphia: C. W. Alexander, 1863), pp. 24–25; 30–31, 44, 67.

5. Rose Greenhow, *My Imprisonment, and the First Year of Abolition Rule at Washington* (London: Richard Bentley, 1863), pp. 7, 93–94.

A handful of contemporary observers believed that Greenhow's patriotism was accompanied by a desire to maintain her unearned social status by proving herself in the business of wartime intrigue. See William E. Doster, *Lincoln and Episodes of the Civil War* (New York: G. P. Putnam & Sons, 1915), pp. 81–83; Jane Ellen Schultz, "Women at the Front: Gender and Genre in Literature of the American Civil War" (Ph.D. diss., University of Michigan, Ann Arbor, 1988), pp. 295–96; and C. Vann Woodward and Elisabeth Muhlenfeld, *The Private Mary Chesnut: The Unpublished Civil War Diaries* (New York: Oxford University Press, 1984), p. 146. See also Edwin C. Fishel, *The Secret War for the Union: The Untold Story of Military Intelligence in the Civil War* (Boston: Houghton Mifflin, 1996), p. 59.

6. Mary Elizabeth Massey, *Bonnet Brigades* (New York: Alfred A. Knopf, 1966), pp. 87–89; Oscar A. Kinchen, *Women Who Spied for the Blue and Gray* (Philadelphia: Dorrance, 1972), pp. 1–2.

7. *New York Herald*, August 3, 1862; from a May 1867 letter from Benjamin F. Butler to Elizabeth Van Lew, quoted in David D. Ryan, *A Yankee Spy in Richmond: The Civil War Diary of "Crazy Bet" Van Lew* (Mechanicsburg, Pa.: Stackpole Books, 1996), pp. 119–20.

8. Alexander, *Pauline of the Potomac*, pp. 46–47, 55. To Grant, Pauline reiterates this position, adding, "I have never yet received from the Government a dollar, and so long as the remnant of my own fortune . . . lasts, so long will I continue to receive nothing" (Charles Wesley Alexander, *Maud of the Mississippi: General Grant's Daring Spy* [Philadelphia: C. W. Alexander, 1863], pp. 28, 100).

9. Alexander, *General Sherman's Indian Spy*, p. 23. Unlike Pauline, Wenonah does accept money to defray her expenses (ibid., p. 25). Presumably the "Indian maiden" does not have a small fortune to tap into in the way that the French aristocrat's daughter does.

As for Mary Murdock, the issue of payment for services does not arise, for perhaps obvious reasons: as depicted, the twisted, tormented creature who is the central character in *The Picket Slayer* does the work of the devil, and therefore her most satisfying reward can only be the letting of her enemy's blood.

10. *The War of the Rebellion: The Official Records of the Union and Confederate Armies* (Washington, D.C.: Government Printing Office, 1881–1902), ser. 1, vol. 29, pt. 2, p. 199 (Mrs. Charles Swartz); ser. 1, vol. 34, pt. 2, p. 213 (Mrs. Byrne); ser. 1, vol. 39, pt. 3, p. 58 (Mary McNell); ser. 1, vol. 49, pt. 2, p. 179 (Mrs. Whitely). (This source hereafter cited as *Official Records*.)

Military officials also describe a number of women who appear in the *Official Records* as "messengers," and I assume that these women were also paid for their work. See, for example, ser. 1, vol. 20, pt. 2, p. 280 (Miss Collins); ser. 1, vol. 20, pt. 2, p. 212 (two Mrs. Smiths); ser. 1, vol. 31, pt. 1, p. 204 (Miss Reed); and ser. 1, vol. 35, pt. 1, p. 493 (Mrs. Fribley). Not all "messengers" provided the quality of intelligence that those sending them hoped for. See the case of Miss Lottie Browning: *Official Records*, ser. 1, vol. 12, pt. 3, p. 166.

11. On Susan Bond, see RG 393, Special Orders, District of South West Missouri, pt. 2, Special Orders No. 260 (September 26, 1864), National Archives, Washington, D.C. (hereafter cited as SO-SWMO); and SO-SWMO, Special Orders No. 306 (November 16, 1864); see also *Official Records*, ser. 1, vol. 41, pt. 4, p. 512. On Rhoden, see RG 110, Provost Marshal General's Bureau, List of Scouts, Guides, Spies and Detectives, box 4, National Archives, Washington, D.C. See also the case of Mary Martin: *Official Records*, ser. 1, vol. 41, pt. 3, p. 216; ser. 1, vol.

41, pt. 3, p. 788; RG 110, Provost Marshal General's Bureau, List of Scouts, Guides, Spies and Detectives, box 4, National Archives, Washington, D.C.; and SO-SWMO, Special Orders No. 260 (September 26, 1864), Special Orders No. 302 (November 12, 1864), and Special Orders No. 304 (November 14, 1864).

12. For Abells, Childers, Nutter, Phillips, Shell, and Myers, see RG 110, Provost Marshal General's Bureau, List of Scouts, Guides, Spies and Detectives, boxes 1, 4, and 5, National Archives, Washington, D.C. (The same source [box 4] includes one of Hester Myers's reports, dated April 8, 1863, from Point of Rocks, Maryland, which she signed "Yours to Command, Hester A. Myers, U. S. Detective.") For Abells, see also Fishel, *The Secret War for the Union*, pp. 253–54, 639. For Hensley, see SO-SWMO, Special Orders No. 220 (August 17, 1864) and Special Orders No. 237 (September 3, 1864).

See also RG 110, Provost Marshal General's Bureau, List of Scouts, Guides, Spies and Detectives, National Archives, Washington, D.C. (Mrs. Brill, Mary Root, Mrs. Alice Williams, Mary Price); RG 393, Special Orders, District of Middle Tennessee, pt. 2, bk. 174 (orders of October 3 and November 29, 1864), National Archives, Washington, D.C. (Ellen Hinson); and RG 393, Special Orders, District of Middle Tennessee, pt. 2, bk. 174 (orders of June 9, 1864), National Archives, Washington, D.C. (Mrs. and Miss Satery).

13. *Official Records*, ser. 1, vol. 47, pt. 2, pp. 395–97. There is no record of Sherman's response.

14. RG 110, Provost Marshal General's Bureau, List of Scouts, Guides, Spies and Detectives, boxes 1 and 5, National Archives, Washington, D.C.

15. On Morris, see *New York Herald*, February 11, 1862; Massey, *Bonnet Brigades*, p. 96; Doster, *Lincoln and Episodes of the Civil War*, p. 83; *Official Records*, ser. 2, vol. 2, pp. 1346–51.

16. *Official Records*, ser. 2, vol. 2, pp. 1349.

17. Ibid., ser. 1, vol. 51, pt. 2, p. 341.

18. RG 110, Provost Marshal General's Bureau, List of Scouts, Guides, Spies and Detectives, box 5, National Archives, Washington, D.C.; Schultz, "Women at the Front," pp. 300–301; Cyrus Bursy to Commissioner of Pensions, September 18, 1890, in RG 15, Records of the Veterans Administration, Emma Smith Porch Pension File, certificate

#276360, National Archives, Washington, D.C. (hereafter cited as Emma Porch Pension File).

19. Deposition for original pension claim, June 16, 1874; Cyrus Bursy to Commissioner of Pensions, September 18, 1890; unnamed document dated March 13, 1896; and report to accompany H.R. 3294, March 4, 1884, all in the Emma Porch Pension File; see also Schultz, "Women at the Front," p. 301.

20. Cyrus Bursy to Commissioner of Pensions, September 18, 1890; Webster Davis to Commissioner of Pensions, July 30, 1898; and Emma Porch to Hon. H. M. Cockrell, February 3, 1896, all in the Emma Porch Pension File.

21. On Baxley, see *Official Records*, ser. 2, vol. 2, p. 1315; Massey, *Bonnet Brigades*, p. 95; Schultz, "Women at the Front," pp. 299–300; Doster, *Lincoln and Episodes of the Civil War*, p. 84. See also Baxley's personal papers at the New York Public Library.

22. *Official Records*, ser. 2, vol. 2, p. 1315.

23. Frank Moore, *Women of the War: Their Heroism and Self-Sacrifice* (Hartford, Conn.: S. S. Scranton, 1866), p. 529.

24. Ibid., pp. 529–30. See also Massey, *Bonnet Brigades*, pp. 79–80; Schultz, "Women at the Front," p. 289; and *New York Times*, April 4, 1915.

25. Linus P. Brockett and Mary C. Vaughan, *Woman's Work in the Civil War: A Record of Heroism, Patriotism, and Patience* (Philadelphia: Zeigler, McCurdy, 1867), p. 770.

26. See, for example, Bell Irvin Wiley, *The Life of Billy Yank: The Common Soldier of the Union* (Baton Rouge: Louisiana State University Press, 1952, 1971), p. 338; Bell Irvin Wiley, *The Life of Johnny Reb: The Common Soldier of the Confederacy* (Baton Rouge: Louisiana State University Press, 1943, 1970, 1978), p. 334; Bell Irvin Wiley, *Confederate Women* (Westport, Conn.: Greenwood Press, 1975), p. 142; Massey, *Bonnet Brigades*, p. 79; Schultz, "Women at the Front," pp. 270, 287–88, 273; John Laffin, *Women in Battle* (New York: Abelard-Schuman, 1967), p. 14; Thomas P. Lowry, *The Story the Soldiers Wouldn't Tell: Sex in the Civil War* (Mechanicsburg, Pa.: Stackpole Books, 1994), p. 122; and Richard C. Hall, *Patriots in Disguise: Women Warriors of the Civil War* (New York: Paragon House, 1993), p. xii.

27. Such was clearly the case with woman soldiers Malinda Blaylock, Florena Budwin, Mary Burns, Amy Clarke alias "Joshua Clarke," Frances

Clayton, Sarah Collins, Catherine Davidson, Frances Day, Marian Green alias "Frank Henderson," Frances Hook, Satronia Smith Hunt, Mary Owens Jenkins, Annie Lillybridge, Elizabeth Niles, Mary Siezgle, Fanny Wilson, Mary Walters, and many others whose names we do not know.

28. See the stories of Amy Clarke alias "Joshua Clarke," Frances Clayton, Frances Day alias "Frank Henderson," Frances Hook, Satronia Smith Hunt, Mary Owens Jenkins, Annie Lillybridge, Fanny Wilson, and Mary Walters.

29. See, for example, Julie Wheelwright, *Amazons and Military Maids: Women Who Dressed as Men in the Pursuit of Life, Liberty and Happiness* (London: Pandora Press, 1989).

30. Wiley, *The Life of Billy Yank*, p. 338. See also Wiley, *The Life of Johnny Reb*, p. 334; Massey, *Bonnet Brigades*, p. 79; Schultz, "Women at the Front," p. 274.

31. B. A. Botkin, *A Civil War Treasury of Tales, Legends, and Folklore* (New York: Random House, 1960), pp. 313–14. See also Wheelwright, *Amazons and Military Maids*, pp. 26–27; Lowry, *The Story the Soldiers Wouldn't Tell*, p. 122.

32. Military Service Record of Henry Fitzallen, in RG 94, Records of the Adjutant General's Office, Compiled Military Service Records, National Archives, Washington, D.C.; *Official Records*, ser. 2, vol. 5, pp. 121–22, 155, 166, 547–48.

33. John Hunt and Bill McIlwain, "The Battling Belles," *American Mercury* 78 (March 1954): pp. 13–15; *Richmond Daily Examiner*, October 31 and November 25, 1864. See also Massey, *Bonnet Brigades*, p. 84; and Lowry, *The Story the Soldiers Wouldn't Tell*, p. 33.

34. Hunt and McIlwain, "The Battling Belles," p. 14. See also Lauren Cook Burgess, ed., *An Uncommon Soldier: The Civil War Letters of Sarah Rosetta Wakeman, Alias Pvt. Lyons Wakeman, 153rd Regiment, New York State Volunteers, 1862–1864* (Pasadena, Md.: MINERVA Center, 1994), p. 6.

35. *Richmond Daily Examiner*, October 31, 1864.

36. Hunt and McIlwain, "The Battling Belles," p. 15.

37. See R. Blacknall to J. N. Beach, August 8, 1872; deposition of Leddy Garrett, August 10, 1872; deposition of Edmund Hill, August 9, 1872; deposition of Jane Dick, August 10, 1872; and deposition of Eugene Eckels, undated; all in RG 107, Records of the Office of the Secretary of War, Records Concerning the Conduct and Loyalty of

Certain Union Army Officers, Civilian Employees of the War Department and U.S. Citizens During the Civil War, National Archives, Washington, D.C. See also Lowry, *The Story the Soldiers Wouldn't Tell*, p. 145.

38. RG 153, Records of the Office of the Judge Advocate General (Army), Court Martial Case File #II 704, Court Martial of Jerome B. Taft, National Archives, Washington, D.C.

39. Ibid. Some testimony in the case suggests that Merrill was initially known in camp not as "Frederick Woods" but as "Charles Johnson." Other evidence suggests that she was involved with the man whom Taft indicated, James Miller. Of course, being the mistress of an officer would by no means preclude Merrill's providing effective service as a soldier herself.

See also the curious history of Annie Jones, for which the most pertinent sources are the *New York Herald*, September 16 and 21, 1863; Lafayette C. Baker, *History of the United States Secret Service* (Philadelphia: L. C. Baker, 1867), pp. 385–87; and Schultz, "Women at the Front," p. 217.

For glimpses of other women who apparently donned soldiers' uniforms for sport, because it pleased the military men with whom they were associated, or for reasons I have not been able to determine, see Lowry, *The Story the Soldiers Wouldn't Tell*, p. 33; *New York Herald*, September 23, 1863; *Frank Leslie's Illustrated Newspaper*, November 5, 1864; and the Lynchburg *Daily Virginian*, October 6, 1864.

40. See Schultz, "Women at the Front," pp. 265–66, 260; Mary Livermore, *My Story of the War* (Hartford, Conn.: A. D. Worthington, 1889), p. 120; Francis Butler Simkins and James Welch Patton, *The Women of the Confederacy* (New York: Garrett & Massie, 1936; reprint, St. Clair Shores, Mich.: Scholarly Press, 1976), p. 81; Wiley, *The Life of Billy Yank*, p. 339; and Janet E. Kaufman, "'Under the Petticoat Flag': Women Soldiers in the Confederate Army," *Southern Studies* 23 (1984): p. 375.

41. Burgess, *An Uncommon Soldier*, p. 6.

42. *The History of Constantius and Pulchera* features the first purely fictional example of a woman disguised as a man in post-Revolutionary American literature. It tells the story of two young lovers—sixteen-year-old Pulchera, the daughter of a wealthy farmer, and Constantius, the son of a wealthy merchant—who have been forcibly separated by Pulchera's

father, who betroths her to the son of a French nobleman. Complicated circumstances during her journey to France lead to Pulchera's assumption of the identity of a male sailor, "Lieutenant Valorus," and as Valorus she goes on to have a series of adventures (storms, shipwrecks, rescues, imprisonments, and dramatic escapes) climaxing in a reunion with her true love, Constantius. (See Anonymous, *The History of Constantius and Pulchera* [n.p., 1795].)

Taking the War of 1812 as its backdrop, Mordecai M. Noah's 1819 play *She Would Be a Soldier* tells the story of Christine, a young woman taught by her soldier father to "love glory when combined with virtue" and to "crack a bottle at twelve paces with a pistol . . . [and] bring down a buck, at any distance," and Lenox, an honest, gallant, and warmhearted infantry lieutenant. Like Pulchera, Christine's father has pledged her to a man other than Lenox, the man she loves. When she discovers her father's plan, her outrage leads her to dress herself in men's clothes and head for Lenox's army camp, where she has a number of adventures in soldier's guise before she and Lenox are reunited. (See Mordecai M. Noah, *She Would Be a Soldier; or, The Plains of Chippewa; An Historical Drama in Three Acts*, printed in Richard Moody, ed., *Dramas from the American Theatre, 1762–1909* [Cleveland, Ohio: World Publishing, 1966], pp. 126–42. See also Jonathan D. Sarna, *Jacksonian Jew: The Two Worlds of Mordecai Noah* [New York: Holmes & Meier, 1981]; and Craig Kleinman, "Pigging the Nation, Staging the Jew in M. M. Noah's *She Would Be a Soldier*," *American Transcendental Quarterly* 10 [September 1996]: pp. 201–17.)

The story of Eliza Allen Billings, published as *The Female Volunteer* in 1851, is similar. With the United States' war with Mexico as its setting, *The Female Volunteer* is at its core a tale of the consequences for true love of parental interference. When Eliza's parents refuse to accept her love for a poor Canadian suitor named William, he joins a volunteer regiment bound for Mexico and she cuts her hair, dons a suit of men's clothes, and follows him under the pseudonym "George Mead." (See Eliza Allen Billings, *The Female Volunteer* [n.p., 1851]).

Needless to say, the theme of the woman soldier or sailor is by no means exclusively American, nor was it exclusively a product of the late eighteenth and early nineteenth centuries. Rather, it was a prominent theme in early modern European literature and song. See Rudolf M. Dekker and Lotte C. van de Pol, *The Tradition of Female Transvestism in Early*

*Modern Europe* (New York: St. Martin's Press, 1989); Dianne Dugaw, *Warrior Women and Popular Balladry, 1650–1850* (New York: Cambridge University Press, 1989). See also Pauline Greenhill, "'Neither a Man nor a Maid': Sexualities and Gendered Meanings in Cross-Dressing Ballads," *Journal of American Folklore* 108 (1995): pp. 156–77.

43. Maturin Murray Ballou, *Fanny Campbell, the Female Pirate Captain: A Tale of the Revolution* (New York: E. D. Long, 1844).

44. Dugaw, *Warrior Women and Popular Balladry, 1650–1850*, p. 1.

45. Fort Scott, Kansas, *Weekly Monitor*, January 17, 1884.

46. Ballou, *Fanny Campbell*, p. 120.

47. Ibid., p. 65.

48. *The Lady Lieutenant: A Wonderful, Startling and Thrilling Narrative of the Adventures of Miss Madeline Moore* . . . .(Philadelphia: Barclay, 1862).

49. There are a few examples of literary women in uniform whose motivations were of a different sort. The first of these is Sally, a "spirited American lass" and the sister of a soldier in the Continental army in William Dunlap's play *The Glory of Columbia; Her Yeomanry*, published in 1803 and considered one of the most popular American plays for the next fifty years. Sally, who follows her soldier brother to camp purely for the fun of it, is a foolish, comical creature, a spirited scamp who proves handy with a musket, but who is also thoroughly ignorant of the seriousness of war and who herself realizes that she is unworthy of a soldier's uniform (see William Dunlap, *The Glory of Columbia; Her Yeomanry: A Play in Five Acts* [New York: D. Longworth, 1803]). Richard Moody calls Dunlap the "father of American drama" (see Moody, *Dramas from the American Theatre*, pp. 87, 90. See also Oral Sumner Coad, *William Dunlap: A Study of His Life and Works and of His Place in Contemporary Culture* [New York: Russell & Russell, 1962], pp. 172–73; and Robert H. Canary, *William Dunlap* [New York: Twayne Publishers, 1970], pp. 99, 101).

Another variation is Lucy Brewer, protagonist of *The Female Marine*, published in several editions following the War of 1812. Lucy Brewer ends up in uniform on board the USS *Constitution* after a wily and ill-intentioned suitor seduces and abandons her and she, in her ignorance and shame, spends three years in a brothel before taking the advice of a young naval officer to escape her situation by disguising herself as a man and joining the military. Through three major engagements Lucy discharges her duties without raising the suspicions of any of her shipmates, although she is nearly discovered at one point when she falls overboard and almost drowns (only at the last moment is she able to persuade her comrades to let her change her own clothes). Brewer claims that her main reason for telling her story is to "induce youths of my sex never to listen to the voice of love, unless sanctioned by paternal approbation: and to resist the impulse of inclination when it runs counter to the precepts of Religion and Virtue" (see *The Female Marine; or, The Adventures of Miss Lucy Brewer* [Boston: Nathaniel Coverly, Jr., 1815; reprint, New York: Da Capo Press, 1966], p. 50). See also Daniel A. Cohen, ed., *The Female Marine and Other Related Works: Narratives of Cross-Dressing and Urban Vice in America's Early Republic* [Amherst: University of Massachusetts Press, 1997]).

For a somewhat similar story and heroine, see *The Life and Sufferings of Miss Emma Cole, Being a Faithful Narrative of Her Life, Written by Herself* (Boston: M. Aurelius, 1844).

A third image of the woman in uniform appears in what was billed as the autobiography of a woman known as "Mountain Charley" when it was published in 1861. This "autobiography" seems to have been loosely based on the true story of a Louisiana woman who married in her mid-teens, was widowed soon thereafter, and subsequently donned male clothing and headed west to find her fortune, taking up a variety of occupations and, after the Civil War broke out, serving under an assumed name with the 5th Wisconsin Infantry. There are several versions of the Mountain Charley story. (See Fred W. Mazzulla and William Kostka, eds., *Mountain Charley; or The Adventures of Mrs. E. J. Guerin, Who Was Thirteen Years in Male Attire* [Norman: University of Oklahoma Press, 1968]. See also the Denver, Colorado, *Rocky Mountain News*, September 10, 1859; the Leadville, Colorado, *Daily Chronicle*, July 15, 1879; and related articles in the Golden, Colorado, *Colorado Transcript*, January 14, February 25, and March 4 and 11, 1885.)

50. C. J. Worthington, ed., *The Woman in Battle: A Narrative of the Exploits, Adventures, and Travels of Madame Loreta Janeta Velazquez* (1876; reprint, New York: Arno Press, 1972), p. 12.

51. Ibid., p. 51.

52. Ibid., p. 69.

53. Ibid., p. 606. In his own preface, publisher Worthington reinforces

Velazquez's position on the appropriateness of her behavior during the war. "Since the author has not seen fit to do so," Worthington writes, "the editor does not feel called upon to argue the question of propriety involved in the appearance of a woman disguised in male attire on the battle-field." Worthington also refuses to condemn Velazquez's assumption of "masculine" characteristics in the pursuit of her wartime career: "Self-reliance, self-esteem, and self-approbation," he writes, "all were necessary for the consummation of such adventures as those herein related" (ibid., p. 7).

54. Jubal A. Early to W. F. Slemons, May 22, 1878, in the Tucker Family Papers, Southern Historical Collection, Louis Round Wilson Library, University of North Carolina, Chapel Hill (hereafter cited as the Tucker Family Papers).

55. Schultz, "Women at the Front," p. 306.

56. As it turns out, some of Early's criticisms of *The Woman in Battle* are persuasive. "After the death of her husband . . ." he wrote, for example, Velazquez

left Pensacola on the 16th of June 1861, for Richmond Va via Montgomery Ala & Columbia S. C.—At the latter place she stopped for several days, and then took "the train bound north" for Richmond, and passed through Lynchburg on her route where she staid [*sic*] one night, thus filling up a gap in the rail-road from Greensboro N. C. to Lynchburg Va, though . . . the road has not really been made until since 1870. (Jubal A. Early to W. F. Slemons, May 22, 1878, in the Tucker Family Papers)

Early certainly caught Velazquez in an error of detail here, as he did elsewhere. However, he was more troubled by Velazquez's discussions of her playful dalliances with other women while she was in the guise of Harry Buford than he was with her confusion of geographical and chronological details. Like both Sarah Emma Edmonds's *Nurse and Spy in the Union Army* (Hartford, Conn.: W. S. Williams, 1865) and Herman Mann's *The Female Review: Life of Deborah Sampson* (Boston: J. K. Wiggin & William Parsons Lunt, 1866; reprint, New York: Arno Press, 1972), *The Woman in Battle* contains several such stories. For Early, the idea of a woman disguising herself as a man and then flirting with other women was repugnant; it spoke well of neither the impostor nor the impostor's targets. Indeed, wrote Early, such stories had the potential to taint the reputation of Southern women generally. (See Jubal A. Early to W. F. Slemons, May 22, 1878, in the Tucker Family Papers.)

57. Schultz, "Women at the Front," pp. 305–6. See also RG 109, War Department Collection of Confederate Records, Applications for Appointments in Military Service, Bound Records, vol. 90, chap. 9, National Archives, Washington, D.C.

For other recent discussions of the authenticity of *The Woman in Battle*, see Massey, *Bonnet Brigades*, p. 82; Sylvia Hoffert, "Madame Loretta [*sic*] Velazquez: Heroine or Hoaxer?," *Civil War Times Illustrated* 17 (June 1978): pp. 24–31; Wheelwright, *Amazons and Military Maids*, pp. 139–40; and Elizabeth Young, "Confederate Counterfeit," in Elaine K. Ginsberg, *Passing and the Fictions of Identity* (Durham, N.C.: Duke University Press, 1996).

58. Louisville, Kentucky, *Daily Journal*, October 9, 1861.

59. Richmond, Virginia, *Whig*, June 19, 1863. See also Massey, *Bonnet Brigades*, p. 83.

60. Richmond, Virginia, *Daily Examiner*, July 2, 1863. See also Massey, *Bonnet Brigades*, p. 83.

61. Hoffert, "Madame Loretta [*sic*] Velazquez," p. 30.

62. *Official Records*, ser. 2, vol. 8, p. 936. See also Massey, *Bonnet Brigades*, p. 83; and RG 110, Provost Marshal General's Bureau, List of Scouts, Guides, Spies, and Detectives, box 6, National Archives, Washington, D.C.

63. Massey has theorized that *The Woman in Battle* instead constitutes a "composite picture of several women's experiences, publicized or rumored at the time and later enlivened by the author's vivid imagination" (Massey, *Bonnet Brigades*, p. 82).

64. Madame L. J. Velazquez to Jubal Early, May 18, 1878, in the Tucker Family Papers.

If Julie Wheelwright is correct, Jubal Early's criticisms of *The Woman in Battle* missed the point entirely, for in fact contemporary readers did not concern themselves with the book's historical accuracy as much as with its entertainment value. "Whatever the official pronouncement of her authenticity," Wheelwright explains, "the warrior heroine appealed to an audience willing to believe in her" (Wheelwright, *Amazons and Military Maids*, p. 140).

65. Worthington, *The Woman in Battle*, p. 42. Later in the book, Velazquez confesses to feeling "no hesitation in saying that I wish I had been created a man instead of a woman . . . but, being a woman, I was bent on making the best of it (ibid., p. 130).

66. Ibid., pp. 33, 37. See also pp. 34–36, in which Velazquez discusses other honored predecessors, including Molly Pitcher but not, interestingly, Deborah Sampson. See also ibid., pp. 86, 95, 99–100.

67. Ibid., pp. 242–43.

68. Madame L. J. Velazquez to Jubal Early, May 18, 1878, in the Tucker Family Papers.

69. Hoffert, "Madame Loretta [*sic*] Velazquez," p. 31.

70. For all its ebullient iconoclasm, *The Woman in Battle* was not a breakthrough work in American literature, and earlier images of women in American military service endured beyond 1876, such as the protagonist in Kate Sherwood's 1885 poem "The Soldier's Ring": a woman who posed as a soldier in order to follow her betrothed into the Union army, fighting at his side until he was killed in action at Antietam. "The Soldier's Ring" reminds us that the image of the woman in Civil War military service which *The Woman in Battle* offered—the bold, strong, economically and otherwise self-interested, morally uncompromised woman under fire—faced stiff and abiding competition in the form of other culturally more acceptable—if not necessarily historically more accurate—images of such women as heartbroken lovers, crazed and/or selfless patriots, or pitiable moral failures. See Kate Sherwood, *Camp-Fire, Memorial Day, and Other Poems* (Chicago: Jansen, McClurg, 1885), pp. 99–107. I thank Professor Nina Silber of Boston University for bringing this poem to my attention.

71. Mann, *The Female Review*, p. xxiii.

72. Deborah Sampson, "An Address Delivered in 1802 in Various Towns in Massachusetts, Rhode Island and New York," in the Deborah Sampson Gannett Papers, Sharon Public Library, Sharon, Mass.

73. Moreover, Sampson's address, although made to sound like an echo of her own thoughts, was in fact a product of Mann's pen. See Eugene Tappan's explanatory remarks in Sampson, "An Address Delivered in 1802."

74. See Lillian Faderman, *Surpassing the Love of Men: Romantic Friendship and Love Between Women from the Renaissance to the Present* (New

York: William Morrow, 1981), p. 60. See also Mann, *The Female Review*, pp. 124, 161–62, 248.

75. When he composed her 1802 address for public consumption, Mann also proposed a sort of protofeminism as a motive in Sampson's enlistment, but he subordinated it completely to her patriotism and even had her apologize for it, at one point having her confess that the story she was about to tell "ought to expel me from the enjoyment of society, from the acknowledgment of my own sex, and from the endearing friendship of the other" (Sampson, "An Address Delivered in 1802," pp. 5–6).

See also Dugaw, *Warrior Women and Popular Balladry*, p. 58.

76. Mann, *The Female Review*, p. xxviii. See also Lucy Freeman and Alma Halbert Bond, *America's First Woman Warrior: The Courage of Deborah Sampson* (New York: Paragon House, 1992), pp. 91, 177.

77. Of course, like many Revolutionary War soldiers, Sampson received no remuneration for her work as a soldier while she was in the service. But I would argue that the fact that she did not collect the money owed to her for her services as a soldier until almost ten years after her discharge reflects not so much a lack of need for the money as a lack of knowledge about how to claim the funds that were overdue in her case. See Mann, *The Female Review*, p. xxiv.

78. Ibid., p. xxviii.

79. Dekker and van de Pol, *The Tradition of Female Transvestism in Early Modern Europe*, pp. 11–16. According to Dekker and van de Pol, when asked, early modern European women most frequently advanced one of two motives for their impostures: the desire to follow a loved one, or patriotism. But the authors caution readers to resist giving such explanations full credence, not least of all because of the contexts in which the women's explanations typically arose. "In many cases," Dekker and van de Pol write,

the women themselves explained their motives, usually to a court of law, and in a few cases in autobiographical writings. But however interesting it is to hear what the women have to say, it is self-evident that they will have emphasized the motives which were to some degree justifiable, which were more or less socially acceptable, or which could be considered as arising from mitigating circumstances, such as . . . patriotism or in order to follow a husband or lover. (Ibid., p. 25)

In fact, Dekker and van de Pol insist that poverty was probably the most powerful driving force behind women's decision to pose as men. In pre-industrial Europe, they write, a man had many options. Women had fewer opportunities, and their wages were always lower. Poor women who sought the same sorts of benefits that the military offered to men simply had to assume male identities in order to attain them (ibid., pp. 32, 102).

80. DeAnne Blanton, "Women Soldiers of the Civil War," *Prologue* 25 (Spring 1993): p. 31; Burgess, *An Uncommon Soldier*, p. 7. See also Schultz, "Women at the Front," p. 264; Wheelwright, *Amazons and Military Maids*, pp. 41–42.

81. Report No. 820, 48th Cong., 1st sess. (to accompany H.R. 5334), p. 1, in RG 15, Records of the Veterans Administraton, Sarah Emma Edmonds·Pension File, application #526889, certificate #232136, National Archives, Washington, D.C.

82. Fort Scott, Kansas, *Weekly Monitor*, January 17, 1884.

83. See also Sylvia G. L. Dannett, *She Rode with the Generals: The True and Incredible Story of Sarah Emma Seelye, Alias Franklin Thompson* (New York: Thomas Nelson & Sons, 1960). Dannett's biography also portrayed its subject as a sexually confused young woman whose father's dismay at not having a son led her to be "so warped about sex and marriage that perhaps in self-protection she acquired more and more the tastes and habits of a boy, eventually choosing the life of a soldier" (ibid., p. 22).

According to Julie Wheelwright, Edmonds joined the army as an outgrowth of her realization that "donning trousers, a transformation as simple as changing a suit of clothes, would transport her to another, more privileged world" (Wheelwright, *Amazons and Military* Maids, p. 25). See also Kathleen De Grave, *Swindler, Spy, Rebel: The Confidence Woman in Nineteenth Century America* (Columbia: University of Missouri Press, 1995).

84. Fort Scott, Kansas, *Weekly Monitor*, January 17, 1884.

85. Ibid.

86. As we know, economic concerns were primary for Edmonds throughout her life. Marriage to Linus Seelye did not bring long-term financial comfort, and when Congress granted Edmonds her veteran's

pension in 1884, it did so "in view of her failing health, and the fact that her husband has no income except from his daily labor, and that she and her family are in indigent circumstances." Shortly before her death, Edmonds, now a widow, sought an increase in her pension, claiming that her disabilities had "increased *four fold*" in the years since 1884. Insisting that "the pension which I receive is not sufficient to pay my Doctor bills, and a person to wait on me," and that "I do not own a foot of land on God's earth—nor a roof to shelter me," Edmonds urged that her pension be increased to thirty dollars per month. It appears that her request was denied. (See Report No. 836, 48th Cong., 1st sess. [to accompany H.R. 5335], p. 1; and Sarah Emma Edmonds Seelye to Mr. Wedderburn, September 24, 1896; both in RG 15, Records of the Veterans Administration, Sarah Emma Edmonds Pension File, application #526889, certificate #232136, National Archives, Washington, D.C.)

87. Burgess, *An Uncommon Soldier*, p. 9.

88. See, for example, Cathy Rogers, "Jennie Comes Marchin' Home," Rockford, Illinois, *Register Star Sunday Magazine*, May 27, 1979, p. 3.

89. Burgess, *An Uncommon Soldier*, p. 12.

90. Moore, *Women of the War*, p. 55.

91. Among the army women and daughters of the regiment discussed here, those who clearly followed loved ones into the service, at least initially, include Annie Etheridge, Kady Brownell, Bridget Divers, Belle Reynolds, Nadine Turchin, Mrs. John Bahr, Ellen Goodridge, Jane Claudia Johnson, and Marie Tepe. Those who remained in the service even after becoming separated—sometimes by choice—from the men they had followed include Annie Etheridge, Bridget Divers, and Marie Tepe. Those who joined the Union and Confederate armies without any apparent connection—at least initially—to a specific man include the Morrison Cavalry's daughter of the regiment, Hannah Ewbank, Lizzie Clawson, the six women with the Garibaldi Guard, the five women with the 25th Pennsylvania Infantry, Sarah Taylor, Lucy Ann Cox, the Irish Brigade's laundress, Elizabeth Finnan, Rose Rooney, Betty Sullivan, Dutch Mary, Eliza Wilson, and Susie King Taylor.

## Afterword

1. Jerome John Robbins Diary, Jerome John Robbins Papers, Michigan Historical Collections, Bentley Historical Library, University of Michigan, Ann Arbor. See also Charles Wesley Alexander, *Pauline of the Potomac; or, General McClellan's Spy* (Philadelphia: Barclay, 1862).

# Selected Bibliography

## Published Materials

Alexander, Charles Wesley. *General Sherman's Indian Spy*. Philadelphia: C. W. Alexander, 1865.

———. *Maud of the Mississippi: General Grant's Daring Spy*. Philadelphia: C. W. Alexander, 1863.

———. *Pauline of the Potomac; or, General McClellan's Spy*. Philadelphia: Barclay, 1862.

———. *The Picket Slayer*. Philadelphia: C. W. Alexander, 1863.

Alexander, Ted, ed. *The 126th Pennsylvania*. Shippensburg, Pa. Beidel Printing House, 1984.

Andrews, Matthew Page. *The Women of the South in War Times*. Baltimore, Md.: Norman, Remington, 1920.

Anonymous, *The History of Constantius and Pulchera*. N.p., 1795.

Austin, Jane Goodwin. *Dora Darling: The Daughter of the Regiment*. Boston: J. E. Tilton, 1865.

Bailey, James H. "Crazy Bet, Union Spy." *Virginia Cavalcade* (Spring 1952): 14–17.

Bakeless, John Edwin. *Spies of the Confederacy*. Philadelphia: J. B. Lippincott, 1970.

Baker, Lafayette Charles. *History of the United States Secret Service*. Philadelphia: L. C. Baker, 1867.

Ballou, Maturin Murray. *Fanny Campbell, the Female Pirate Captain: A Tale of the Revolution*. New York: E. D. Long, 1844.

Barber, John W. *Historical Collections of New Jersey: Past and Present*. New Haven, Conn: John W. Barber, 1868.

Barton, George. *The World's Greatest Military Spies and Secret Service Agents*. Boston: Page, 1918.

Beard, Mary R. *Woman as Force in History*. New York: Macmillan, 1946.

Beers, Fannie A. *Memories: A Record of Personal Experience and Adventure During Four Years of War*. Philadelphia: J. B. Lippincott, 1888.

Beymer, William Gilmore. *On Hazardous Service: Scouts and Spies of the North and South*. New York: Harper & Brothers, 1912.

Biddle, Edward W. "Historical Address at the Unveiling of Molly Pitcher Monument in Carlisle, Pennsylvania, June 28, 1916." Carlisle, Pa.: Hamilton Library Association, 1916.

Billings, Eliza Allen. *The Female Volunteer; or, The Life and Wonderful Adventures of Miss Eliza Allen, A Young Lady of Eastport, Maine*. N.p., 1851.

Blanton, DeAnne. "Women Soldiers of the Civil War." *Prologue* 25 (Spring 1993): 27–33.

Blessing, Patrick. *The Irish in America: A Guide to the Literature and the Manuscript Collections*. Washington, D.C.: Catholic University of America Press, 1992.

Blumenthal, Walter Hart. *Women Camp Followers of the American Revolution*. Philadelphia: George S. MacManus, 1952.

Boritt, Gabor S. *War Comes Again: Comparative Vistas on the Civil War and World War II*. New York: Oxford University Press, 1995.

Botkin, B. A. *A Civil War Treasury of Tales, Legends, and Folklore*. New York: Random House, 1960.

Boudinot, Elias. *Journal or Historical Recollections of American Events During the Revolutionary War*. Philadelphia: Frederick Bourquin, 1894.

Bourne, Jody. "Woman Recalls Saunemin's Best-Known Civil War Vet." *Dwight* (Illinois) *Star and Herald*, March 21, 1991.

Bradford, Sarah. *Harriet Tubman: The Moses of Her People*. New York: Carol Publishing, 1991.

Brockett, Linus. P. *The Camp, the Battlefield, and the Hospital; or, Light and Shadows of the Great Rebellion*. Philadelphia: National Publishing, 1866.

———, and Mary C. Vaughan. *Woman's Work in the Civil War: A Record of Heroism, Patriotism, and Patience*. Philadelphia: Zeigler, McCurdy, 1867.

Brooks, Fred. "Shiloh Mystery Woman." *Civil War Times Illustrated* 17 (August 1978): 29.

Buel, Joy Day, and Richard Buel, Jr. *The Way of Duty: A Woman and Her Family in Revolutionary America*. New York: W. W. Norton, 1985.

Bullough, Vern L., and Bonnie Bullough. *Cross Dressing, Sex, and Gender*. Philadelphia: University of Pennsylvania Press, 1993.

Burger, Nash K. *Confederate Spy: Rose O'Neale Greenhow*. New York: Franklin Watts, 1967.

Burgess, Lauren Cook, ed. *An Uncommon Soldier: The Civil War Letters of Sarah Rosetta Wakeman, Alias Pvt. Lyons Wakeman, 153rd Regiment, New York State Volunteers, 1862–1864*. Pasadena, Md.: MINERVA Center, 1994.

Carter, Robert Goldthwaite. *Four Brothers in Blue*. 1913. Reprint. Austin: University of Texas Press, 1978.

Chase, George Wingate. *The History of Haverhill, Massachusetts, from Its First Settlement, in 1640, to the Year 1860*. Haverhill, Mass.: published by the author, 1861.

Clark, Harry Hayden, ed. *Transitions in American Literary History*. New York: Octagon Books, 1975.

Clausius, Gerhard. "The Little Soldier of the 95th: Albert D. J. Cashier." *Journal of the Illinois State Historical Society* 51 (Winter 1958): 380–87.

Clayton, Ellen C. *Female Warriors: Memorials of Female Valour and Heroism, from the Mythological Ages to the Present Era*. 2 vols. London: Tinsley Brothers, 1879.

Clement, J., ed. *Noble Deeds of American Women; with Biographical Sketches of Some of the More Prominent*. New York: George H. Derby, 1851; reprint, Williamstown, Mass.: Corner House Publishers, 1975.

Clinton, Catherine, and Nina Silber, eds. *Divided Houses: Gender and the Civil War*. New York: Oxford University Press, 1992.

Coad, Oral Sumner. *William Dunlap: A Study of His Life and Works and of His Place in Contemporary Culture*. New York: Russell & Russell, 1962.

Cohen, Daniel A., ed. *The Female Marine and Other Related Works: Narratives of Cross-Dressing and Urban Vice in America's Early Republic*. Amherst: University of Massachusetts Press, 1997.

Cole, Adelaide M. "Anne Bailey: Woman of Courage." *DAR Magazine* 114 (1980): 322–25.

Compton, Piers. *Colonel's Lady and Camp-Follower: The Story of Women in the Crimean War*. New York: St. Martin's Press, 1970.

Conklin, Eileen F. *Women at Gettysburg, 1863*. Gettysburg, Pa.: Thomas Publications, 1993.

Conrad, Earl. *Harriet Tubman*. Washington, D.C.: Associated Publishers, 1943.

Creighton, Margaret S., and Lisa Norling. *Iron Men, Wooden Women: Gender and Seafaring in the Atlantic World, 1700–1920*. Baltimore, Md.: Johns Hopkins University Press, 1996.

Crotty, Daniel G. *Four Years Campaigning in the Army of the Potomac*. Grand Rapids, Mich.: Dygert Brothers, Printers and Binders, 1874.

Dannett, Sylvia G. L. *She Rode with the Generals: The True and Incredible Story of Sarah Emma Seelye, Alias Franklin Thompson*. New York: Thomas Nelson & Sons, 1960.

Darrach, Henry. "Lydia Darragh, of the Revolution." *Pennsylvania Magazine of History and Biography* 23 (April 1899): 86–91.

———. *Lydia Darragh: One of the Heroines of the Revolution*. Philadelphia: City History Society of Philadelphia, 1916.

Davis, Curtis Carroll. "The Civil War's Most Over-Rated Spy." *West Virginia History* 27 (October 1965): 1–9.

———. "Companions of Crisis: The Spy Memoir as a Social Document." *Civil War History* 10 (December 1964): 385–400.

———. "Effie Goldsborough: Confederate Courier." *Civil War Times Illustrated* 7 (April 1968): 29–31.

———. "'The Pet of the Confederacy' Still? Fresh Findings about Belle Boyd." *Maryland Historical Magazine* 78 (Spring 1983): 35–53.

———, ed. *Belle Boyd in Camp and Prison, Written by Herself*. New York: Thomas Yoseloff, 1968.

Davis, Natalie Zemon. "Women on Top." In her *Society and Culture in Early Modern France*. Stanford, Calif.: Stanford University Press, 1965.

Davis, William C., ed. *The Image of War, 1861–1865*. Vol. 1, *Shadows of the Storm*. Garden City, N.Y.: Doubleday, 1981.

De Grave, Kathleen. *Swindler, Spy, Rebel: The Confidence Woman in Nineteenth Century America*. Columbia: University of Missouri Press, 1995.

Dekker, Rudolf M., and Lotte C. van de Pol. *The Tradition of Female Transvestism in Early Modern Europe*. New York: St. Martin's Press, 1989.

De Leon, T. C. *Belles, Beaux and Brains of the 60's*. New York: G. W. Dillingham, 1907.

De Pauw, Linda Grant. *Fortunes of War: New Jersey Women and the American Revolution*. Trenton: New Jersey Historical Commission, 1975.

———. *Founding Mothers: Women in America in the Revolutionary Era*. Boston: Houghton Mifflin, 1975.

———. *Four Traditions: Women of New York During the American Revolution*. Albany: New York State American Revolution Bicentennial Commission, 1974.

———. "Women in Combat: The Revolutionary War Experience." *Armed Forces and Society* 7 (Winter 1991): 209–26.

Destler, Chester McArthur, ed. "The Second Michigan Volunteer Infantry Joins the Army of the Potomac." *Michigan History* 41 (1957): 385–412.

Dexter, Elisabeth Anthony. *Colonial Women of Affairs: Women in Business and the Professions in America Before 1776*. Boston: Houghton Mifflin, 1924. Reprint. Clifton, N.J.: Augustus M. Kelley, 1972.

Dornbusch, C. E. *Military Bibliography of the Civil War*. 4 vols. New York: New York Public Library, 1961–72.

Doster, William E. *Lincoln & Episodes of the Civil War*. New York: G. P. Putnam & Sons, 1915.

Douglas, Henry Kyd. *I Rode with Stonewall*. Chapel Hill: University of North Carolina Press, 1940.

Dugaw, Dianne. *Warrior Women and Popular Balladry, 1650–1850*. New York: Cambridge University Press, 1989.

Dunlap, William. "The Glory of Columbia; Her Yeomanry: A Play in Five Acts." New York: D. Longworth, 1803.

Edmonds, S. Emma E. *Unsexed; or, The Female Soldier: The Thrilling Adventures, Experiences and Escapes of a Woman, as Nurse, Spy and Scout, in Hospitals, Camp and Battlefields*. Philadelphia: Philadelphia Publishing, 1864.

Egle, William Henry. *Some Pennsylvania Women During the War of the Revolution*. Harrisburg, Pa.: Harrisburg Publishing, 1898.

Ellet, Elizabeth F. *Women of the American Revolution*. 2 vols. Philadelphia: George W. Jacobs, 1900.

Erauso, Catalina de. *Lieutenant Nun: Memoir of a Basque Transvestite in the New World*. Boston: Beacon Press, 1996.

Eskew, Garnett Laidlaw. *Willard's of Washington: The Epic of a Capital Caravansary*. New York: Coward-McCann, 1954.

Evans, Elizabeth. *Weathering the Storm: Women of the American Revolution*. New York: Charles Scribner's Sons, 1975.

Ewing, Elizabeth. *Women in Uniform Through the Centuries*. London: B. T. Batsford, 1975.

Faderman, Lillian. *Surpassing the Love of Men: Romantic Friendship and Love Between Women from the Renaissance to the Present*. New York: William Morrow, 1981.

Feinberg, Leslie. *Transgender Warriors: Making History from Joan of Arc to RuPaul*. Boston: Beacon Press, 1996.

*The Female Marine; or The Adventures of Miss Lucy Brewer*. Boston: Nathaniel Coverly, Jr., 1817; reprint, New York: Da Capo Press, 1966.

Fielding, Henry. *The Female Husband, and Other Writings*. Liverpool, England: Liverpool University Press, 1960.

Fishel, Edwin C. *The Secret War for the Union: The Untold Story of Military Intelligence in the Civil War*. Boston: Houghton Mifflin, 1996.

Fornell, Earl W. "A Woman in the Union Army." *American-German Review* 26–27 (February–March 1961): 13–15.

Freeman, Lucy, and Alma Halbert Bond. *America's First Woman Warrior: The Courage of Deborah Sampson*. New York: Paragon House, 1992.

Funderburg, Anne. "Women of the Confederacy." *Southern Partisan* 14 (second quarter 1994): 18–22.

Galbraith, Loretta, and William Galbraith, eds. *A Lost Heroine of the Confederacy: The Diaries and Letters of Belle Edmondson*. Jackson: University Press of Mississippi, 1900.

Garber, Marjorie. *Vested Interests: Cross-Dressing and Cultural Anxiety*. New York: Routledge, 1992.

Garrison, Webb. "Southern Women Helped Soldiers in Gray." *Atlanta Constitution*, November 26, 1989.

Ginsberg, Elaine K. *Passing and the Fictions of Identity*. Durham, N.C.: Duke University Press, 1996.

Greenbie, Marjorie Barstow. *My Dear Lady: The Story of Anna Ella Carroll, the "Great Unrecognized Member of Lincoln's Cabinet."* New York: Whittlesey House, 1940; reprint, New York: Arno Press, 1974.

Greenhill, Pauline. "'Neither a Man nor a Maid': Sexualities and Gendered Meanings in Cross-Dressing Ballads." *Journal of American Folklore* 108 (1995): 156–77.

Greenhow, Rose. *My Imprisonment, and the First Year of Abolition Rule at Washington*. London: Richard Bentley, 1863.

Haas, Paul H. "A Volunteer Nurse in the Civil War: The Diary of Harriet Douglas Whetten." *Wisconsin Magazine of History* 48 (Winter 1964–65): 205–21.

Hacker, Barton C. "Women and Military Institutions in Early Modern Europe: A Reconnaissance." *Signs* 6 (Summer 1981): 643–71.

Hall, Edward Hagaman. *Margaret Corbin: Heroine of the Battle of Fort Washington, 16 November 1776*. New York: American Scenic and Historic Preservation Society, 1932.

Hall, Richard C. *Patriots in Disguise: Women Warriors of the Civil War*. New York: Paragon House, 1993.

Halttunen, Karen. *Confidence Men and Painted Women: A Study of Middle-Class Culture in America, 1830–1870*. New Haven: Yale University Press, 1982.

Hanson, John. *Historical Sketch of the Old Sixth Regiment of Massachusetts Volunteers During Its Three Campaigns in 1861, 1862, 1863 & 1864*. Boston: Lee & Shepard, 1866.

Harris, Joel Chandler. *Stories of Georgia*. New York: American Book Company, 1896.

Haynie, J. Henry. *The Nineteenth Illinois*. Chicago, Ill.: M. A. Donohue, 1912.

Herek, Raymond J. "A Woman in Regimentals." *Civil War Times Illustrated* 22 (January 1984): 31.

Hergesheimer, Joseph. *Swords and Roses*. New York: Alfred A. Knopf, 1929.

Hodgson, Joseph. *The Confederate Vivandière; or, The Battle of Leesburg*. Montgomery, Ala.: John M. Floyd, Book and Job Printer, 1862.

Hoffert, Sylvia. "Madame Loretta Velazquez: Heroine or Hoaxer?" *Civil War Times Illustrated* 17 (June 1978): 24–31.

Hoffman, Ronald, and Peter Albert, eds. *Women in the Age of the American Revolution.* Charlottesville: University Press of Virginia, 1989.

Holmes, Jeanne. *Women in the Military.* Novato, Calif.: Presidio Press, 1982.

Hopley, Mrs. James R. "Anne Sargent Bailey." *Ohio Archaeological and Historical Quarterly* 16 (1907): 340–47.

Houghton, Edwin B. *The Campaigns of the Seventeenth Maine.* Portland, Maine: Short & Loring, 1866.

Hunt, John, and Bill McIlwain. "The Battling Belles." *American Mercury* 78 (March 1954): 13–15.

Hurn, Ethel Alice. *Wisconsin Women in the War Between the States.* Madison: Wisconsin History Commission, 1911.

Inness, Sherrie. "Girls Will Be Boys and Boys Will Be Girls: Cross-Dressing in Popular Turn-of-the-Century College Fiction." *Journal of American Culture* 18 (1995): 15–23.

Jacquette, Henrietta Stratton, ed. *South After Gettysburg: Letters of Cornelia Hancock from the Army of the Potomac, 1863–1865.* Freeport, N.Y.: Books for Libraries Press, 1971.

James, Edward T., and Janet W. James, eds. *Notable American Women, 1607–1950: A Biographical Dictionary.* 3 vols. Cambridge, Mass.: Belknap Press, 1971.

Johnson, Bradley T. "Memoir of Jane Claudia Johnson." *Southern Historical Society Papers* 29 (1901): 33–42.

Jones, J. B. *A Rebel War Clerk's Diary.* New York: Sagamore Press, 1958.

Jones, Terry L. *Lee's Tigers: The Louisiana Infantry in the Army of Northern Virginia.* Baton Rouge: Louisiana State University Press, 1987.

Kane, Harnett T. *Spies for the Blue and Gray.* Garden City, N.Y.: Hanover House, 1954.

Kaufman, Janet E. "'Under the Petticoat Flag': Women Soldiers in the Confederate Army." *Southern Studies* 23 (1984): 363–75.

Kerber, Linda K. *Women of the Republic: Intellect and Ideology in Revolutionary America.* Chapel Hill: University of North Carolina Press, 1980.

Ketchum, Richard, ed. *American Heritage Pictorial History of the Civil War.* Vol. 2. Garden City, N.Y.: Doubleday, 1960.

Kilgore, H. D. *The Story of Hannah Duston.* Haverhill, Mass.: Duston-Dustin Family Association, 1959.

Kinchen, Oscar A. *Women Who Spied for the Blue and Gray*. Philadelphia: Dorrance, 1972.

Kittle, Laurie. "A Female Marine Aboard the Constitution." *Marine Corps Gazette* 64 (February 1980): 53–56.

Klaver, Carol. "An Introduction to the Legend of Molly Pitcher." *MINERVA: Quarterly Report on Women and the Military* 12 (Summer 1994): 36–61.

Klein, Randolph. "Heroines of the Revolution: Mary Ludwig Hays, the Heroine of Monmouth, and Margaret Cochran Corbin, the Heroine of Fort Washington." *Journal of American History* 16 (January 1922): 31–35.

Kleinman, Craig. "Pigging the Nation, Staging the Jew in M. M. Noah's *She Would Be a Soldier*." *American Transcendental Quarterly* 10 (September 1996): 201–17.

*The Lady Lieutenant: A Wonderful, Startling and Thrilling Narrative of the Adventures of Miss Madeline Moore. . . .* Philadelphia: Barclay, 1862.

Laffin, John. *Women in Battle*. New York: Abelard-Schuman, 1967.

Lammers, Pat, and Amy Boyce. "A Female in the Ranks." *Civil War Times Illustrated* 22 (January 1984): 24–30.

Landis, John. *A Short History of Molly Pitcher: The Heroine of the Battle of Monmouth*. Carlisle, Pa.: Corman Printing, 1905.

Lanier, W. A. "Mad Ann Bailey's Cabin Located on Hill Three Miles Below Gallipolis on River." *Gallipolis* (Ohio) *Daily Tribune*, November 11, 1947.

Larson, C. Kay. "Bonny Yank and Ginny Reb." *MINERVA: Quarterly Report on Women and the Military* 8 (Spring 1990): 33–48.

Leech, Margaret. *Reveille in Washington, 1860–1865*. New York: Harper & Brothers, 1941.

Leonard, Patrick J. "Ann Bailey: Mystery Woman Warrior of 1777." *MINERVA: Quarterly Report on Women and the Military* 11 (Fall/Winter 1993): 1–4.

Lewis, Virgil A. "Anne Bailey." *Ohio Archaeological and Historical Quarterly* 17 (1908): 44–47.

*The Life and Sufferings of Miss Emma Cole, Being a Faithful Narrative of Her Life, Written by Herself*. Boston: M. Aurelius, 1844.

Linderman, Gerald F. *Embattled Courage: The Experience of Combat in the American Civil War*. New York: Free Press, 1987.

Livermore, Mary. *My Story of the War*. Hartford, Conn.: A. D. Worthington, 1889.

Long, E. B. "Anna Ella Carroll: Exaggerated Heroine?" *Civil War Times Illustrated* 14 (July 1975): 28–35.

Lord, Walter, ed. *The Fremantle Diary*. Boston: Little, Brown, 1954.

Lowry, Thomas P. *The Story the Soldiers Wouldn't Tell: Sex in the Civil War*. Mechanicsburg, Pa.: Stackpole Books, 1994.

Mahony, D. A. *The Prisoner of State*. New York: G. W. Carleton, 1863.

Mann, Herman. *The Female Review: Life of Deborah Sampson*. Boston: J. K. Wiggin & Wm. Parsons Lunt, 1866; reprint, New York: Arno Press, 1972.

Martin, Joseph Plumb. *Private Yankee Doodle: Being a Narrative of Some of the Adventures, Dangers and Sufferings of a Revolutionary Soldier*. New York: Eastern Acorn Press, 1979.

Massey, Mary Elizabeth. *Bonnet Brigades*. New York: Alfred A. Knopf, 1966.

Mast, Greg. "'Sam' Blaylock, 26th North Carolina Troops." *Military Images* 11 (July–August 1989): 10.

Mazzulla, Fred W., and William Kostka, eds. *Mountain Charlie; or, The Adventures of Mrs. E. J. Guerin, Who Was Thirteen Years in Male Attire*. Norman: University of Oklahoma Press, 1968.

McElligott, Mary Ellen, ed. "'A Monotony Full of Sadness': The Diary of Nadine Turchin, May, 1863–April, 1864." *Journal of the Illinois State Historical Society* 70 (1977): 27–89.

McLaughlin, Megan. "The Woman Warrior: Gender, Warfare and Society in Medieval Europe." *Women's Studies* 17 (1990): 193–209.

McPherson, James M. *Ordeal by Fire: The Civil War and Reconstruction*. New York: Alfred A. Knopf, 1982.

Meyer, Eugene L. "The Odyssey of Pvt. Rosetta Wakeman, Union Army." *Smithsonian* 24 (January 1994): 96–104.

*Michigan Women in the Civil War*. Lansing: Michigan Civil War Centennial Observance Commission, 1963.

Miller, Francis Trevelyan, ed. *Photographic History of the Civil War*. 10 vols. New York: Thomas Yoseloff, 1957.

Mills, H. Sinclair. *The Vivandière: History, Tradition, Uniform and Service*. Collinswood, N.J.: Civil War Historicals, 1988.

Moody, Pauline. "Massachusetts's Deborah Sampson." Sharon, Mass.: privately printed, 1975.

Moody, Richard, ed. *Dramas from the American Theatre, 1762–1909*. Cleveland, Ohio: World Publishing, 1966.

Moore, Frank, *Women of the War: Their Heroism and Self-Sacrifice*. Hartford, Conn.: S. S. Scranton, 1866.

Norton, Mary Beth. *Liberty's Daughters: The Revolutionary Experience of American Women, 1750–1800*. Boston: Little, Brown, 1980.

Nulton, Karen Sue. "The Social Civil War." Ph.D. diss., Rutgers University, New Brunswick, N.J., 1992.

Parker, Amelia Campbell. "Revolutionary Heroine Interred in West Point Cemetery." *Daughters of the American Revolution Magazine* 60 (June 1926): 347–52.

Pinkerton, Allan. *The Spy of the Rebellion: Being a True History of the Spy System of the United States Army During the Late Rebellion*. New York: G. W. Carleton, 1883.

Proctor, Samuel, and Louis Schmier, eds. *Jews of the South: Selected Essays from the Southern Jewish Historical Society*. Macon, Ga.: Mercer University Press, 1984.

Quinn, Arthur Hobson. *The Literature of the American People: An Historical Critical Survey*. New York: Appleton-Century-Crofts, 1951.

Racine, Philip N., ed. *"Unspoiled Heart": The Journal of Charles Mattocks of the 17th Maine*. Knoxville: University of Tennessee Press, 1994.

Richardson, Albert D. *The Secret Service: The Field, the Dungeon, and the Escape*. Hartford, Conn.: American Publishing, 1865.

Richman, Irwin. "Pauline Cushman: She Was a Heroine but Not a Lady." *Civil War Times Illustrated* 7 (February 1969): 38–44.

Robertson, John. *Michigan in the War*. Lansing, Mich.: W. S. George, State Printers, 1882.

Ross, Ishbel. *Rebel Rose: Life of Rose O'Neal Greenhow, Confederate Spy*. New York: Harper & Brothers, 1954.

Rowson, Susannah Haswell. *Charlotte Temple*. New York: Oxford University Press, 1986.

Ryan, David D., ed. *A Yankee Spy in Richmond: The Civil War Diary of "Crazy Bet" Van Lew*. Mechanicsburg, Pa.: Stackpole Books, 1996.

St. Clair, A. Mulholland. *The Story of the 116th Regiment, Pennsylvania Infantry*. Philadelphia: F. McManus, Jr., 1899.

Salmonson, Jessica Amanda. *The Encyclopedia of Amazons: Women Warriors from Antiquity to the Modern Era*. New York: Anchor Books, 1991.

Samuels, Shirley, ed. *The Culture of Sentiment: Race, Gender, and Sentimentality in Nineteenth-Century America*. New York: Oxford University Press, 1992.

Sarmiento, F. L. *Life of Pauline Cushman, the Celebrated Union Spy and Scout*. Philadelphia: John E. Potter, 1865.

Sarna, Jonathan D. *Jacksonian Jew: The Two Worlds of Mordecai Noah*. New York: Holmes & Meier, 1981.

Scarborough, Ruth. *Belle Boyd: Siren of the South*. Macon, Ga.: Mercer University Press, 1983.

Schultz, Jane Ellen. "Women at the Front: Gender and Genre in Literature of the American Civil War." Ph.D. diss., University of Michigan, Ann Arbor, 1988.

Sherwood, Kate. *Camp-Fire, Memorial Day, and Other Poems*. Chicago: Jansen, McClurg, 1885.

Sigaud, Louis. *Belle Boyd: Confederate Spy*. Richmond, Va.: Dietz Press, 1944.

Silliker, Ruth L., ed. *The Rebel Yell & the Yankee Hurrah: The Civil War Journal of a Maine Volunteer*. Camden, Maine: Down East Books, 1985.

Simkins, Francis Butler, and James Welch Patton. *The Women of the Confederacy*. New York: Garrett & Massie, 1936; reprint, St. Clair Shores, Mich.: Scholarly Press, 1976.

Smith, Thomas T., ed. *Daughter of the Regiment: Memoirs of a Childhood in the Frontier Army, 1878–1898*. Lincoln: University of Nebraska Press, 1996.

Sparks, David S., ed. *Inside Lincoln's Army: The Diary of Marsena Rudolph Patrick, Provost Marshal General, Army of the Potomac*. New York: Thomas Yoseloff, 1964.

Sperry, Rachel, "A Brief Reply to the Late Writings of Louisa Baker [alias] Lucy Brewer. . . ." Boston: Nathaniel Coverly, Jr., 1816.

Spiller, Robert E., et al., eds. *Literary History of the United States*. New York: Macmillan, 1953.

Stanley, Jo, ed. *Bold in Her Breeches: Women Pirates Across the Ages*. London: Pandora Press, 1995.

Stickley, Julia Ward. "The Records of Deborah Sampson Gannett, Woman Soldier of the Revolution." *Prologue* 4 (Winter 1972): 233–41.

Stryker, William S. *The Battle of Monmouth*. Princeton, N.J.: Princeton University Press, 1927.

Sutler, Boyd B. "Nancy Hart, Lady Bushwhacker." *Civil War Times* 1 (January 1960): 7.

Talmadge, Marian, and Iris Gilmore. *Emma Edmonds: Nurse and Spy*. New York: G. P. Putnam's Sons, 1970.

Taylor, Richard. *Destruction and Reconstruction: Personal Experiences of the Late War*. New York: Longman's, Green, 1955.

Taylor, Susie King. *A Black Woman's Civil War Memoirs: Reminiscences of My Life in Camp with the 33rd U.S. Colored Troops, Late 1st South Carolina Volunteers*. New York: Markus Wiener Publishing, 1988.

"They Also Served." *Civil War Times Illustrated* 17 (August 1978): 41.

Trustram, Myna. *Women of the Regiment: Marriage and the Victorian Army*. Cambridge: Cambridge University Press, 1984.

Turtledove, Harry. *Guns of the South*. New York: Ballantine Books, 1992.

Underwood, J. L. *The Women of the Confederacy*. New York: Neale Publishing, 1906.

*The War of the Rebellion: The Official Records of the Union and Confederate Armies*. 130 volumes. Washington, D.C.: Government Printing Office, 1881–1902.

Watson, John F. *Historic Tales of Olden Time, Concerning the Early Settlement and Progress of Philadelphia and Pennsylvania*. Philadelphia: E. Littell and Thomas Holden, 1833.

Weinert, Richard P. "Federal Spies in Richmond." *Civil War Times Illustrated* 4 (February 1965): 28–34.

Wheelock, Julia S. *The Boys in White: The Experience of a Hospital Agent in and Around Washington*. New York: Lange & Hillman, 1870.

Wheelwright, Julie. *Amazons and Military Maids: Women Who Dressed as Men in the Pursuit of Life, Liberty and Happiness*. London: Pandora Press, 1989.

———. *The Fatal Lover: Mata Hari and the Myth of Women in Espionage*. London: Collins & Brown, 1992.

———. "Poisoned Honey: The Myth of Women in Espionage." *Queen's Quarterly* 100 (Summer 1993): 291–309.

Wiley, Bell Irvin. *Confederate Women*. Westport, Conn.: Greenwood Press, 1975.

———. *The Life of Billy Yank: The Common Soldier of the Union*. Baton Rouge: Louisiana State University Press, 1952, 1971.

———. *The Life of Johnny Reb: The Common Soldier of the Confederacy*. Baton Rouge: Louisiana State University Press, 1943, 1970, 1978.

Wood, Leonora. *Belle Boyd: Famous Spy of the Confederate States Army.* Keyser, W.Va.: Mountain Echo, 1940.

Woodward, C. Vann, and Elisabeth Muhlenfeld. *The Private Mary Chesnut: The Unpublished Civil War Diaries.* New York: Oxford University Press, 1984.

Worthington, C. J., ed. *The Woman in Battle: A Narrative of the Exploits, Adventures, and Travels of Madame Loreta Janeta Velazquez.* 1876. Reprint. New York: Arno Press, 1972.

Wright, Richardson. *Forgotten Ladies: Nine Portraits from the American Family Album.* Philadelphia: J. B. Lippincott, 1928.

Young, Agatha. *The Women and the Crisis: Women of the North in the Civil War.* New York: McDowell, Obolensky, 1959.


## Archival Materials

John C. Babcock Papers. Library of Congress, Washington, D.C.

William F. Broaddus Diary. Library of Virginia, Richmond, Va.

Deborah Sampson Gannett Papers. Sharon Public Library, Sharon, Mass.

Frank Moore Papers. William R. Perkins Library, Duke University, Durham, N.C.

Eugenia Phillips Papers. Philip Phillips Family Papers. Library of Congress, Washington, D.C.

RG 15. Records of the Veterans Administration. Kady Brownell Pension File. Certificate #279843. National Archives, Washington, D.C.

RG 15. Records of the Veterans Administration. Robert S. Brownell Pension File. Application #6135. Certificate #23495. National Archives, Washington, D. C.

RG 15. Records of the Veterans Administration. Albert D. J. Cashier Pension File. Application #755646. Certificate #1001132. National Archives, Washington, D.C.

RG 15. Records of the Veterans Administration. Deborah Sampson Gannett Pension File. Certificate #32722. National Archives, Washington, D.C.

RG 15. Records of the Veterans Administration. Charles E. Hooks Pension File. Application #40925. Certificate #25505. National Archives, Washington, D.C.

RG 15. Records of the Veterans Administration. Emma A. Porch Pension File. Certificate #276360. National Archives, Washington, D.C.

RG 15. Records of the Veterans Administration. Ephraim Sampson Pension File. Certificate #W11053. National Archives, Washington, D.C.

RG 15. Records of the Veterans Administration. Sarah Emma Edmonds Pension File. Application #526889. Certificate #232136. National Archives, Washington, D.C.

RG 15. Records of the Veterans Administration. John B. Turchin Pension File. Application #744629. Certificate #532315. National Archives, Washington, D.C.

RG 94. Records of the Adjutant General's Office. Administrative Precedent File ("Frech File") #3H36. National Archives, Washington, D.C.

RG 94. Records of the Adjutant General's Office. AGO Document File Record Cards. #1502399. National Archives, Washington, D.C.

RG 94. Records of the Adjutant General's Office. Carded Medical Records, Mexican and Civil Wars. National Archives, Washington, D.C.

RG 94. Records of the Adjutant General's Office. Compiled Military Service Records. National Archives, Washington, D.C.

RG 94. Records of the Adjutant General's Office. Hospital Registers, Civil War. National Archives, Washington, D.C.

RG 94. Records of the Adjutant General's Office. Records and Pension Office Document File #184934. National Archives, Washington, D.C.

RG 94. Records of the Adjutant General's Office. Records and Pension Office Record Cards. #439572; #184934Y1. National Archives, Washington, D.C.

RG 107. Records of the Office of the Secretary of War. Records Concerning the Conduct and Loyalty of Certain Union Army Officers, Civilian Employees of the War Department and U.S. Citizens During the Civil War. National Archives, Washington, D.C.

RG 109. Letters Received by the Confederate Secretary of War, 1861–1865. National Archives, Washington, D.C.

RG 109. Union Provost Marshal's File of Two- or More-Named Papers Relating to Citizens. National Archives, Washington, D.C.

RG 109. War Department Collection of Confederate Records. Bound Records. National Archives, Washington, D.C.

RG 109. War Department Collection of Confederate Records. Compiled Military Service Records.

RG 110. Provost Marshal General's Bureau, List of Scouts, Guides, Spies and Detectives. National Archives, Washington, D.C.

RG 153. Records of the Office of the Judge Advocate General (Army). Court Martial Case #II 704, Court Martial of Jerome B. Taft. National Archives, Washington, D.C.

RG 393. Special Orders, District of Middle Tennessee. Pt. 2, Bk. 174. National Archives, Washington, D.C.

RG 393. Special Orders, District of South West Missouri. Pt. 2. National Archives, Washington, D.C.

Jerome John Robbins Papers. Michigan Historical Collections, Bentley Historical Library, University of Michigan, Ann Arbor.

Julia Ward Stickley Files on Deborah Sampson Gannett, 1786–1990. Massachusetts State Archives, Boston.

Rebecca Usher Papers. Collection 9, Maine Historical Society, Portland.

Elizabeth Van Lew Papers. Manuscripts Division, New York Public Library.

John A. Vinton Papers. New Hampshire Antiquarian Society, Hopkinton.

Antonia Ford Willard Papers. Willard Family Papers. Library of Congress, Washington, D.C.

## Newspapers and Journals

*Brooklyn Daily Times*

*Cairo* (Illinois) *City Gazette*

*Cincinnati Dollar Times*

*Cleveland Plain Dealer*

*Detroit Advertiser and Tribune*

*Detroit Free Press*

*Detroit Journal*

*Detroit Post and Tribune*

*Dwight* (Illinois) *Star and Herald*

*Fayetteville* (North Carolina) *Observer*

*Fincher's Trades Review*

*Fort Scott* (Kansas) *Weekly Monitor*

*Frank Leslie's Illustrated Weekly*

*Harper's Weekly*

*Jackson Mississippian*
*La Grange* (Georgia) *Daily News*
*Lansing* (Michigan) *State Republican*
*Louisville* (Kentucky) *Daily Journal*
*Lynchburg Daily Virginian*
*Maysville* (Kentucky) *Dollar Weekly Bulletin*
*Memphis Bulletin*
*Nashville Dispatch*
*New York Daily News*
*New York Evening Express*
*New York Herald*
*New York Sun*
*New York Times*
*New York Tribune*
*Owensburg* (Kentucky) *Monitor*
*Pennsylvania Mercury and Universal Advertiser*
*Philadelphia Inquirer*
*Philadelphia North American*
*Philadelphia Times*
*Pittsfield* (Illinois) *Republican*
*Richmond Daily Examiner*
*Richmond Daily Whig*
*Richmond Enquirer*
*Richmond Sentinel*
*The Sibyl*
*Vicksburg* (Mississippi) *Herald*
*Washington Chronicle*
*Washington Evening Star*
*Washington Republican*
*Wellsburg* (West Virginia) *Herald*
*Wilmington* (Virginia) *Journal*

# Index

Page numbers in *italics* refer to illustrations.